The South English Legendary

EARLY ENGLISH TEXT SOCIETY

Original Series No. 244

1959 (for 1957), reprinted 1969

PRICE 30s.

The South English Legendary

EDITED BY
CHARLOTTE D'EVELYN
AND
ANNA J. MILL

VOLUME III

Introduction and Glossary by
CHARLOTTE D'EVELYN

Published for
THE EARLY ENGLISH TEXT SOCIETY
by the
OXFORD UNIVERSITY PRESS
LONDON NEW YORK TORONTO

OXFORD
UNIVERSITY PRESS

Great Clarendon Street, Oxford OX2 6DP
United Kingdom

Oxford University Press is a department of the University of Oxford.
It furthers the University's objective of excellence in research, scholarship,
and education by publishing worldwide. Oxford is a registered trade mark of
Oxford University Press in the UK and in certain other countries

© The Early English Text Society 1959

The moral rights of the authors have been asserted

Database right Oxford University Press (maker)

First Edition published in 1959
Reprinted 1969

All rights reserved. No part of this publication may be reproduced,
stored in a retrieval system, or transmitted, in any form or by any means,
without the prior permission in writing of Oxford University Press,
or as expressly permitted by law, or under terms agreed with the appropriate
reprographics rights organization. Enquiries concerning reproduction
outside the scope of the above should be sent to the Rights Department,
Oxford University Press, at the address above

You must not circulate this book in any other form
and you must impose this same condition on any acquirer

Published in the United States of America by Oxford University Press
198 Madison Avenue, New York, NY 10016, United States of America

British Library Cataloguing in Publication Data
Data available

Library of Congress Cataloging in Publication Data
Data available

Original Series, 244

ISBN 978-0-19-722244-7

FOREWORD

THE following introduction is concerned primarily not with the larger problems of *The South English Legendary* as a whole but with the particular problems of the four manuscripts used in this edition. These problems involve, however, some comparison with the earliest MS., Laud 108, in Horstmann's edition, for the purpose of determining the nature of the distinction commonly made between the 'Laud text' and the 'Harley text' of certain legends, e.g. of St. Paul, of St. Bridget, of St. Thomas à Becket. Not the mechanical disorder of MS. Laud 108 but the state of its text should offer the most satisfactory clues to the early history of *The South English Legendary*. Detailed studies of individual legends, one hopes, will continue to be made. It is an easy prophecy that their combined results will bring to light a wide range of contact of *The South English Legendary* with earlier hagiographical writings and, especially in its English legends, with local sources and traditions.

To the acknowledgement of assistance already made in the Foreword of Vol. I it is a pleasant duty to add here thanks to Professor Francis L. Utley and to Mr. A. I. Doyle for information about manuscripts of *The South English Legendary* previously unreported. The glossary has benefited from the interest and fertile suggestions of Professor Bruce Dickins. Professor Ruth J. Dean has given help with French words. Mr. Burchfield's solicitous supervision has helped materially to bring the volume nearer to that unattainable goal of perfect correctness in print.

C. D'E.

South Hadley, Massachusetts
  15 January 1959

To my brother
NORMAN F. D'EVELYN

CONTENTS

FOREWORD vii

ERRATA xi

INTRODUCTION
   I. The Manuscripts of *The South English Legendary* 1
   II. The Manuscripts used in the Present Edition 3
   III. Relationship of the Manuscripts used in the Present Edition 6
   IV. The Text of MSS. C and H 11
   V. MS. Laud 108 and MSS. C and H 15
   VI. Conclusion: The Value of *The South English Legendary* 24

APPENDIXES
   I. Bibliography 27
   II. Table of Contents, MS. C 29
   III. Table of Contents, MS. H 31
   IV. List of Legends, MS. A 33
   V. List of Legends, MS. J 35
   VI. Items previously printed from MSS. C, H, A, and J 37

NOTE ON THE GLOSSARY 40

GLOSSARY 41

ERRATA

Vol. I. p. 11, l. 85 var.	*for* þuse	*read* þulke
p. 47, l. 6	,, valeize	,, valeiȝe
p. 111, l. 28 var.	,, men	,, men *add.*
p. 120, ll. 54, 57	,, plestre	,, plastre
p. 129, l. 15	,, dawes	,, dawes ·
p. 151, l. 80	,, Te	,, þe
p. 237, l. 485 var.	,, [*letter*	,, *letter*
Vol. II. p. 387, l. 90	*for* Leine	*read* Lenie
p. 443, l. 1	,, Efleuè	,, Eflleue
p. 496, l. 111 var.	,, sped	,, sped . . . (*rest cut*)
p. 503, l. 351	,, roueisouns	,, Roueisouns
p. 540	,, 253	,, 235
p. 609, l. 500 var.	,, 500–22	,, 499–522
p. 656, l. 1424	,, ouercaste	,, ouercast

INTRODUCTION

1. *The Manuscripts of 'The South English Legendary'*[1]

CARLETON BROWN's *Register of Middle English Religious and Didactic Verse* (ii, p. ix)[2] notes that the S.E.L. is preserved in 34 manuscripts, 'not counting MSS. which incorporate single selections'. Brown and Robbins's *Index of Middle English Verse* (Appendix V, p. 737) repeats this number without the qualifying statement. These 34 manuscripts are indexed in the *Register* (ii. 448) and include 9 manuscripts classified as 'Fragments'. Added to the 34 is a further list of 13 manuscripts—the number should be 15^3—containing 'pieces from [the S.E.L.], occurring separately'. To this total should be added two other manuscripts, both incomplete, Winchester MS. 33a[4] and P.R.O. MS. C. 47/34/1, no. 5.[5] This brings

---

[1] Abbreviated in the Introduction as 'the *S.E.L.*'
[2] For fuller bibliographical statement of works cited in this introduction, see Appendix I, Bibliography.
[3] Two MSS. are not listed: B.M. Addit. 22283, f. 83^a, col. 2: St. Michael, Part III, recorded under Item 2220 (ii. 332), and Camb. Univ. Ee. 2. 15, f. 94^b: St. Augustine of Canterbury, recorded under Item 1769 (ii. 259).
[4] Wells, *Manual*, 9th Supplement (1951), 1815. For information about this MS. and the securing of a rotograph of it I am indebted to Professor Francis L. Utley. The MS., dated 15th century, contains the following S.E.L. items: f. 1^a Adam; f. 4^a Noah; f. 5^b Abraham; f. 7^a Rebecca; f. 9^a Joseph (for these five items see *Index* 3973); f. 12^a Pilate (*Index* 2755); f. 15^b Judas (*Index* 1809); f. 17^b St. Oswald the Bishop (*Index* 3035); f. 20^b St. Edward the King (*Index* 2890); f. 24^a St. Cuthbert (*Index* 2880); f. 25^a St. Mary of Egypt (*Index* 2990); f. 30^a St. Gregory (*Index* 2910); f. 31^b SS. Philip and James (*Index* 3048); f. 33^a De festis mobilibus per annum (*Index* 791); f. 33^a Lent (*Index* 1859); f. 35^b Easter (*Index* 3384); f. 36^b Litany (*Index* 1911); f. 37^a St. Peter (*Index* 3046); f. 38^a St. Paul (*Index* 3041); f. 39^a St. Matthias (*Index* 3026); f. 39^b Invention of the Cross (*Index* 3387); f. 45^a Exaltation of the Cross (*Index* 3388); f. 47^a last half blank; f. 47^b blank; f. 48^a (incorrectly numbered 47 in photostat) the fruit called Christendom = Banna Sanctorum (*Index* 2304); f. 49^a Circumcision (*Index* 4266); f. 49^b Epiphany (*Index* 3813); f. 49^b SS. Fabian and Sebastian (*Index* 2895); f. 51^b St. Agnes (*Index* 2850).
[5] Information about this MS. I owe to Mr. A. I. Doyle. It is dated early 14th century and contains the following items: f. 1^a Banna Sanctorum (*Index* 2304), the opening couplet cut off at the top margin; f. 1^b 3eresday (Circumcision, *Index* 4266); f. 1^b Twelfth Day (Epiphany, *Index* 3813); f. 2^a St. Hilary (*Index* 2912), ll. 1–89. Several pages are missing between f. 2^a and f. 3^a. The latter begins with St. Julian the Hospitaller (*Index* 2950), l. 44; f. 4^a St. Bride, longer version (*Index* 2872), ll. 1–82. Small coloured drawings, busts and full-length figures, ornament the margins at the beginning of Twelfth Day, St. Hilary, and St. Bride.

the present number of known manuscripts of the *S.E.L.* up to 51. Of the fragmentary manuscripts of the *S.E.L.* two, Gray's Inn MS. 20 and B.M. Addit. MS. 24078, are literally in shreds and patches. Single items, or small blocks of items, preserved in many manuscripts, are of definite value for the study of individual legends and may offer clues for the solution of problems connected with the *S.E.L.*, but in relation to the study of the full text they too are 'fragments'. Considering the nature of the *S.E.L.*, completeness can be only a relative term. The earliest MS., Laud 108 (S.C. Bodl. 1486), dated end of the thirteenth century, now contains 59 items;[1] one of the latest, Bodl. 779 (S.C. Bodl. 2567), dated *c.* 1400, includes 135 items.[2] The *S.E.L.* obviously expanded as it circulated. This fact helps to disguise the original plan, purpose, and extent of the work.

Horstmann's pioneer efforts in listing manuscripts of the *S.E.L.* and comparing their contents brought out the fact that this work was a composite, including, besides saints' legends proper, material on Old Testament history, the life of Christ, and the feasts of the Church. And this material appeared in different order and amount and sometimes in different metrical form in the various manuscripts. To clear a way through this jungle of variations Horstmann worked out a rough pattern of relationships among the various manuscripts, taking into account content and order and metrical differences and noting in a more general way textual characteristics.[3] The content of MS. Laud 108 (L) shows no pattern. MS. Harley 2277 (H) and MS. Corpus Christi College, Cambridge, 145 (C), with a minimum of *temporale* material, present the saints' legends in general in the order

[1] E.E.T.S. o.s. 87, pp. v f. and xiii. Horstmann, following the numbering of the MS., gives the original number as 67. The first 7 items are now missing; the 9th (Infancy of Christ) is not a part of the *S.E.L.* The statement of the number of items in a given MS. may vary in different listings of its contents, even by the same person. Horstmann, for example, gives a separate number to each of the three parts of St. Michael where they occur consecutively in H 2277 and C 145, but he lists all three parts as one item for MS. Stowe 949 (E.E.T.S. o.s. 87, pp. xv f.). Again Horstmann does not itemize the miracles of the Virgin which follow the legend of St. Theophilus in H 2277 (ibid., p. xv), whereas in the *Register*, i. 326, each miracle is listed separately.

[2] E.E.T.S. o.s. 87, pp. xxii f. The total number of items listed for this MS. in the *Register*, i. 29 f., is larger, since, among other variations, the legends of SS. Philip and James and of SS. Fabian and Sebastian are treated as two items by Horstmann but as four in the *Register*.

[3] See particularly *Altenglische Legenden* (Paderborn, 1875), pp. iii–xxxviii, and E.E.T.S. o.s. 87, pp. vii–xxiv. For a general summary of these groupings, based on Horstmann, see Wells, *Manual* (New Haven, 1916), pp. 294 f.

of the calendar, beginning with 3eresday, 1 January, and ending with St. Thomas of Canterbury, 29 December.[1] This arrangement provides the pattern for most of the extant manuscripts which preserve the beginning of the legendary material. Three manuscripts, however—Pepys 2344, Egerton 1993, Bodl. Addit. C 36 (S.C. Bodl. 30236)—with minor differences, follow the order of the church year.[2] In later manuscripts the *temporale* material and the number of saints' lives are increased. In no two manuscripts is the list of saints' lives exactly duplicated in number and order.

Editors of separate legends or *temporale* material have worked out the manuscript relations for these particular items: for St. Brendan (Bälz, p. ii), for St. Juliana (Schleich, p. 25), for the Southern Passion (Beatrice D. Brown, p. xxx), for St. Thomas of Canterbury (Thiemke, p. viii), for St. Ursula and the 11,000 Virgins (Schubel, p. 133). As one would expect, the pattern of grouping changes for each of these legends. One factor which these five groupings have in common is the absence of direct dependence of one manuscript upon another.[3] The manuscripts studied are related only through hypothetical common ancestors—a result which confirms the fact of the diversity of the extant manuscripts already apparent in Horstmann's more cursory comparison.

II. *The Manuscripts used in the Present Edition*

1. *British Museum MS. Harley 2277 (H)*

The importance of Harley 2277 as the earliest orderly text of the *S.E.L.* has long been recognized. The manuscript has been frequently described and its contents listed.[4] Many of its items have been

---

[1] Both MSS. add after St. Thomas of Canterbury the legends of Judas and Pilate—in this case not saintly or in the calendar. MS. C has appended also a life of St. Guthlac, but in a later hand.

[2] See *Register*, i. 126, 219, 288. Minnie E. Wells, 'The Structural Development of the S.E.L.', *J.E.G.P.* xli (1942), pp. 320 f., argues in favour of this as the original order.

[3] Only in the *stemma* for St. Brendan is direct relation between two MSS. indicated and one of these, the alleged dependence of Bodl. 779 (S.C. 2567) on Trinity College, Oxford, 57, is challenged by Mrs. Brown (loc. cit., note 36).

[4] See Wanley, *A Catalogue of the Harl. MSS. in the British Museum* (London, 1808), ii. 637; Horstmann, *Alteng. Leg.* (1875), p. iv; Horstmann, E.E.T.S. o.s. 87, p. xiv; *Register*, i. 324; Wells, *Manual*, p. 294. A list of contents written in the same hand as the text is given on f. 232[b] of the MS. See Appendix III.

printed.[1] The text is legibly written, 38 to 40 lines to a page, but, to judge by its numerous errors, somewhat carelessly copied. The margins, in later times, have been much scribbled over. Wanley identified the John Sanford whose name frequently appears in the margin as a member of 'the Family of Sanford of Comberslery in Somersetshire, during the Reign of Queen Elizabeth'.[2] 'About 1300' is the date generally accepted for Harley 2277.[3] Miss Serjeantson's study of West-Midland dialects assigns it to Gloucestershire.[4]

2. *Corpus Christi College, Cambridge, MS.* 145 (*C*)

MS. Corpus Christi College, Cambridge, 145 was unknown to Horstmann when he printed his first account of the *S.E.L.* manuscripts. It was brought to the attention of students by Zupitza's detailed record of its contents.[5] Zupitza (following Nasmith) noted three different hands in the text.[6] The main part of the legendary, ff. 1ᵃ–210ᵇ, is written in the first hand, 40 lines to the page. At f. 210ᵇ a second hand, 32 lines to the page, copies the life of St. Guthlac. At f. 214ᵃ a third hand, crowding 50 to 60 and more lines to the page, begins the legend of Judas followed by that of Pilate (f. 215ᵃ) and by the conclusion of the legend of St. Thomas of Canterbury and his Translation (f. 217ᵃ). The text of the first hand has been frequently altered—the *o* in the combination *eo* erased, *u* changed to *y*. These alterations, as Zupitza noted,[7] seem to have been made by the scribe of the second hand. This second hand has occasionally added marginal titles and page-headings and has supplied a table of contents (f. iiᵇ).[8]

The text is clearly, even gracefully, written. Red and blue capital letters and paragraph marks furnish the only decoration. The caesural pause is indicated by a raised dot and a daub of red on the following word, but this rubrication stops (except for ff. 210ᵇ–211ᵃ) after f. 110ᵃ.

---

[1] See Appendix VI.   [2] Wanley, op. cit. ii. 639.

[3] Wanley, op. cit. ii. 637, dated the handwriting before 1320. Horstmann, *Alteng. Leg.* (1875), p. iv, set the date *c.* 1300. It is so dated in Ward, *Catalogue of Romances* (London, 1893), ii. 551; *Register*, i. 324, and by the editors of separate items of the *S.E.L.*: Bälz, p. i; B. D. Brown, p. xvii; Schubel, p. 147; Thiemke, p. 1.   [4] *R.E.S.* iii (1927), 322.

[5] *Anglia*, i (1878), 392 f. For later listings of its contents see Horstmann, *Alteng. Leg.* N.F. (1881), p. xlv; E.E.T.S. o.s. 87, p. xiv; *Register*, i. 206; Wells, *Manual*, p. 294.   [6] *Anglia*, i. 393, 408.

[7] *Anglia*, i. 393. Horstmann, *Alteng. Leg.* N.F. (1881), p. xlvi, makes a similar statement.   [8] See Appendix II.

INTRODUCTION 5

The date of the manuscript, that is, the date of the first hand, is generally accepted as early fourteenth century.[1] James characterizes the third hand as 'a hand of the original time, writing more closely'. The second hand he describes as 'later'.[2]

On the lower margins of ff. 1ᵇ and 2ᵃ a note in Latin states that this manuscript was given to the church of St. Mary 'de Suthewyk' by John Kateryngton, canon of that church. James identifies the church as Southwick Priory, [Hampshire], and dates the note as 'of cent. XIV–XV'.[3] MS. C is one of those presented to Corpus Christi College by Archbishop Parker.

Only two items, the legends of the 11,000 Virgins and of St. Guthlac, have been printed in full from this manuscript.[4]

3. *Ashmole 43 (S.C. Bodl. 6924) (A)*

Ashmole 43[5] begins incompletely at f. 4 in the legend of St. Wulfstan. Its last folios, 259–69, are badly mutilated. The text itself is written clearly and evenly, 40 lines to a page, with the initial letters of each line set off in red from the rest of the text. The list of contents, more extensive than that of H and C, is available in Horstmann and Brown.[6] The manuscript has been dated variously as '*c.* 1300', '*c.* 1310', 'first half of the 14th century', but 'second quarter of the 14th century' may be considered the accepted period.[7]

[1] See M. R. James, *A Descriptive Catalogue of the Manuscripts in the Library of Corpus Christi College, Cambridge* (Cambridge, 1912), p. 331; *Register*, i. 206. Zupitza, *Anglia*, i. 393, dated the manuscript end of the 14th century. Horstmann, *Alteng. Leg.* N.F. (1881), p. xlv, assigned it to the beginning of the 14th century. In E.E.T.S. O.S. 87, p. ix, he specified the date more exactly as *c.* 1320. Wells, *Manual*, p. 294, follows this later statement.

[2] James, loc. cit.; W. F. Bolton, *The Middle English and Latin Poems of Saint Guthlac*, p. 168.

[3] Ibid. The note is quoted by James and by Zupitza, *Anglia*, i. 393. On Southwick Priory see Dugdale, *Monasticon Anglicanum* (London, 1846), vi. 243; *The Victoria History of the Counties of England, Hampshire*, ii (London, 1903), pp. 164–8.   [4] See Appendix VI.

[5] For full description see W. H. Black, *A Descriptive, Analytical, and Critical Catalogue of the MSS. bequeathed unto the University of Oxford by Elias Ashmole, Esq.* (Oxford, 1845), p. 646; Madan, Craster, Denholm-Young, *A Summary Catalogue of Western MSS. in the Bodleian Library at Oxford* (Oxford, 1937), II. ii. 1123; Horstmann, *Alteng. Leg.* (Paderborn, 1875), p. vii; Grace E. Moore, *The Middle English Verse Life of Edward the Confessor* (Philadelphia, 1942), p. iii.

[6] Horstmann, op. cit. p. viii, and E.E.T.S. O.S. 87, p. xiv; *Register*, i. 83.

[7] See *Summary Cat. of Western MSS*, loc. cit.; *Register*, loc. cit.; Wells, *Manual*, 1st Supplement (New Haven, 1919), p. 961, where it is stated, 'Ashmole 43 may be of 1325–1350', modifying the date '*c.* 1300' recorded in the

B

Several items from Ashmole 43 have been printed and its text has been used as the base for recent critical editions of separate legends.[1]

4. *British Museum MS. Cotton Julius D. IX (J)*

MS. Cotton Julius D. IX is the most extensive in content of the S.E.L. manuscripts under discussion.[2] It is dated fifteenth century.[3] Its small octavo pages are solidly written, with the number of lines varying from 32 to 42 to a page. Marginal notes are few and the separate items are most commonly marked not by title but by chapter and Roman numeral. A few items from this text have been printed.[4]

III. *Relationship of the Manuscripts used in the Present Edition*

In content and arrangement MSS. C and H and MSS. A and J have been considered 'pairs'. What these correspondences involve in each pair and between the two pairs needs to be indicated in some detail.

1. *The Relationship of MSS. C and H*

The close relationship between MSS. C and H was noted in passing by Zupitza.[5] Horstmann[6] pointed out in more detail their agreement in content, and expressed his opinion that the text of C would correct the errors of H. In their original state the two manuscripts

---

original *Manual* (New Haven, 1916), p. 295. The earlier dating is apparently based on that given in the old catalogue of Ashmolean MSS. (see p. 5, note 5, above) which states (p. 64) that Ashmole 43 is 'written in a small fair hand about the year 1300'. The official copy of this catalogue in the Bodleian has a marginal annotation (p. 64), 'Macray thinks in the 2nd quarter of the 14th cent. July 1887'. Horstmann, E.E.T.S. o.s. 87, p. xiv, gives the date as '*c.* 1310' and is followed by Thiemke, p. 1, and Schubel, p. 133. The dating, first half of the 14th century, is given without comment by Bälz, p. i.

[1] See Appendix VI.

[2] For the description of J see *B.M. Cat. of Cott. MSS.*, p. 16; Horstmann, *Alteng. Leg.* (1875), p. xxvi; Moore, *The ME. Verse Life of Edward the Confessor*, p. v. The list of contents is given in E.E.T.S. o.s. 87, p. xiv; *Register*, i. 269.

[3] *B.M. Cat. of Cotton MSS.*, loc. cit.; Ward, *Catalogue of Romances*, ii, dates the MS. 'XVth century' (p. 480 and p. 738) and 'early XVth century' (p. 554); Horstmann, *Alteng. Leg.* (1875), p. xxvi, accepts 15th century as the date but in E.E.T.S. o.s. 87, p. xiv, suggests '*c.* 1370?'; *Register*, i. 269, and Wells, *Manual*, p. 295, give the date as 15th century.

[4] See Appendix VI.   [5] *Anglia*, i. 392.

[6] *Alteng. Leg.* N.F. (1881), pp. xlv f.

INTRODUCTION

apparently contained the same number of legends in the same order. In their present state each supplies almost completely the other's loss of material. Horstmann gave concrete expression to this apparent supplementary relation by combining the contents of H and C in a single list, characterizing the joint collection as the 'First complete annus festivalis, in the order of the year'.[1]

In analysing the contents of this C–H list the material presumably once common to both manuscripts but now lost through damage should first be noted. Through damage H has lost completely the first twenty-five items and ll. 1–24 of the 26th item, St. Benedict. Between f. 11 and f. 12 several leaves are missing in the account of the Passion.[2] One leaf, containing 78 lines of the early history of the Cross, is lost between f. 37 and f. 38. Between f. 105 and f. 106 material is missing, covering, by comparison with C, the conclusion of SS. Martha and Fronton (38 ll.), the whole of St. Oswald (44 ll.), and the beginning of St. Lawrence (6 ll.). Between f. 176 and f. 177 one leaf is lost containing the conclusion of St. Andrew (76 ll.) and the beginning of St. Nicholas (4 ll.). The next gap occurs between f. 188 and f. 189, where one leaf (80 ll.) from the beginning of St. Thomas the Apostle is lost. Finally between f. 193 and f. 194 several leaves covering ll. 27–286 of St. John the Evangelist are missing. The loss of material in H is chiefly due to damage. Within the text the dropping of a line or couplet, rarely of any larger number of lines, occasionally occurs.[3]

Unlike H, MS. C has lost through damage only one large section of material. Between f. 168 and f. 169 leaves are missing which include the end of SS. Simon and Jude (18 ll.), the next twelve items (Nos. 71–82), as given in H, and the first part of St. Thomas the Apostle (286 ll.). On the other hand, unlike H, C never contained the larger part of the *temporale* material covering the Passion, Ascension, and Pentecost. The text skips from Lent (f. 51ª) directly to Easter (f. 51ª), and then to St. Mary of Egypt (f. 51ᵇ), where the legendary proper begins again. C makes the small omissions usual with all copyists.[4]

Matching the losses and important omissions in both manuscripts it is apparent that H and C supplement each other's defects in all but two instances. The loss through damage in H of a large section

---

[1] E.E.T.S. o.s. 87, p. xiv. See Table of Contents of the present edition. Items are cited according to the numbering of the present edition.
[2] See Beatrice D. Brown, E.E.T.S. o.s. 169, p. xviii, who calculates the loss as 'probably twelve leaves (912 vv.)'.
[3] These small omissions are noted in the variant readings.
[4] See variant readings *passim*.

on the Passion corresponds to the omission of this material in C; the loss through damage in H of portions of the text of St. Andrew and St. Nicholas corresponds to a similar loss through damage in C. On the other hand, C supplies the twenty-five items missing through damage at the beginning of H and H supplies the twelve items missing through damage in C. With the single exception of the section on the Passion the arrangement and content of H and C seem to have been identical.

2. *The Relationship of MSS. A and J*

That A and J formed a clearly similar pair of manuscripts was first stated by Horstmann,[1] who later combined their contents, as he had done with MSS. C and H, in a single list.[2] Following the order of the year the two manuscripts run almost parallel throughout the main body of the text, that is, from Wulfstan (19 Jan.) to Thomas of Canterbury (29 Dec.).[3] The divergences in this part of the text are minor: (1) J omits the legends of Swithun, Kenelm, Frideswide, and Oswald the King; (2) J substitutes the legend of Ailbriȝt (Ethelbert, 20 May) for that of Alban (22 June), both out of order in their contexts; (3) J inverts the legends of Leonard (6 Nov.) and Eustace (2 Nov.), restoring the right order; (4) J adds in their proper places the legends of Jakes (James, 27 Nov.) and Birinus (3 Dec.) and includes the miracle of Edward the Confessor's ring at the end of the legend of John the Evangelist; (5) A adds in the proper place the prologue and feast of the Conception of the Virgin (8 Dec.).

The chief differences between A and J are additions made after the legend of Thomas of Canterbury (29 Dec.) in what seems to be an appendix in each manuscript. These additions destroy the normal order of the text. In A the legend of Edward the Confessor (5 Jan.) follows immediately that of Thomas of Canterbury and is left incomplete through mutilation of the manuscript.[4] In J nine items are added after Thomas of Canterbury: Egwin (30 Dec.), Silvester (31 Dec.), Ailbriȝt (20 May, already given in the main body of the

---

[1] *Alteng. Leg.* (Paderborn, 1875), p. xxvi; *Alteng. Leg.* N.F. (1881), p. xliv; see summary in Wells, *Manual*, p. 295.

[2] E.E.T.S. o.s. 87, p. xiv.

[3] See Appendixes IV and V. MS. A, as already noted, has lost completely the first four items and ends incompletely.

[4] Moore, *The Middle English Verse Life of Edward the Confessor*, iv, calculates that '160 lines, or two folios' of the legend are missing.

text), Ignatius (6 Feb.),[1] Frideswide (19 Oct.) which J had omitted from its proper place, Part III of Michael, Edward the Confessor (5 Jan.), Guthlac (11 Apr.), four miracles of the Virgin preceding the legend of Theophilus (4 Feb.?). By these additions J has brought its contents in line with A's in only two particulars: the restoration of Frideswide and the addition of Edward the Confessor. The mutilated condition of A leaves one in doubt whether A like J contained several items after the legend of Thomas of Canterbury. It is apparent at least from the position of the one surviving addition in A that A and J were not running as closely parallel here as in the main body of the text. Apart from these appended legends the two manuscripts may properly be regarded as paired in content and arrangement.

3. *The relationship of MSS. AJ and MSS. CH*

A comparison of the content and arrangement of the two groups, AJ and CH, makes it clear that both follow the same general pattern —a calendar of feasts and legends in the order of the year. The variations within this pattern are only such as would naturally occur with so flexible a framework. The changes for instance in J, the latest manuscript of the four, keep the text a legendary still rather than a *temporale* and underline through the addition of the lives of Ailbri3t and Egwin the English colouring of the collection. The differences between the two groups include a few rearrangements of material, several omissions, and a number of additions. Apart from the 'appended' legends in A and J, to be considered later, these changes are specifically as follows:

Rearrangements. (1) AJ make one item of the three parts of the legend of the Holy Rood—Early History, Invention (3 May), and Exaltation (14 Sept.), thus disregarding the calendar order. (2) On the other hand, AJ separate the first two parts of the legend of St. Michael—Part I in monte Gargano (29 Sept.) and Part II in monte Tomba (16 Oct.), thus bringing Part II into its proper chronological place.[2] Part III of St. Michael, the well-known 'scientific' summary which has no connexion with the saint and no place in the calendar, is omitted in AJ at this point. J includes it, as already noted, in the

[1] This legend is not recorded elsewhere in *S.E.L.* MSS. See *Index* 461, No. 2914.
[2] Part I (29 Sept.) of St. Michael is slightly out of order in AJ because of the addition in both these MSS. of the legend of Justine (7 Oct.) between Matthew (21 Sept.) and Part I of St. Michael. See p. 10, note 2, below.

appendix. (3) The legend of St. Alban (22 June) is shifted in A to a place after St. Quentin (31 Oct.). J substitutes in the same place the legend of St. Ailbriʒt (20 May). (4) The legend of St. Oswald the King (5 Aug.) is inserted in A after St. John the Evangelist (27 Dec.). J omits St. Oswald.

Omissions. (1) The legend of Longinus (15 Mar.) is dropped by AJ.[1] (2) The account of the Passion, partially lost in H and omitted entirely in C, is also omitted in AJ. (3) The legend of Theophilus (4 Feb.?) with its six accompanying miracles of the Virgin is omitted in the main body of the text by AJ. J adds the legend and four miracles in the appendix. (4) In the legend of St. James (25 July) AJ give only one miracle, that of the Forsworn Pilgrims, for the three in CH. (5) The legend of St. Martha (29 July) is omitted in AJ. (6) The legends of Judas and Pilate added in CH at the end of the collection are omitted in AJ. (7) J omits the legends of St. Swithun and St. Kenelm and A omits the miracle of Edward the Confessor's Ring which in CH and J concludes the legend of St. John the Evangelist. These particular omissions, in one not both manuscripts, may be purely scribal and accidental, and may not indicate, therefore, any real variation in the amount of material in CH and AJ. Of all these omissions, the second, that of the Passion, is the most extensive and distinctive and sets H apart from the other three manuscripts.

Additions. Additions make up the greater number of differences between AJ and CH. In the main body of the text AJ have added nine legends, with one exception, each properly placed in the calendar: Seven Sleepers (27 July), Hippolitus (13 Aug.), Justine (7 Oct.),[2] Leger (2 Oct.), Francis (4 Oct.), Faith (6 Oct.), Eustace (2 Nov.),[3] Brice (13 Nov.), Cecilia (22 Nov.). A alone has in proper order Frideswide (19 Oct.)[4] and the Conception of the Virgin with its prologue (8 Dec.). J alone adds in proper order Jakes (27 Nov.) and Birinus (3 Dec.) and, as noted above, substitutes Ailbriʒt (20 May) for A's Alban (22 June), both out of place.

In the appendix A and J add Edward the Confessor (5 Jan.)— A immediately after Thomas of Canterbury (29 Dec.), J among other

[1] This section of the text is lost in H.
[2] In both A and J Justine is added between St. Matthew (21 Sept.) and Part I of St. Michael (29 Sept.).
[3] Eustace (2 Nov.) and Leonard (6 Nov.) are reversed in order in J.
[4] As noted above, p. 9, J includes Frideswide in the appendix, from which one may assume that that legend is not an addition by A only but an omission by J.

INTRODUCTION

items out of order. The additional items in the appendix of J include only five not found in CH: Egwin (30 Dec.), Silvester (31 Dec.), Ailbri3t (22 May), Ignatius (1 Feb.), and Guthlac (11 Apr.).[1] Two items in the appendix of J, Part II of St. Michael and Theophilus with four miracles of the Virgin, bring the contents of J more in line with that of CH.

In sum, A and J together contain nineteen items not found in CH. These additions outbalance the few omissions in AJ compared with CH. Two points are noteworthy. First, among all the additions only one, the Conception of the Virgin, given in A alone, is *temporale* material. Second, of the eleven items added by both A and J five are already extant in Laud 108, the earliest surviving text.[2] In other words, AJ preserve original material not incorporated in the earlier CH. CH establish the framework but not the content of the early S.E.L.

IV. *The Text of MSS. C and H*

It is unfortunate that the early MS. H is both incomplete and carelessly copied. Its incompleteness, as already noted, is filled out satisfactorily by C. Its carelessness, also, is usually remedied by the text of C. But C, though more fairly copied than H, makes its own mistakes and transmits in turn doubtful readings. Neither manuscript can claim to be a good copy of the original. The following examples are typical of the variations between the two texts, and show, further, that H and C are independent copies. Complete readings of A and J are added for comparison.

1. *St. Alphege*, ll. 31–32 (I, p. 149)

    C. And nyme Alfe þe godeman · þat abbot is of Baþe
       And schere him & make him bissop · of Wynchestre raþe
    H. And nym Alphe þe gode man.· þat priour is of Baþe
       Smyre him and make him bischop.· at Wircestre wel raþe
    A. & nym alfe þe gode mon.· þat abbod is of baþe
       Smere him & make him biscop.· of Wynchestre raþe
    J. & nym alfe þe gode man. þat abbot is of baþe
       nime him & make him bischop. of Winchestre raþe

---

[1] Guthlac, as noted above, p. 4, is added in MS. C by a later hand.
[2] Laud has Hippolytus, Leger, Francis, Faith, Eustace; it lacks the Seven Sleepers, Justine, Brice, Fridesuide, Edward the Confessor. Cecilia is added in a later hand.

With reference to the ceremony of consecrating Alphege bishop H's reading 'Smyre him' is preferable to C's reading 'schere him' and is confirmed by A. J's fifteenth-century text has lost the reading and merely repeats the verb of l. 31. On the other hand, C's reading 'Wynchestre' for H's 'Wircestre' is factually correct and is confirmed by A and J.

2. *St. Theophilus, Miracle of Sir Emmery*, ll. 345-6 (I, p. 233)

   C. Þo hi come toward þe stede · þe deuel wel ȝare i seie
      Ac þo þe deuel oure Leuedi sei · he gan to grede heie
   H. Þo hi come toward þe stede: þe deuel was ȝare bifore
      Ac þo deuel oure leuedi iseȝ : he gan to grede sore
   A. Legend omitted
   J. Þo hi come touard þe stude þe deuel wel ȝare hi seie
      ac þo þe deuel our ladi isei. he gan to grede heie

In this case the variation between H and C in the second half of the lines represents independent readings, with C's reading confirmed by J.

3. *St. Matthew*, ll. 5-6 (II, p. 397)

   C. For as [oure] Louerd ȝeode ouerlond · sein Matheu he sei bicas
      Is mester do of tollares craft · for tollare he was
   H. For as oure louerd ȝeode ouer lond: seint Matheu he seȝ bicas
      His mester do of fissching: iwoned as he was
   A. Vor as our lord ouer lond eode: S. matheu he sei bicas
      His mester do of walkyng: vor walkare he was
   J. for as our lord ouer lond eode sein Matheu he sei bicas
      his mester do of walking for walkere he was

Of the three variant statements of St. Matthew's craft only C's is correct. St. Matthew was neither a fisher as H states, nor a walker as A J state, but a toller. A J's variant can be explained. The original *tollere* may have been miscopied or misread as *follere* (OE. *fullere*) or its dialectal form *uollere*. *Follere* is a synonym for *walkere* (OE. *wealcere*). *Tollares craft* in this way may become *uolleres craft* or *walkyng*.[1] The confusion in the text began early. Laud 108 shows a transitional stage in the wrong reading: 'his mester don of walkingue: for a follare he was'.[2] There is no apparent explanation for H's

---

[1] For a similar substitution see SS. Philip and James, I, p. 166, l. 87. C reads *Mid a uoulares perche*; H *Mid a folleres perche*; A *Myd a walkares perche*; J *Wit an walkeris sparþe*.

[2] E.E.T.S. o.s. 87, p. 77, l. 6. Horstmann notes in the margin, '*al*. tollare'.

reading, except that it may be an attempt to clear up a confused statement by substituting the craft of Simon and Andrew, fishers.

4. *St. John the Evangelist*, ll. 495-6 (II, p. 609).

   C. Non oþer þing of sein Ion · me nemiʒte an eorþe finde
      Al clene ich wene in heuene he is · þer nis no lyme bihinde
   H. Non oþer þing of seint Iohn: me nemiʒte an vrþe fynde
      Al clene i^c wene in heuene he is: þer nebileuede noþing bihynde
   A. Non oþer þing of S. Ion: me ne miʒte on erþe fynde
      Al clene i^c wene in heuene he is: þer nys noþing bihinde
   J. Non oþer þing of sein Ion · me ne myʒte an erþe finde
      Al clene ich wene in heuen he is þer nis no lime behinde

The variant readings in the second half of the second line are equally intelligible and equally indecisive as to the original reading. The cross-agreements, C with J and H with A, are a reminder that CH and AJ are not necessarily stable groupings.

5. *St. Thomas of Canterbury*, ll. 1051-4 (II, p. 644).

   C. Þis holyman wel mildeliche · out of þis court gan gon
      Þe kyng and al þat mid him was · wraþþede ham anon
      Hi cride on þis holyman · and belwede echon
      Mid as gret noise as al þe toun · biset were mid hore fon
   H. Þis holi man out of þis court: wel myldeliche gan gon
      Þat king & alle þat wiþ him were: wraþþede him anon
      Wiþ also grete noyse as al þe toun biset were wiþ here fon
      Þis holi man him wende forþ: as stille as eni ston
   A. Þis holimon out of þis court: wel mildelich gan gon
      Þe kyng & alle þat wiþ him were: wraþþede hem anon
      Hi cride on þis holi mon: & volwede vchon
      Myd a gret noise as all þe toun: biset were wiþ hore fon
   J. Þis holiman wel mildeliche out of þis court gan gon
      Þe king & al þat wit him were wraþþeþ hom anon
      Hi cride on þis holiman & belweþe echon
      Wit as grete [noise *om.*] as al þe toun biset were wit hor fon

The significant variations here are in the third line. H omits l. 1053, copies l. 1054 in its place, and adds a wholly conventional statement which interrupts the text and anticipates l. 1059. A's variant is the substitution of *volwede* (followed) for *belwede* (bellowed), which spoils the meaning. In both places the probably correct readings are preserved by C and J.

This sampling can only suggest the kind and amount of variation between the texts of C and H. In these five instances, the reading of C is preferable in two cases (3, 5); the reading of H in one case (1); the readings indecisive in two cases (2, 4).[1] Even in these comparatively early copies of the *S.E.L.* one is confronted with a corrupt and variable text as well as mutilated manuscripts. Neither C nor H will give a wholly satisfactory or complete text of the *S.E.L.*, but in general C seems to have the advantage over H in both respects.

The fact that in comparatively recent editions of separate legends of the *S.E.L.*[2] Ashmole 43 has been chosen for the text even where H or C was available raises the question whether A should not be selected in preference to the combination of H and C as representative of the whole work. It should be noted, first, that in each case the editors of these separate legends date A earlier than the date now generally accepted.[3] This presumed earlier dating would of itself give A an initial advantage which in fact cannot be claimed for that manuscript. In the second place the superiority of A in a single legend does not necessarily extend to the whole text. It is a characteristic of A in many legends to make continual omissions. For example, in comparison with C, in the legend of St. Patrick A omits 96 lines;[4] in comparison with CH, in St. Bartholomew, 54 lines; in St. Matthew, 38 lines; in St. Michael, Part II, 74 lines; in comparison with H, in All Souls, 137 lines; in St. Martin, 98 lines. These omissions vary in extent from single couplets to a passage of 88 lines (ll. 541-628) dropped in the legend of St. Patrick. Not all of them are arbitrary or careless omissions made by the scribe of A. MS. J shares many of them. For instance, J makes the same long omission just referred to in St. Patrick but does not make the series of short omissions which mark the text of A in All Souls. In other words, in comparison with CH and J the text of A in several items is noticeably shortened.[5] In this respect the text of A is no better representative of the *S.E.L.* than that of CH.

[1] A close comparison of the complete text of St. Alphege and of St. Mary of Egypt gives similar results.
[2] St. Brendan, edited by Bälz, 1909; St. Juliana, edited by Schleich, 1927; St. Thomas of Canterbury, edited by Thiemke, 1919.
[3] Bälz, p. i, 'erste Halfte XIV Jh.'; Schleich, p. 19, 'um 1300'; Thiemke, p. i, '*ca.* 1310'. See p. 5, note 7, above.
[4] The specific lines omitted in each of the examples given above are recorded in the variant readings.
[5] Another instance of A's shortened texts is the legend of St. Eustace (not in CH), which runs to 331 lines in Laud (E.E.T.S. o.s. 87, p. 393), to 326 lines in J, to 213 lines in A.

INTRODUCTION 15

In the reading of individual lines, as the variants show, A frequently supports H in the correction of obvious errors in C. On the other hand A in many cases offers readings unlike those of CH. Which manuscript in these instances is correct is another problem, the problem of the critical text.

v. *MS. Laud 108 and MSS. C and H*

As the earliest surviving manuscript of the *S.E.L.*, Laud 108 is naturally of special importance. In spite of its incompleteness and disorder it foreshadows the pattern and content of the later *S.E.L.* And in the text of certain of the individual legends Laud offers variations that raise and complicate the whole question of origins and original text. It has been customary, for example, to speak of the 'Laud text' and the 'Harley text' of the life of St. Thomas of Canterbury[1] and of the 'shorter' and 'longer' versions of the life of St. Bridget in Laud and Corpus respectively.[2] These points of difference need further clarification.

First, in regard to order, while Laud as it stands is obviously without plan, a plan similar to that of MSS. C and H lies behind its disorder. The 'prologue' attached in L to the legend of St. Fabian makes this fact clear:[3]

> Al þis bok is i-maked of holi dawes: and of holie mannes liues
> Þat soffreden for ore louerdes loue: pinene manie and riue,
> Þat ne spareden for none eiȝe: godes weorkes to wurche;
> Of ȝwas liues ȝwane heore feste fallez: men redez in holi churche.
> Þei ich of alle ne mouwe nouȝt telle: ichulle telle of some,
> Ase euerech feste after oþur: In þe ȝere doth come.—
> Þe furste feste þat in þe ȝere comez: we cleopiez ȝeres-dai . . .[4]

The prologue is followed by brief statements on the feast of the Circumcision (4 ll.) and of Epiphany (12 ll.) and a four-line life of St. Fabian. The first line of this prologue summarizes the content of the work—feast-days and saints' legends; the sixth and seventh lines indicate the order—1 January the starting-point. This is the same order as that of MS. C and presumably of MS. H. The distinction

---
[1] *Index* 116, No. 728.
[2] *Index* 153, Nos. 2871 and 2872.
[3] See Minnie E. Wells, *P.M.L.A.* li (1936), 340 f.
[4] E.E.T.S. o.s. 87, p. 177, ll. 1 f.

between the actual arrangement of material in L and in CH is merely that of order and disorder, not of different pattern.

In regard to content, MSS. CH add to both the *temporale* and the *sanctorale* material in Laud. The Annunciation (No. 27) and the movable feasts, Septuagesima (No. 28), Lent (No. 29), Easter (No. 30), and Rogationtide (No. 35), are included in MSS. CH.[1] Both C and H contain the Assumption (No. 60), but that feast apparently was originally in MS. L also, according to a marginal note of the fifteenth century on f. 10: 'verte ad istud signum + in isto libro in principio libri et ibi inveniet plus de passione domini post assumptionem ste. Mariae.'[2]

The additions in MSS. CH compared with Laud are more extensive in the *sanctorale* material. They include twenty-six lives of saints,[3] six miracles of the Virgin following the legend of St. Theophilus (No. 45), two lives of 'traitors', Judas (No. 89) and Pilate (No. 90). The inclusion of additional English saints, Aldhelm, Alphege, Chad, Oswald the Bishop, Swithun, and of the Celtic St. Patrick, emphasizes the local colouring of the whole collection.

Of the seven omissions of saints' lives in MSS. CH as compared with Laud,[4] that of chief interest, because of the proposed assignment of the authorship of the *S.E.L.* to the friars,[5] is the absence of the lives of both St. Francis and St. Dominic. There is a gap in MS. H between f. 105 and f. 106 where the life of St. Dominic would fit chronologically—his day is 4 August—but MS. C in the correspond-

[1] MS. H, as noted above, p. 7, contains also the Passion, incomplete through loss of leaves.
[2] Horstmann, *Archiv*, xlix (1872), 397, and *Leben Jesu* (Münster, 1873), p. 69. The evidence that this note might seem to furnish for claiming that MS. L also contained the *S.E.L.* version of the Passion is not decisive, since the note follows an incomplete text not of the *S.E.L. Passion* but of the so-called 'long life of Christ', distinct from the *Passion* but early confused with it. See Beatrice D. Brown, E.E.T.S. o.s. 169, p. viii and note 4. The same ambiguity of content would not apply to the Assumption.
[3] Listed alphabetically these are Aldhelm (No. 42), Alphege (No. 32), Anastasia (No. 84), Andrew (No. 80), Benedict (No. 26), Chad (No. 20), Christina (No. 54), Denys (No. 67), Giles (No. 62), Hilary (No. 4), Jerome (No. 66), Juliana (No. 17), Longinus (No. 22), Luke (No. 68), Margaret (No. 52), Martha (No. 57), Oswald the Bishop (No. 19), Patrick (No. 23), Peter the Dominican (No. 36), Peter (No. 48), Quentin (No. 71), Simon and Jude (No. 70), Stephen (No. 85), Swithun (No. 50), Valentine (No. 16).
[4] These are Dominic, Eustace, Faith, Francis, Hippolytus, Leger, Silvester.
[5] See Beatrice D. Brown, E.E.T.S. o.s. 169, pp. xciii f.; Minnie E. Wells, *P.M.L.A.* li. 359 f.; H. G. Pfander, *The Popular Sermon of the Medieval Friar in England*, p. 12 and note 42; W. A. Hinnebusch, *The Early English Friars Preachers*, p. 310.

ing section of text is undamaged and does not include St. Dominic. No mutilation occurs in either manuscript at the point where the life of St. Francis (4 Oct.) belongs. The argument for friar authorship in general does not depend primarily on the presence or absence of the lives of the two founders. The argument for Dominican as against Franciscan authorship in part does.[1] The elimination of both lives, if it were intentional, at this early stage in the growth of the S.E.L. would seem to remove any trace of possible discrimination between the two orders. But on the other hand, both C and H contain the life of St. Peter the Dominican preacher and martyr (No. 36), which fact, if the canon of contents of the S.E.L. were not so uncertain, might be counted as a trace of Dominican sympathy.

The essential differences between MS. L and MSS. CH are not these mechanical divergences of order and disorder, omission or addition of separate items, but the variations in content of items common to both groups. The items particularly in question are (1) Prologue and St. Fabian (L No. 28 and C Nos. 1, 2, 3, 6); (2) St. Bridget (L No. 32, C No. 12); (3) St. Edward the Elder (L No. 17, C No. 24); (4) Conversion of St. Paul (L No. 31, C No. 49); (5) St. Thomas of Canterbury (L No. 27, C No. 87).[2] In the case of St. Edward and of the Conversion of St. Paul, the difference is merely one of length, of a longer or shorter version. In the other cases more complex variations of content make the Laud and Corpus–Harley copies almost different versions.

To take the simpler cases first: the life of St. Edward the Elder in MS. L runs to 232 lines; in MS. C[3] to 262 lines. MS. C adds a passage of 24 lines (93–116) on St. Dunstan's prophecy of disaster for St. Edward's successor. These lines are inserted after l. 90 of the Laud text. Four scattered couplets are also added in MS. C, after ll. 2, 78, 158, 204 respectively of MS. L, making a total addition of 32 lines. One couplet in MS. L (ll. 39–40) is omitted in MS. C. Throughout the text common to both L and C only two pairs of rimes differ.[4] The variations in wording within the lines are not unusual or

---

[1] See Beatrice D. Brown, op. cit., p. cx; Minnie E. Wells, op. cit., p. 359.

[2] The legend of St. Mary Magdalene is not included in this comparison. The Laud text, as is well known, is an entirely different text written partially in stanzas, not couplets. See E.E.T.S. o.s. 87, p. 462 and note.

[3] MS. H is defective in the section including this legend.

[4] (1) C ll. 31–32, *wiþ eny þing*: *imad king* = L ll. 29–30, *in ani manere*: *kyng were*. (2) C ll. 209–10, *leide þere*: *verst arere* = L ll. 181–2, *huy ladde*: *a-rerd hadde*.

sufficiently extensive to constitute the texts of MS. L and MS. C different versions of the St. Edward legend, except in a rather small variation in the length of the two texts.[1]

The legend of St. Paul presents a similar kind of variation. MS. L gives only the Conversion (74 ll.); MSS. CH the Conversion and the later life (284 ll.). In the section on the Conversion MSS. CH add 4 lines (C 13–16) after Laud's l. 12 and at the point of transition from the Conversion to the later life substitute a different couplet (C 67–68) for Laud's ll. 63–64. Otherwise within this section the texts are similar in content and wording, with only one variation in rimes.[2] Here as in the legend of St. Edward the essential difference is addition of material. But in this case the addition is made not within the text but to the text. Apparently MSS. CH combine two festivals of St. Paul, the Conversion (25 Jan.) and the Commemoration (30 June).[3]

In the legend of St. Bridget the variations seem somewhat more complicated. MS. L contains the so-called 'shorter version' of 58 lines; MS. C the 'longer version' of 270 lines.[4] Of MS. L's 58 lines, forty are clearly paralleled in MS. C;[5] twelve (ll. 25–36) recount a miracle of St. Bridget not included in MS. C; six (ll. 1–6) are completely divergent from the text of MS. C. In the 40 lines which correspond the rime-words with one exception (L ll. 7–8 and C ll. 143–4) are the same, the wording practically the same in several lines, sufficiently similar in the rest to indicate a common source. At the points in the narrative of MS. L where MS. C has additional material,[6] the breaks are clean cut between one incident and the next. Only the divergent opening lines 1–6 suggest a different source for MS. L and MS. C.

[1] The newly reported Winchester MS. (see p. 1 above) agrees in length, 232 lines, with Laud, omitting the 24-line prophecy. It also agrees with L in the rimes listed in the preceding note. But like MS. C it has an additional couplet after Laud l. 158 (= C ll. 185–6).
[2] C ll. 51–52, *wel bliþe: he herede God fale siþe* = L ll. 47–48, *wel bliþe: ech ȝwyle him þouȝte fiue*. In the points of difference noted above the Winchester MS. agrees with Laud and like Laud contains only the Conversion.
[3] No MS. of the *S.E.L.* contains a life of Paul without the Conversion; see *Index* 483, No. 3041.
[4] See *Index* 453, Nos. 2871 and 2872. MS. H is defective in this section.
[5] L ll. 7–24 = C ll. 145–60; L ll. 37–42 = C ll. 165–70; L ll. 43–58 = C ll. 253–66, 269–70.
[6] The additional lines in MS. C are 7–142; 161–4 at the conclusion of an incident common to both texts; 171–252; 267–8 in the conventional conclusion of the legend.

INTRODUCTION

L reads:

> Seinte Bride of hei3e men: In scotlond heo cam,
> Of riche men and of gret power: In lawe of cristindom.
> Þis Maide bi-gan wel 3ong: to beo of porture hende;
> Þare ne scholde vil dede ne word: neuere fram hire wende.
> heo bigan ore louerd crist to serui: in worde and in dede;
> 3wane hire 3ongue felawes weren atþe plei3: hire oresones heo seide.
>
> (E.E.T.S. o.s. 87, p. 192)

C reads:

> Sein Bride þat holi maide · of Irlonde was
> Bi3ute he[o] was in spousbruche · in a wonder cas
> Duptak was hure uader name · þat ispoused hadde a wif
> In luþer bileue of paynime · hi ladde hore lif
> A seruant he hadde inis hous · Broksek was hure name
> Þis Duptak biso3te hure · of lecherie and ssame
>
> (I, p. 37)

The lines in MS. L are conventional and general. Except for the reference to Scotland they might apply to any precocious saint-to-be. In contradiction to the statements in MS. C, MS. L implies that St. Bridget was born of Christian parents, omits the names of her father and mother and stepmother, and avoids any reference to her pagan and unhallowed begetting. In fact the whole early history of St. Bridget and her stepfather, the magician, is dropped. MS. L begins the story at the point where St. Bridget, as a grown girl, is put in charge of her mother's dairy. At this point, also, the material common to MS. L and MS. C begins. And here occurs the only difference in rime-pairs between their common text.

L reads:

> hire moder louede hire swiþe wel: þat, þo heo was of elde,
> Al hire chese and al hire milk: heo bi-tok hire to welde,
>
> (E.E.T.S. o.s. 87, p. 192, ll. 7–8)

C reads:

> Hure moder & eke hure hosebonde · toke þe maide to welde
> Chese and botere & hore kun · atom and eke auelde
>
> (I, p. 42, ll. 143–4)

The variant half-line, 'þat, þo heo was of elde', obviously serves in MS. L as a link between the opening lines and the later story of St. Bridget. The transition is sudden enough. MS. L in the opening section, and throughout the legend, gives the impression of piecemeal composition. The question rises in one's mind whether these opening lines were not 'made up' to introduce this highly selective and abbreviated account. Who made them up, the scribe of MS. L or of his copy, only a fuller knowledge of the direct sources of the S.E.L. legend can decide. The fact remains that these opening lines are the only significant variants between the texts of MS. L and MS. C. They seem to have little authority compared with the text of MS. C. The chief divergence remains one of amount of material.

Again, in the legend of St. Thomas of Canterbury a distinction is commonly made between the Laud and Harley (Corpus–Harley) texts. The legend may be divided into three sections: Section I, a brief account of the parents of St. Thomas, his English father, Gilbert, and his Saracen mother, Alisaundre; Section II, an extensive life of St. Thomas; Section III, a brief account of the translation of the Saint. The legend, furthermore, has three different openings. The Laud text begins with the lines:

> Wolle ȝe nouþe i-heore þis englische tale: þat is here i-write
> Of seint Thomas of Caunterburi: al-hou he was bi-ȝite?[1]

The Corpus text begins:

> Gilberd was sein Thomas fader · þat triwe man was & god...[2]

The third opening, which is found in manuscripts representative of both Laud and Corpus–Harley texts, is as follows:

> Engelond glad þou beo: vor þou miȝt wel eþe
> & al holi chirche also: for one monnes deþe
> Þe erchebiscop S. Thomas: þat hire wel dere boȝte
> Wiþ his derworþe brayn: þat þe scharpe swerd soȝte.[3]

Before discussing this variable third opening the chief distinction between the Laud and CH texts should be pointed out. In the Laud text Section I[4] totals 202 lines. After the introductory couplet, addressed to the audience, Section I recounts the story of Thomas's

---

[1] E.E.T.S. o.s. 87, p. 106, ll. 1–2. See *Register*, ii. 397, No. 2677; *Index* 669, No. 4171. The opening lines of Laud are also printed by Thiemke, p. 1.
[2] E.E.T.S. 236, p. 610, l. 1. See *Register*, ii. 93, No. 565; *Index* 144, No. 907.
[3] E.E.T.S. 236, p. 610, l. 1, variant reading quoted from Ashm. 43. See *Register*, ii. 78, No. 461; *Index* 116, No. 728. The text of Ashm. 43 is also printed in Thiemke, pp. 14 f.
[4] Thiemke prints two texts of Section I: pp. 1 f. Fassung a from Laud 108; pp. 14 f. Fassung b from Ashm. 43. See his discussion, p. iii.

INTRODUCTION

parentage and birth and ends with a couplet also addressed to the audience:

> Of is fader and of is moder: ȝe habbez i-heord telle,
> Acke of seint thomas him-selue: þat beste cometh nou to spelle.[1]

Between Section I and Section II the Laud text inserts the quatrain addressed to England, just referred to as the third opening, and then continues with the long story of St. Thomas (Section II, 2,198 ll.) and his translation (Section III, 74 ll.).

In the CH text, Section I is without formal introduction. It begins directly with naming Thomas's father, Gilbert, tells in 148 lines the story of his parents and his birth, and without break continues with the life of St. Thomas (Section II, 2,296 ll.) and his translation (Section III, 74 ll.).

In both the Laud and the CH texts the general outline of the story of St. Thomas's parents is similar. Details, however, frequently vary. The Laud text (l. 141), for example, says that the Saracen princess was christened 'Alisaundre'; the CH text gives her no name. Moreover, the actual wording of the two texts is quite distinct. The 202 lines of the Laud text and the 148 lines of the CH text have only five rime-pairs in common, and even in these few instances, the correspondence in wording is limited usually to these riming words.[2] Occasionally there is an echo of wording between the two texts[3] and

---

[1] E.E.T.S., o.s. 87, p. 112, ll. 201–2; Thiemke, p. 13.

[2] The examples from Laud quoted from E.E.T.S. o.s. 87.

The examples from CH quoted from E.E.T.S. 236.

(1) L 13–14
heo hadden i-beo so longue,
In bendes swiþe strongue,

CH 9–10
to of swinke hore me[te] stronge
hi liuede ham þoȝte to longe

(2) L 39–40
onder-fonge: for þe loue of þe,
treweliche weddi me.

CH 39–40
bileue for loue of þe
ȝif þou wolt spousi me

(3) L 61–62
ne speken no-þe-mo;
to londone for-to go.

CH 51–52
he and oþer mo
me ne miȝte ham noȝt ofgo

(4) L 143–4
wel glad of him heo was.
he bi-ȝat seint thomas.

CH 119–20
bitwene ham biȝete was
þe holy sein Thomas

(5) L 173–4
þat he hadde In þouȝt
þare-a-ȝein heo nolde beo nouȝt

CH 135–6
ȝif þou hast wille & þoȝt
ne bilef it for me noȝt

[3] Cf. L 147–8: *Anon-riȝtes a-morewe: so gret wille him nam/to þe holi londe for-to gon: þat he cam evore fram*/with CH 121–2: *Þis Gilberd anon amorwe · so gret wille him com to/To wende eft to þe Holy Lond · þat he nuste wat do.* See also L 83–84 and CH 91–92; L 93–94 and CH 95–96.

in two instances a first half-line in one is the second half-line in the other.¹ In the Laud text the last lines of Section I (ll. 188–202) tell of Gilbert's return to London and of the precocity of the young Thomas. Some of this information is repeated in Laud in the early lines of Section II (ll. 208 f.). In the CH text (ll. 148–52) there is no break between Sections I and II and no repetition of material. Early in Section II the Laud text (at l. 211) and the CH text (at l. 153) begin to run parallel and so continue throughout the rest of the legend. The difference in amount of material in Section II and III is just under 100 lines (L = 2,275 lines; CH = 2,370 lines), a comparatively small proportion considering the total number of lines. Changes in rime-pairs also are relatively few, so that one may say a common groundwork of text is preserved in both Laud and CH. Within the lines the readings often vary widely but not to the extent of constituting different versions. The marked divergences between the Laud and CH texts, in amount of material, rime-pairs, and wording, occur only in Section I, the story of St. Thomas's parents.

To return to the third opening, the quatrain beginning 'Engelond glad þou beo'.² These lines are used with four different connexions. (1) In two manuscripts, A and J, they introduce Section I, the story of Gilbert, in the CH version.³ (2) In one manuscript, Stowe 949, they introduce Section I in the Laud version.⁴ (3) In three manuscripts, Laud 108 (S.C. 1486), Vernon (S.C. 3938), and Lambeth 223, they serve as the link between Sections I and II, that is, between the story of Gilbert in the Laud version and the life of St. Thomas.⁵ (4) In one

---

¹ L 31 (1st half): *And of ȝwat bi-leue he were*: CH 30 (2nd half): *& wat hare bileue were*. See also L 124 and CH 106.

² See p. 20 above. For the list of MSS. with this beginning see *Register*, ii. 78, No. 461; *Index* 116, No. 728. For corrections to be made in these entries see notes 3 and 5 below. Thiemke, pp. 13 and 14, prints the Laud and Ashmole 43 texts of the quatrain with variant readings from other MSS. of the legend of St. Thomas known to him. He does not include Bodl. Add. MS. C. 220 (S.C. 29430) or Camb. Univ. Add. MS. 3039. The exact use of the quatrain in these two MSS. has still to be checked.

³ The *Register* and *Index* (see note 5) state that the MSS. listed under the opening in question are 'Laud' texts 'without the introductory section (202 vv.) dealing with Gilbert, St. Thomas's father'. This might mean that such MSS. had the Harley text of Section I. But the statement in the cross-reference, *Register*, No. 2677, and *Index*, No. 4171, is quite definite: 'which omit the story of Gilbert.' In that case the statement under No. 461 and No. 728 is incorrect for MSS. A, J, and Stowe 949.

⁴ See Thiemke, p. 1, variants on ll. 1–2, and p. 13, variants on ll. 203–8. See note 3 above.

⁵ For the readings in these three MSS. see Thiemke, p. 14, variants on ll. 1–4.

INTRODUCTION

manuscript, Laud Misc. 463 (S.C. 1596), they introduce directly Section II, the life of St. Thomas, omitting the story of Gilbert.

In the shifting position of this quatrain the fact and something of the process of manipulation of material in the *S.E.L.* are evident. The preservation of these lines in Laud indicates that they belong to an early stage in the shaping of the material. Their use in Laud, it has been noted, is an interruption and leads to the repetition of statements about the young Thomas. In the next earliest manuscripts, CH, the quatrain is dropped altogether; there is a different version of the Gilbert story with no interruptions or repetitions. When the quatrain reappears in Ashmole 43 it is attached to this CH version of the Gilbert story. It is not clear whether Laud represents the first fumbling approach to this smoother text, or a corruption of it. It is clear that the story of Gilbert with its variant opening and closing lines has undergone the chief revision in this legend and constitutes the real distinction between the Laud and Harley (CH) versions.[1]

Finally, to put first things last, the differences between the Prologue and St. Fabian in MS. L and in MSS. CH should be pointed out. In MS. L the introductory material, out of place as already noted,[2] consists of an embryonic prologue of 6 lines, followed by brief accounts of the feasts of '3eres Day' and Epiphany and a 4-line life of St. Fabian. This 6-line prologue has nothing in common with the 68-line *Banna Sanctorum* of MS. C, except its function, a general statement of the subject of the work. None of the 4 lines which constitute the account of '3eres Day' in MS. L is repeated in the 28 lines given to that feast in MS. C.[3] Both MS. L and MS. C devote 12 lines to the feast of Epiphany without correspondence in a single line and with only one rime in common.[4] The 4-line life of St. Fabian in MS. L has no resemblance in text to the 24-line life in MS. C.[5]

Since the quatrain on these three cases occurs within the text, not at the beginning, the MSS. in question are not included in the *Register* under No. 461 or in the *Index* under No. 728.

[1] The omission of the story of Gilbert altogether in MS. Laud Misc. 463 (S.C. 1596) is apparently a unique and late revision.

[2] See p. 15 above.

[3] E.E.T.S. o.s. 87, p. 177, ll. 7–10; E.E.T.S. 235, No. 2.

[4] E.E.T.S. o.s. 87, p. 178, ll. 11–22; E.E.T.S. 235, No. 3. The corresponding rimes are L 21–22 and C 3–4.

[5] E.E.T.S. o.s. 87, p. 178, ll. 23–26; E.E.T.S. 235, No. 6. The distinction between longer and shorter versions of SS. Fabian and Sebastian noted in the *Register*, ii. 267, Nos. 1810 and 1811, and in the *Index* 458, Nos. 2895 and 2896

To summarize these differences between certain items common to MS. L and MS. C (or CH), it is clear that in some instances (St. Edward the Elder, St. Paul, St. Bridget) the difference is primarily one of more or less material; in others (St. Fabian, '3eres Day', Epiphany, Section I of St. Thomas), of different handling of similar material; in one case (Prologue) of completely different material. The incompleteness in every case lies with MS. L. Here a knowledge of exact sources might determine whether the scribe of MS. L is responsible for such omissions. The inadequacies of other items, such as the Laud Prologue and St. Fabian, and the inexpertness of the Laud link between Sections I and II of St. Thomas suggest various and unsatisfactory explanations: deficient source, poor copy, unskilful composer. When to all these differences are added the extensive variants in the readings of single lines throughout the text it is obvious that the place of MS. Laud in the history of the text of the *S.E.L.* is extremely uncertain and that the problems of the *S.E.L.* whether textual or literary must be worked out piecemeal through the study of separate items.

vi. *Conclusion: The Value of the 'S.E.L.'*

The *S.E.L.* is and will remain a rich field for scholarly research which will materially increase knowledge of its manuscripts, text, authorship, sources, and affiliation with other medieval writings. That research will be well bestowed. The *S.E.L.* is a valuable repository of information on more than one aspect of medieval culture. But primarily it is a human document quite consciously aimed at getting and holding the interest of its audience. That the author was a friar—or friars—and the audience laymen has been effectively argued.[1] The material this friar preacher put before his hearers— true stories of God's 'hardy knights'—had and still has its appeal as story and biography as well as ideal and example.

In range of time these stories extend from the days of Christ and

---

applies only to the life of St. Fabian. In both MSS. L and C the life of St. Sebastian runs to 90 lines with only slight variations in the wordings. A small error in the listing of the MSS. of the short life of St. Fabian should be noted: Lambeth MS. 223, f. 53ª, contains the 4-line life, beginning 'Saynt ffabian xiij 3ere: Pope was in Rome', and should therefore be listed under No. 1811 in the *Register* and under No. 2896 in the *Index*.

[1] See p. 16 above.

the Apostles to the almost contemporary period of St. Thomas and St. Edmund, archbishops of Canterbury. Their variety is equally wide. Some of the legends, such as those of Fabian and Sebastian, Valentine, Oswald the King, are mere sketches. Some of the early martyrdoms—those of Lucy, Agnes, Christina, for example—tend to follow a standard pattern: conversion and conflict with orthodoxy, torture, and triumph. But it is variety, both in incident and in character, that impresses even the modern reader of this collection. Muscular Christianity finds an early and cheerful exponent in St. Christopher; St. Bridget displays innocent ingenuity in her charitable if high-handed disposal of her parents' property; in St. Bartholomew, Christian comeliness is portrayed and its opposite in the fiend he exorcizes; the aged St. John the Evangelist, playing with his partridge, meets the taunts of the young worldling with Christian benevolence and wisdom.

The collection of this varied material has included some subject-matter not properly saint's legend. The second part of *St. Michael* deals principally with the fallen angels in their later role of evil spirits; the third part, as is well known, is a summary of medieval natural science and physiology. *St. Brendan* is a wonder-voyage and *St. Patrick* a visit to Purgatory. The material in *All Saints* and *All Souls* is largely propaganda to encourage offerings in commemoration of souls and saints. The stories of Pilate and Judas, among the most interesting of the legends, are early, if perhaps unintentional, studies of criminal tendencies abetted by environment and circumstance. And in *St. Thomas à Becket* and to a lesser degree in *St. Edmund Rich* history encroaches on legend.

To the interest of this subject-matter the passing comments of the narrator add their flavour. Whether such comment is original with the author or transferred from his source is still an open question. It belongs in part to the technique of oral delivery. Conventional is the pious concluding prayer in which the audience is invited to join; less commonplace, the call for show of interest and approval in such lines as these:

Nou an alle deuelwey · and necome he neuere aȝen
Wy sitte ȝe so stille · wi ne segge ȝe amen[1]

Bantering asides purposely belittle the audience. Referring to the

---

[1] *St. Peter* (No. 48), ll. 391–2. See also *St. Alphege* (No. 32), ll. 117–18; *St. Benedict* (No. 26), ll. 45–46; *St. James* (No. 55), ll. 384–6.

three riddles which the devil in disguise puts to St. Andrew in disguise the narrator comments:

> Nou wo worþe is pol so wis: & sorwe him come to
> Ichot þer nys non of ȝou: þat couþe aposy so[1]

And understatement is a common device for emphasis. St. Edmund reprimands rather than rewards the messengers who have brought him news of his election as archbishop, and the narrator remarks:

> Here ȝiftes hi miȝte eþe bere: þat seint Edmund hem caste[2]

Throughout the work the narrator is concerned to keep the contact between his subject and his audience alive and personal.

No one will claim that the *S.E.L.* is a work of art. Yet it has the marks of literary workmanship. It begins, in the form represented by MSS. C and H, with a show of conventional medieval rhetoric. The *Banna Sanctorum* is a carefully worked-out symbol of Christendom, represented first as the 'new fruit' of God's garden watered by the blood of saints and martyrs; and then as Christ's territory or kingdom defended in battle by the same blood of saints and martyrs. The last of the saints' legends, that of St. Thomas of Canterbury, ends with a similar piece of medieval rhetoric, the climax of fateful Tuesdays which marked St. Thomas's career. But it is not from such evidences of formal art that the stories of the *S.E.L.* derive, in varying degree, their effectiveness. It is rather their simplicity and directness, and a certain hardness and heartiness on the part of both their saints and their sinners, that give these legends the perennial appeal of the good fight well fought.

---

[1] *St. Andrew* (No. 80), ll. 213–14. See also *St Jerome* (No. 66), ll. 73–74; *St. Michael* (No. 65), l. 150; *11,000 Virgins* (No. 69), ll. 57–58.

[2] *St. Edmund* (No. 76), l. 429. See also *St. Edmund* (No. 76), ll. 423-4; *All Souls* (No. 73), l. 190; *St. Lucy* (No. 82), ll. 133-4.

APPENDIX I

Bibliography

BÄLZ, MARTHA. *Die ME. Brendanlegende des Gloucesterlegendars*, Berlin, 1909.
BIRCH, WALTER DE GRAY. *Memorials of Saint Guthlac of Crowland*, Wisbech, 1881.
BLACK, WILLIAM HENRY. *The Life and Martyrdom of Thomas Beket, Archbishop of Canterbury*, Percy Soc. LIX, London, 1845.
BOLTON, WHITNEY FRENCH. *The Middle English and Latin Poems of Saint Guthlac*, Princeton Univ. diss., 1955, Microfilm Publication No. 13669. (See *Dissertation Abstracts XV*, No. 11 (1955), p. 2201.)
BROWN, BEATRICE DAW. *The Southern Passion*, E.E.T.S. o.s. 169, London, 1927.
BROWN, CARLETON. 'The *Cursor Mundi* and the "Southern Passion"', *M.L.N.* xxvi (1911), 15.
—— *A Register of Middle English Religious & Didactic Verse*, 2 vols., Oxford, 1916, 1920.
—— and ROBBINS, ROSSELL HOPE. *The Index of Middle English Verse*, New York, 1943.
COCKAYNE, OSWALD. *Þe Liflade of St. Juliana*, E.E.T.S. o.s. 51, London, 1872.
—— *Seinte Marherete, The Meiden ant Martyr, in Old English*, E.E.T.S. o.s. 13, London, 1866.
FORSTMANN, H. 'Untersuchungen zur Guthlac-Legende', *Bonner Beiträge zur Anglistik*, xii (1902), 1.
FURNIVALL, FREDERICK J. *Early English Poems and Lives of Saints*, Berlin, 1862.
—— *Originals and Analogues of Some of Chaucer's Canterbury Tales*, Chaucer Soc. 2nd Series, 10, Part II, No. 12, London, 1875.
HEUSER, W. *Die Kildare-Gedichte*, Bonner Beiträge zur Anglistik, xiv, Bonn, 1904.
HINNEBUSCH, WILLIAM A. *The Early English Friars Preachers*, Instit. hist. ff. praed. Romae ad s. Sabinae, Dissert. Hist. XIV, Rome, 1951.
HORSTMANN, CARL. *Altenglische Legenden*, Paderborn, 1875.
—— *Altenglische Legenden*, Neue Folge, Heilbronn, 1881.
—— 'Die altenglische Legende von St. Brendan', *Archiv f. d. Studium d. neueren Sprachen u. Literaturen*, liii (1874), 17.
—— *Leben Jesu, ein Fragment, und Kindheit Jesu*, Münster, 1873.
—— 'Die Legenden des MS. Laud 108', *Archiv f. d. Studium d. neueren Sprachen u. Literaturen*, xlix (1872), 395.
—— *The Early South-English Legendary*, E.E.T.S. o.s. 87, London, 1887.

JACOBUS DE VORAGINE. *Legenda Aurea*, ed. Th. Graesse, Dresden, 1846.
LILJEGREN, S. B. 'Four Middle English Versions of the Legend of the Eleven Thousand Virgins', *Englische Studien*, lvii (1923), 85.
LOVEWELL, BERTHA ELLEN. *The Life of St. Cecilia*, Yale Studies in English, III, Boston, 1898.
MÄTZNER, EDUARD. *Altenglische Sprachproben*, Berlin, 1867.
MCCANN, DOM JUSTIN. 'Early English Verses on St. Benedict', *Downside Review*, xli (1923), 44.
MOORE, GRACE E. *The Middle English Verse Life of Edward the Confessor*, Univ. of Pennsylvania diss., Philadelphia, 1942.
MORRIS, RICHARD. *Legends of the Holy Rood*, E.E.T.S. o.s. 46, London, 1871.
—— and SKEAT, W. W. *Specimens of Early English*, Part II, 2nd edition, Oxford, 1889.
PFANDER, HOMER G. *The Popular Sermon of the Medieval Friar in England*, New York Univ. diss., New York, 1937.
SAMPSON, GEORGE. *The Cambridge Book of Prose and Verse*, Cambridge, 1924.
SCHLEICH, G. 'Die Gloucestershire-Legende der heiligen Juliane', *Archiv f. d. Studium d. neueren Sprachen u. Literaturen*, cli (1927), 19.
SCHUBEL, FRIEDRICH. *Die südenglische Legende von den elftausend Jungfrauen*, Greifswalder Beiträge zur Literatur- und Stilforschung, 21, Greifswald, 1938.
SERJEANTSON, MARY S. 'The Dialects of the West Midlands in Middle English', *R.E.S.* iii (1927), 54, 186, 319.
THIEMKE, HERMANN. *Die ME. Thomas Beket-Legende des Gloucesterlegendars*, Palaestra, 131, Berlin, 1919.
TRYON, RUTH WILSON. 'Miracles of Our Lady in Middle English Verse', *P.M.L.A.* xxxviii (1923), 308.
WARD, H. L. D. *Catalogue of Romances in the Department of MSS. in the British Museum*, ii, London, 1893.
WELLS, JOHN EDWIN. *A Manual of the Writings in Middle English 1050–1400*, New Haven, 1916.
—— Supplements 1–8, New Haven, 1919–41; Supplement 9, ed. Beatrice Daw Brown, Eleanor K. Heningham, and Francis Lee Utley, New Haven, 1951.
WELLS, MINNIE E. 'The Structural Development of the South English Legendary', *J.E.G.P.* xli (1942), 320.
WRIGHT, THOMAS. *Popular Treatises on Science written during the Middle Ages*, London, 1841.
—— *St. Brandan: A Medieval Legend of the Sea in English Verse and Prose*, Percy Soc. XIV, London, 1844.
WÜLCKER, RICHARD PAUL. *Altenglisches Lesebuch*, Halle, 1874.
ZUPITZA, J. 'Zwei Mittelenglischen Legendenhandschriften', *Anglia*, i (1878), 392.

APPENDIX II

Table of Contents in Corpus Christi College, Cambridge, MS. 145
(Written in red by the second hand)[1]

f. ii^b col. 1
[*First item illegible*]
Circumcisio domini (1 Jan.)
Epiphania domini (6 Jan.)
de Sancto Hillario (14 Jan.)
de Sancto Wolstano (19 Jan.)
de Sancto Fabiano (20 Jan.)
de Sancto Sebastiano (20 Jan.)
de Sancta Agneta (21 Jan.)
de Sancta Agneta secunda
de Sancto Vincencio (22 Jan.)
de Sancto Iuliano (27 Jan.)
de Sancto Iuliano (?27 Jan.)
de Sancta Brigida (1 Feb.)
de Sancto Blasio (3 Feb.)
de Sancta Agatha (5 Feb.)
de Sancta Scolastica (10 Feb.)
de Sancto Valentino (14 Feb.)
de Sancta Iuliana (16 Feb.)
de Sancto Matheo (24 Feb.)
de Sancto Oswaldo (28 Feb.)
de Sancto Ceddo (2 Mar.)
de Sancto Grigorio (12 Mar.)
de Sancto Longino (15 Mar.)
de Sancto Patricio (17 Mar.)
de Sancto Edwardo (18 Mar.)
de Sancto Cudberto (20 Mar.)
de Sancto Benedicto (21 Mar.)
de Anunciacione dominica
   (25 Mar.)
de Septuagesima
de Quinquagesima
de Quatragesima
de Pasca

de Sancta Maria egipciaca
   (2 Apr.)
de Sancto Alphego (19 Apr.)
de Sancto Georgeo (23 Apr.)
de Sancto Marco (25 Apr.)
de Letenia maiore
de Letenia minore
de Sancto Petre predicatore
   (29 Apr.)
de Sancto Philippo (1 May)
de Sancto Iacabo (1 May)
de Invencione crucis (3 May)
de Sancto Curiaco (4 May)
de Sancto Brendano (16 May)
de Sancto Donstano (19 May)
de Sancto Aldelmo (25 May)
de Sancto Augustino Anglorum
   (28 May)
de Sancto Barnaba (11 June)

f. ii^b col. 2
de Sancto Theophilo (?4 Feb.)
Miracula sancte Marie
de Sancto Albano (22 June)
decollacio Sancti Iohannis Baptiste (24 June, *for* 29 Aug.)
de Sancto Petro (29 June)
de ad uincula eius (1 Aug.)
de cathedra eius (22 Feb.)
de Sancto Paulo converso
   (25 Jan., 29 June)
de Sancto Swithino (15 July)
Translatio eius (15 July)
de Sancto Kinelmo (17 July)

---

[1] Contractions have been expanded and dates added.

de Sancta Margareta (20 July)
de Sancta Maria Magdelena
  (22 July)
de Sancta Cristina (24 July)
de Sancto Jacobo (25 July)
de Sancto Cristoforo (25 July)
de Sancta Martha (29 July)
de Sancto Oswaldo (9 Aug.)
de Sancto Laurencio (10 Aug.)
de Assumptione [Virginis][1]
  (15 Aug.)
de Sancto Bartho[lomeo][1]
  (24 Aug.)
de Sancto Egideo (1 Sept.)
de Exultacione Crucis (14 Sept.)
de Sancto Matheo (21 Sept.)
de Sancto Michaele archangelo
  (29 Sept., 8 May)
de Sancto Michaele in monte
  (29 Sept.)
de Inferno
de Sancto Ieronimo (30 Sept.)
de Sancto Dionisio (9 Oct.)
de Sancto Luco (18 Oct.)
de xj Mᵃ virginum (21 Oct.)
de Sancto Simone (28 Oct.)

de Sancto Iuda (28 Oct.)
de Sancto Quintino (31 Oct.)
ffestiuitas omnium Sanctorum
  (1 Nov.)
Commemoracio animarum
  (2 Nov.)
de Sancto Leonardo (6 Nov.)
de Sancto Martino (11 Nov.)
de Sancto Edmundo (16 Nov.)
de Sancto Edmundo rege
  (20 Nov.)
de Sancto Clemente (23 Nov.)
de Sancta Katarina (25 Nov.)
de Sancto Andrea (30 Nov.)
de Sancto Nicholao (6 Dec.)
de Sancta Lucia (13 Dec.)
de Sancto Thoma apostolo
  (21 Dec.)
de Sancta Anastacia (25 Dec.)
de Sancto Steffano (26 Dec.)
de Invencione eius (3 Aug.)
de Sancto Iohanne ewangelista
  (27 Dec.)
de Sancto Thoma (29 Dec.)
de translacione eius (7 July)
de Sancto Guthlaco (11 Apr.)

[1] Text blurred.

APPENDIX III

Table of Contents in British Museum MS. Harley 2277[1]

f. 232^b   In isto libro continentur vite sanctorum subscriptorum ✓ et alie Historie similiter subscripte.

        Circumcisio domini
        Epiphania domini
        Sanctorum
col. 1 Hillarij
        Wolstani
        Fabiani
        Sabastiani
        Agnetis
        Vincencij
        Iuliani confessoris
        Iuliani hospitis
        Brigide
        Blasij
        Agathe
        Scolastice
        Valentini
        Iuliane virginis
        Mathie apostoli
        Oswaldi
        Cedde confessoris
        Gregorij
        Longij
        Patricij
        Edwardi Iuuenis
        Cutberti
        Benedicti
        Concepcio sancte Marie
        Quadragesima
        Qualiter debemus
          Iuiunare
        Pascha et Passio domini
          et Ewangeliste
        Marie Egepciace
        Alphegi martiris

Georgij martiris
Marci Ewangeliste
Letania Maior et minor
Rogaciones
Philippi et Iacobi
col. 2 Jacobi
Inuencio Crucis
Quiriaci
Brendani
Dunstani
Aldelmi
Augustini
Barnabe
Teodoli
Miracula de sancta Maria
Alboni
Iohannis Baptiste
Sancti Petri apostoli
Pauli Apostoli
Swithini
Kenelmi Regis
Margarete
Magdalene
Cristine
Iacobi apostoli
Miracula eius
Cristofori
Marthe
Oswaldi
Laurencij
Assumpcio Marie
Bartholomei
Egidij
Exaltacio Crucis

[1] Written in three columns; contractions have been expanded.

APPENDIX III

col. 2	Miracula eius	Clementis
	Mathei Ewangeliste	Miracula eius
	Michaelis (*twice*)	Katerine
col. 3	Natura angelorum	Andree
	et elementorum	Miracula eius
	et nature humane	Nicholai
	et nature anime	Miracula eius
	Ierom (*in red, faint*)	Lucie
	Dionisij	Thome apostoli
	Luce	Anastasie
	xj$^{mil.}$ virginum	Stephani
	Simonis et Iude	Iohannis Ewangeliste
	Quintini	Miracula eius
	Omnium sanctorum	Thome Martiris Cantuariensis
	Omnium animarum	[*space in MS.*]
	Leonardi	Maledictorum Iude et Pilati
	Martini	
	Eadmundi confessoris	
	Eadmundi Regis	

APPENDIX IV

List of Legends in Bodleian MS. Ashmole 43 (S.C. 6924)

[MS. imperfect]
- f. 4ᵃ St. Wulfstan l. 85
- f. 6ᵃ St. Fabian
- f. 6ᵃ St. Sebastian
- f. 7ᵇ St. Agnes
- f. 9ᵃ Miracle of the Emperor's Daughter
- f. 10ᵃ St. Vincent
- f. 12ᵇ St. Julian the Confessor
- f. 13ᵃ St. Julian the Hospitaller
- f. 15ᵃ St. Bride (Bridget)
- f. 18ᵇ St. Blaise
- f. 21ᵇ St. Agatha
- f. 23ᵇ St. Scholastica
- f. 24ᵃ St. Valentine
- f. 25ᵃ St. Juliana
- f. 28ᵃ St. Matthias
- f. 28ᵇ St. Oswald the Bishop
- f. 31ᵇ St. Chad
- f. 32ᵇ St. Gregory the Great
- f. 34ᵃ St. Patrick
- f. 41ᵇ St. Edward the Elder
- f. 45ᵃ St. Cuthbert
- f. 46ᵃ St. Benedict
- f. 48ᵇ The Annunciation
- f. 48ᵇ Septuagesima
- f. 49ᵃ Lent
- f. 51ᵃ Easter
- f. 52ᵃ St. Mary of Egypt
- f. 56ᵃ St. Alphege
- f. 59ᵃ St. George
- f. 60ᵇ St. Mark
- f. 61ᵃ Rogationtide
- f. 62ᵃ St. Peter the Dominican
- f. 62ᵇ St. Philip and St. James
- f. 63ᵇ The Holy Cross
  - *a.* Early History
- f. 66ᵃ   *b.* Invention
- f. 68ᵃ   *c.* Exaltation
- f. 71ᵃ St. Quiriac
- f. 71ᵇ St. Brendan
- f. 80ᵇ St. Dunstan
- f. 83ᵃ St. Aldhelm
- f. 84ᵃ St. Augustine of Canterbury
- f. 85ᵇ St. Barnabas
- f. 87ᵃ St. John the Baptist
- f. 88ᵇ St. Peter
- f. 95ᵃ St. Paul (Conversion and Commemoration)
- f. 98ᵇ St. Swithun
- f. 100ᵃ St. Kenelm
- f. 104ᵇ St. Margaret
- f. 108ᵃ St. Mary Magdalene
- f. 112ᵇ St. Christina
- f. 117ᵃ St. James the Greater
- f. 119ᵇ Miracle of the Forsworn Pilgrims
- f. 120ᵃ St. Christopher
- f. 122ᵇ Seven Sleepers
- f. 124ᵇ St. Lawrence
- f. 127ᵃ St. Hippolytus
- f. 128ᵃ The Assumption of the Virgin
- f. 131ᵃ St. Bartholomew
- f. 134ᵇ St. Giles
- f. 136ᵃ St. Matthew
- f. 137ᵇ St. Justin
- f. 138ᵃ St. Michael   Part I
- f. 139ᵇ St. Jerome
- f. 141ᵇ St. Leger
- f. 142ᵇ St. Francis
- f. 149ᵃ St. Faith
- f. 150ᵇ St. Denys
- f. 151ᵇ St. Michael   Part II
- f. 154ᵃ St. Luke
- f. 155ᵇ St. Frideswide
- f. 157ᵇ The Eleven Thousand Virgins

f. 160ᵃ SS. Simon and Jude	f. 199ᵃ St. Andrew
f. 162ᵇ St. Quentin	f. 200ᵇ Miracle of the 3 Riddles
f. 164ᵇ St. Alban	f. 202ᵃ St. Nicholas (4 miracles)
f. 165ᵇ All Saints	f. 208ᵇ Prologue to Conceptio Mariae
f. 166ᵇ All Souls	
f. 169ᵇ St. Eustace	f. 209ᵇ Conceptio Mariae
f. 172ᵇ St. Leonard (4 miracles)	f. 212ᵃ St. Lucy
f. 174ᵃ St. Martin	f. 214ᵃ St. Thomas the Apostle
f. 176ᵃ St. Brice	f. 219ᵃ St. Anastasia
f. 177ᵃ St. Edmund Rich	f. 220ᵇ St. Stephen
f. 184ᵇ St. Edmund the King	f. 222ᵃ St. John the Evangelist
f. 185ᵇ St. Cecilia	f. 228ᵃ St. Oswald the King
f. 188ᵇ St. Clement	f. 228ᵇ St. Thomas à Becket
f. 195ᵃ Miracle of Child Preserved under the Sea	f. 259ᵃ Translation of St. Thomas
	f. 260ᵃ St. Edward the Confessor
f. 195ᵇ St. Katherine	[*incomplete: MS. damaged*]

APPENDIX V

List of Legends in British Museum MS. Cotton Julius D. IX[1]

f. 1ᵃ	Prologue	f. 52ᵇ c. 28	Lent
f. 2ᵃ c. 1	3eres day	f. 54ᵇ c. 29	Easter
f. 2ᵇ c. 2	Twelfth day	f. 55ᵇ c. 30	St. Mary of Egypt
f. 2ᵇ c. 3	St. Hilary	f. 60ᵃ c. 31	St. Alphege
f. 4ᵃ c. 4	St. Wulfstan	f. 63ᵃ c. 32	St. George
f. 7ᵃ c. 5	St. Fabian	f. 64ᵃ c. 33	St. Mark
f. 7ᵇ c. 6	St. Sebastian	f. 64ᵇ c. 34	Rogationtide
f. 9ᵃ c. 7	St. Agnes	f. 65ᵇ c. 35	St. Peter the Dominican
f. 10ᵇ	Miracle of the Emperor's Daughter	f. 65ᵇ c. 36	St. Philip
f. 11ᵇ c. 8	St. Vincent	f. 66ᵃ c. 37	St. James the Less
f. 14ᵃ c. 9	St. Julian the Confessor	f. 67ᵃ c. 38	The Holy Cross *a.* Early History
f. 14ᵇ c. 10	St. Julian the Hospitaller	f. 69ᵇ f. 71ᵇ c. 39	*b.* Invention *c.* Exaltation
f. 16ᵇ c. 11	St. Bridget	f. 74ᵃ c. 40	St. Quiriac
f. 20ᵇ [c. 12]	St. Blaise	f. 74ᵇ c. 41	St. Brendan
f. 23ᵇ [c. 13]	St. Agatha	f. 83ᵇ c. 42	St. Dunstan
f. 25ᵃ c. 14	St. Scholastica	f. 86ᵇ c. 43	St. Aldhelm
f. 26ᵃ c. 15	St. Valentine	f. 87ᵇ c. 44	St. Augustine of Canterbury
f. 27ᵃ c. 16	St. Juliana	f. 89ᵃ c. 45	St. Barnabas
f. 30ᵃ c. 17	St. Matthias	f. 90ᵃ c. 46	St. John the Baptist
f. 30ᵇ c. 18	St. Oswald the Bishop	f. 92ᵃ c. 47	St. Peter
f. 33ᵇ c. 19	St. Chad	f. 98ᵇ c. 48	St. Paul (Conversion and Commemoration)
f. 35ᵃ c. 20	St. Gregory the Great		
f. 36ᵃ c. 21	St. Patrick	f. 101ᵇ c. 49	St. Margaret
f. 44ᵇ c. 22	St. Edward the Elder	f. 105ᵇ c. 50	St. Mary Magdalene
		f. 110ᵃ c. 51	St. Christina
f. 48ᵃ c. 23	St. Cuthbert	f. 114ᵇ c. 52	St. James the Greater
f. 49ᵇ c. 24	St. Benedict		
f. 52ᵃ c. 25	The Annunciation	f. 117ᵃ	Miracle of the Forsworn Pilgrims
f. 52ᵃ c. 26	Movable Feasts		
f. 52ᵇ c. 27	Septuagesima	f. 118ᵃ c. 53	St. Christopher

[1] The separate legends are marked in the MS. by chapter numbers (Roman), not by titles.

APPENDIX V

f. 120ᵇ c. 54	Seven Sleepers	
f. 122ᵇ c. 55	St. Lawrence	
f. 125ᵃ c. 56	St. Hippolytus	
f. 126ᵃ c. 57	The Assumption of the Virgin	
f. 129ᵃ c. 58	St. Bartholomew	
f. 132ᵇ c. 59	St. Giles	
f. 134ᵃ c. 60	St. Matthew	
f. 135ᵇ c. 61	St. Justin	
f. 136ᵃ c. 62	St. Michael Part I	
f. 137ᵃ c. 63	St. Jerome	
f. 139ᵃ c. 64	St. Leger	
f. 140ᵃ c. 65	St. Francis	
f. 146ᵃ c. 66	St. Faith	
f. 147ᵇ c. 67	St. Denys	
f. 149ᵇ c. 68	St. Michael Part II	
f. 152ᵇ c. 69	St. Luke	
f. 153ᵇ c. 70	The Eleven Thousand Virgins	
f. 156ᵃ c. 71	SS. Simon and Jude	
f. 158ᵇ c. 72	St. Quentin	
f. 160ᵇ c. 73	St. Ailbriʒt [Ethelberht]	
f. 161ᵇ c. 74	All Saints	
f. 163ᵃ c. 75	All Souls	
f. 167ᵇ c. 76	St. Leonard (4 miracles)	
f. 172ᵃ c. 77	St. Eustace	
f. 173ᵇ c. 78	St. Martin	
f. 177ᵃ c. 79	St. Brice	
f. 178ᵃ c. 80	St. Edmund Rich	
f. 185ᵇ c. 81	St. Edmund the King	
f. 187ᵃ c. 82	St. Cecilia	
f. 190ᵃ c. 83	St. Clement	
f. 197ᵃ	Miracle of the Child Preserved under the Sea	
f. 197ᵃ c. 84	St. Katherine	
f. 201ᵇ c. 85	St. James Intercisus	
f. 202ᵇ c. 86	St. Andrew	
f. 204ᵃ	Miracle of the 3 Riddles	
f. 205ᵇ c. 87	St. Birinus	
f. 207ᵃ c. 88	St. Nicholas (4 miracles)	
f. 214ᵃ c. 89	St. Lucy	
f. 216ᵇ c. 90	St. Thomas the Apostle	
f. 222ᵇ c. 91	St. Anastasia	
f. 224ᵃ c. 92	St. Stephen	
f. 225ᵇ c. 93	St. John the Evangelist	
f. 230ᵃ	Miracle of King Edward's Ring	
f. 232ᵇ [c. 94]	St. Thomas à Becket	
f. 265ᵇ	Translation of St. Thomas	
f. 266ᵇ c. 95	St. Egwin	
f. 268ᵇ c. 96	St. Silvester	
f. 271ᵇ c. 97	St. Ailbriʒt [Ethelberht, *repeated, see* c. 73]	
f. 272ᵇ c. 98	St. Ignatius	
f. 273ᵇ c. 99	St. Frideswide	
f. 276ᵃ c. 100	St. Michael Part III	
f. 281ᵃ c. 101	St. Edward the Confessor	
f. 297ᵇ c. 102	St. Guthlac	
f. 301ᵇ c. 103	Miracle of the Jewish Boy	
f. 302ᵃ c. 104	Miracle of the Devil in Service	
f. 302ᵇ c. 105	Miracle of Emmery	
f. 304ᵃ c. 106	Miracle of Ave Maria	
f. 304ᵃ c. 107	St. Theophilus	

APPENDIX VI

Items previously printed from MSS. C, H, A, and J[1]

A. From MS. CCCC 145
  1. Banna Sanctorum (*Index* 2304)
      Zupitza, *Anglia*, i. 393, ll. 1–16, 57–68.
  2. 11,000 Virgins (*Index* 721)
      Schubel, *Die südengl. Legende v. d. elftausend Jungfrauen*, p. 178.
  3. St. Guthlac (*Index* 2911)
      Birch, *Memorials of St. Guthlac*, xxix, ll. 1–24.
      Forstmann, *Bonner Beit.* xii. 32, ll. 1–24.
      Bolton, *The Middle English and Latin Poems of Saint Guthlac*, pp. 221 ff.

B. From MS. Harl. 2277
  1. St. Andrew (*Index* 2848)
      Furnivall, *Early English Poems*, 98, ll. 1–108.
  2. St. Brendan (*Index* 2868)
      Wright, *St. Brandan*, Percy Soc. XIV. 1.
      Sampson, *Cambridge Book of Prose and Verse*, p. 345 (ll. 151–222 from Wright).
  3. St. Christopher (*Index* 2878)
      Furnivall, *Early English Poems*, p. 59.
      Mätzner, *Altengl. Sprachproben*, i. 194 (from Furnivall).
  4. St. Dunstan (*Index* 2884)
      Furnivall, *Early English Poems*, p. 34.
      Mätzner, *Altengl. Sprachproben*, i. 171 (from Furnivall).
      Morris and Skeat, *Specimens*, ii. 19, ll. 1–92.
  5. 11,000 Virgins (*Index* 721)
      Furnivall, *Early English Poems*, p. 66.
      Liljegren, *Eng. St.* lvii. 103.
      Schubel, *Die südengl. Legende v. d. elftausend Jungfrauen*, p. 151.
  6. St. Edmund Rich of Canterbury (*Index* 2886)
      Furnivall, *Early English Poems*, p. 71.
  7. St. Edmund the King (*Index* 2887)
      Furnivall, *Early English Poems*, p. 87.

[1] Arranged alphabetically under each MS. Extracts of less than 10 lines are not included. Index numbers are from Brown and Robbins, *The Index of Middle English Verse*.

APPENDIX VI

8. St. James the Apostle (*Index* 2918)
   Furnivall, *Early English Poems*, p. 57 (Miracle of young man of Lyons).
9. St. John the Evangelist (*Index* 2932)
   Furnivall, *Early English Poems*, p. 106 (Miracle of St. Edward's Ring).
10. Judas (*Index* 1809)
    Furnivall, *Early English Poems*, p. 107.
    Wülcker, *Altengl. Lesebuch*, i. 18 (from Furnivall).
11. St. Katherine (*Index* 2954)
    Furnivall, *Early English Poems*, p. 90.
    Wülcker, *Altengl. Lesebuch*, i. 12 (from Furnivall).
12. St. Kenelm (*Index* 2956)
    Furnivall, *Early English Poems*, p. 47.
13. St. Lucy (*Index* 2961)
    Furnivall, *Early English Poems*, p. 101.
14. St. Margaret (*Index* 2987)
    Cockayne, E.E.T.S. o.s. 13, p. 24.
    Mätzner, *Altengl. Sprachproben*, p. 200 (from Cockayne).
15. St. Michael, Part III (*Index* 3029 and 3453)
    Wright, *Popular Treatises on Science*, p. 132.
    Mätzner, *Altengl. Sprachproben*, p. 137 (from Wright).
16. The Passion (*Index* 483)
    Brown, C., *M.L.N.* xxvi. 16, 135 scattered lines.
17. Pilate (*Index* 2755)
    Furnivall, *Early English Poems*, p. 111.
18. St. Swithun (*Index* 3060)
    Furnivall, *Early English Poems*, p. 43.
19. St. Theophilus, Six Miracles of Our Lady (*Index* 50, 56, 57, 58, 59, 1788)
    Furnivall, *Early English Poems*, p. 40 (No. 57), p. 42 (No. 1788).
    Tryon, *P.M.L.A.* xxxviii. 313 (No. 50), 314 (No. 56), 316 (No. 59), 319 (No. 58).
20. St. Thomas of Canterbury (*Index* 907)
    Black, Percy Soc. LIX. 1.
    Mätzner, *Altengl. Sprachproben*, 177, ll. 1787 to end (from Black).
21. St. Thomas of Canterbury, Translation (*Index* 3064)
    Black, Percy Soc. LIX. 123.
    Mätzner, *Altengl. Sprachproben*, p. 192 (from Black).

C. From MS. Ashmole 43 (S.C. 6924)
   1. St. Benedict (*Index* 2860)
      McCann, *Downside Review*, xli (1923), 48.

APPENDIX VI

2. St. Brendan (*Index* 2868)
   Horstmann, *Archiv*, liii. 17.
   Bälz, *Die ME. Brendanlegende des Gloucesterlegendars*, p. 1.
3. St. Cecilia (*Index* 2873)
   Lovewell, *The Life of St. Cecilia*, p. 72.
   Furnivall, *Originals and Analogues*, p. 208.
4. Conceptio Marie and Prologue (*Index* 2632)
   Horstmann, *Altengl. Legenden* (1875), p. 64.
5. 11,000 Virgins (*Index* 721)
   Schubel, *Die südengl. Legende v. d. elftausend Jungfrauen*, p. 162.
6. The Holy Cross
   a. Early History (*Index* 3389)
      Morris, E.E.T.S. o.s. 46, p. 18.
   b. Invention (*Index* 82)
      Morris, E.E.T.S. o.s. 46, p. 36.
   c. Exaltation (*Index* 3388)
      Morris, E.E.T.S. o.s. 46, p. 48.
7. St. Juliana (*Index* 2951)
   Cockayne, E.E.T.S. o.s. 51, p. 81.
   Schleich, *Archiv*, cli. 25.
8. St. Patrick (*Index* 3037)
   Horstmann, *Altengl. Legenden* (1875), p. 151.
9. St. Quiriac (*Index* 3051)
   Morris, E.E.T.S. o.s. 46, p. 58.
10. St. Thomas of Canterbury (*Index* 728 and 3064)
    Thiemke, *Palaestra* 131, p. 14.
    Funke, *A Middle English Reader* (Berne, 1944), p. 56, ll. 2103-90 (from Thiemke).

D. From MS. Cott. Julius D. IX
   1. St. Edward the Confessor (*Index* 2888)
      Moore, *The ME. Verse Life of Edward the Confessor*, p. 1.
   2. 11,000 Virgins (*Index* 721)
      Liljegren, *Eng. St.* lvii. 98.
      Schubel, *Die südengl. Legende v. d. elftausend Jungfrauen*, p. 228.
   3. St. Eustace (*Index* 2894)
      Horstmann, E.E.T.S. o.s. 87, p. 395, ll. 86-179.
   4. St. Guthlac (*Index* 2911)
      Birch, *Memorials of Saint Guthlac*, xxix, ll. 1-24; xxx, ll. 105-24.
      Forstmann, *Bonner Beit.* xii. 22.
      Bolton, *The Middle English and Latin Poems of Saint Guthlac*, p. 184.

NOTE ON THE GLOSSARY

This glossary records primarily the more unusual words and the more unusual meanings of common words found in *The South English Legendary*. But occasionally familiar words, verbs in particular, are included when the variety of their forms is of interest. Occasionally, too, the early appearance of the word, determined by quotation from *The South English Legendary* in the *Oxford English Dictionary* and in those parts of the *Middle English Dictionary* now in print, is the criterion for its selection. Because of the length of the text, usually only two examples of any form are cited and not all the variations of any form or word are included. The opportunity has been taken, however, of noting in the glossary some differences in spelling in the control manuscripts purposely omitted from the variant readings, see for example, *hasewe, hucche*; and of giving, when they are available, readings from three instead of from two control manuscripts where the word in question is doubtful or unusual, see for example, *chikene, Gibolot*. French phrases, which are few, are included in the English glossary, for example, *as armes* under *arme, iambeleue*.

In a few instances the text of MS. Laud 108 is used for illustration, quoted in Horstmann's edition, E.E.T.S. o.s. 87, by page and line, for example under *chikene*. The *Legenda Aurea* of Jacobus de Voragine is also cited as *L.A.*, by page, from Graesse's edition (Dresden, 1846), for example under *weie*. References to other authorities are self-explanatory.

In the arrangement of the glossary initial ȝ is given a separate section following *g*; *þ*, a separate section following *t*; initial *v* and *u* are listed together under *v*; *y*, initial and medial, is treated as *i*. Hyphens, not admitted in the printed text, are used in the glossary wherever necessary to connect prefixes and stems and also the parts of compound words. Words are referred to by page (large figures) and line (small figures), thus 42/54. Emended words are marked with an asterisk.

GLOSSARY

a *pron.* see **he**.
abenche *adv.* on a bench, in court 536/91.
abigge, abugge *v. inf.* pay for, atone for 564/424, 131/88; **abuþ** *pr.* 131/76; **abo(u)ȝte** *pt.* 73/52, 467/121; **aboȝt** *pp.* 20/39.
ablenche *v. inf.* flinch from 99/394.
ablende *v. pt.* made blind 320/158, 530/444; **ablend(e)** *pp.* 70/20, 26; *a.* 327/364, 372/208.
ablode *a.* and *adv.* with blood, bloody 84/94, 572/11.
abode *n.* delay 233/342.
abowe *v. inf.* bend, submit 295/108, 340/14; **aboup** *pr.* 654/1339.
abreide *v. pt.* awoke 515/20.
abusmare *adv.* scornfully 272/217, 603/321.
abusseþ *v. pr.* hides 655/1388, probably for *pt.* as in var. H; **abuschepe** *pt.* J.
ac, ok *conj.* but 153/142, 141.
acale *pp.* chilled, cold 46/253, 463/15; see **of-cale**.
acces *n.* attack (of fever) 219/59, 414/385.
accolit *n.* acolyte, novice 485/53.
acely, *v. inf.* seal 223/65; **acelede** *pt.* 223/68.
achoke *v. inf.* choke 430/58.
acontes *n. pl.* reckoning, report 42/146, 396/195; **acountes** 606/400, 616/164.
aconti *v. inf.* report 222/34.
acorda(u)nt *a.* matching 148/333, 464/38.
acorie *v. inf.* suffer for 344/119; **acoreþ** *pr.* 410/248.
acoupede *v. pt.* accused 635/771.
acrois *adv.* with arms extended, crosswise 350/59.
acused(e) *v. pt.* charged 622/369, 656/1401; **acused** *pp.* 362/125.
adeolwey *adv.* to destruction 91/174; **an alle deuelwey** 260/391; **in þe deueles weie** 264/510; **deuelwey** 91/168.
adrawe *pp.* drawn 484/42, var. **idraue** J.
adrenche *v. inf.* drown, sink 52/150, 213/72; **adreinte** *pt.* 244/61; **adreint** *pp.* 343/100.
adrinke *v. inf.* drown 77/179; **adronk** *pt.* 562/378; **adronke** *pp.* 138/52.

afalle *v. inf.* fall, fall upon 487/114; **aualle** *pp.* 166/79.
afare *pp.* departed 539/177.
afere *v. inf.* frighten 67/157, 73/65; **aferde** *pt.* 10/68.
afflicciouns *n. pl.* suffering 458/57.
afingred *pp.* starved, hungry 126/137, 194/418.
afischeþ, avisseþ *adv.* fishing 468/133, 594/20.
aforcede *v. pt. reflex.* exerted 10/56, 32/9.
after-tale *n.* second thoughts 630/619.
agaste *v. pt.* terrified, was afraid 90/147, 196/471; *pp.* 151/80.
agonne *v. pt. pl.* succeeded 482/155.
agreiþed *pp.* arrayed 578/191, 193.
agrise *v. inf.* fear, be terrified 239/40; **agros** *pt.* 141/152; **agrise** *pp.* 587/54.
aȝe *adv.* again 13/161, 121/94.
aȝend see **ȝend** *a.*
aȝen-soukynge *n.* sucking back 454 163.
aȝenward *adv.* backward 116/199.
ake *v. inf.* ache 17/40; **akeþ** *pr. pl.* 26/33; **ok** *pt.* 433/149.
akeleþ *v. pr. pl.* cool 364/169; **akelde** *pt.* 459/94.
aker-staf *n.* plough-staff 470/186.
alblasters *n. pl.* cross-bow men 2/25.
alblastre *n.* cross-bow 348/208.
alclyne *n.* ? treasure-chest 467/124; see var. Other variants are: **halle clene** Laud 108 424/120; **al clene** B.M. Egerton 2891; **ale clene** Trin. Camb. 605. Passage om. in 7 MSS. Word may be connected with Sp. *alcancia*, a box in which to hide money; see Dozy and Engelmann, *Glossaire des mots espagnols et portugais dérivés de l'arabe*, 2nd edit., 1869, p. 84. I owe this reference to Professor Bruce Dickins.
aldai *adv.* all day long 112/66; every day, commonly 348/1, 658/1466.
alegge *v.¹ inf.* inveigh against 6/46; **aleggi** state in court 656/1402.
alegge *v.² inf.* alleviate 106/590; reduce 555/162, 673/1934; **alegge** *pr. subj.* 664/1646.
alyt *n.* one chosen to office, bishopelect 74/101, var. **elit** A; **o(or e)lyȝt** J.
allinge *adv.* wholly 286/218.
allonge *a.* in phr. ~ **niȝt** all night long 200/597; ~ **day** 623/394.

GLOSSARY

almesfol *a.* charitable 665/1682.
alonde *adv.* in this country, here 83/83, 664/1653; on land 349/21.
alosed *pp.* praised 444/39, 500/248.
aloute *v. inf.* bow down 86/26, 174/200; alotte *pt. pl.* 47/19.
alowe *adv.* low down 592/63.
am, amsulue *pron.* see hi.
amad *a.* crazed 63/28, 587/41.
amaystrede *v. pt.* subdued 699/61.
ambes-as *n.* see as *n.*
amonte *v. inf.* mean, be worth 175/232; amonteþ *pr.* 106/603.
amore *adv.* any more 433/143.
amorwe *adv.* next morning 200/593, 249/71.
amte, amti *a.* empty 95/293, 130/52.
anapped *pp.* drowsy 501/281.
anemne *v. inf.* name 286/208; anemnede *pt.* 341/20.
aneþeri *v. inf.* degrade 638/850.
aneue *adv.* in the evening 495/70.
angle *n.* corner 91/158.
angwise *n.* extreme suffering 24/158; angwises *pl.* 615/134; *fin* ~ sharp distress of mind 585/421.
anhansed *pp.* exalted 390/2.
anhongred *pp.* hungry 463/8.
anhonteþ *adv.* hunting 111/45, 284/150.
anouward(e) *prep.* on top of 16/F8, 104/555.
answeriare *n.* one who answers 550/220.
anuy *n.* discomfort, trouble 193/396, 663/1624; *fin* ~ chagrin 327/352.
anuye *v. inf.* distress, vex 296/146, 330/68; anuyd *pp.* 6/31, 168/34.
apaid *pp.* satisfied 557/226.
apays *adv.* in peace 488/148.
ape *n.* fool 262/426, 273/269.
apeiri *v. inf.* harm, weaken 453/129; aperri lose value 475/340; apeirede *pt. pl.* 641/952; apeired *pp.* 469/168.
apel *n.* appeal to higher court 629/594, 595.
apert *a.* open, plain 14/174, 379/162; ready 25/6.
aperte *adv.* openly 155/207.
aperteliche *adv.* clearly, publicly 209/158, 211/14.
apoysene *v. inf.* poison 126/133; apoisened *pp.* 126/134, 601/234.
aposy *v. inf.* set questions, question 549/214; aposede *pt.* 25/11.
aprochi *v. inf.* come near 569/118.
aquiti *v. inf.* pay 137/39.
aranced *pp.* mutilated 220/93, var. iranced H A J.

areche *v. inf.* reach, attain 246/123, 411/289.
aredi *a.* prepared 2/27.
areng, arenk *adv.* in order, in a row 3/68, 189/274.
arere *v. inf.* raise 2/41; arereþ *pr.* incites 411/285, var. for þrouweþ J, 411/295; arerede *pt.* 411/294.
arere *adv.* to the rear 330/68.
arewe *a.* cowardly 456/7; aru weak 424/669 var. J; *arwere *comp.* 52/157.
arewe *adv.* one after another 413/365.
arme *n.* weapon 158/84, 679/2097; armes *pl.* 215/41; *as* ~ to arms! 371/177.
army *v. inf.* furnish with arms 2/45, 678/2090; armed(e) *pt.* 2/43, 47; iarmed *pp.* 265/18.
arnde *v.* see eorne.
aroute *v. inf.* turn aside, escape 163/17, 349/26; see atroute.
arsmetrike *n.* science of numbers 500/224.
arst *adv.* first, before that 58/131, 355/187.
art *n.* trickery 122/17; cunning 258/336; scholastic learning 499/222; artȝ *pl.* fields of learning 533/4.
as *n.* ace (in dice) 62/16; ambes-as double ace, bad luck 39/72, 196/494.
as *pron.* see he.
asaile, asaili *v. inf.* attack 92/188, 410/273; asailede *pt.* 194/430; assaillede *pt. pl.* 469/182.
asake *v. inf.* deny 704/195.
aschende *v. pt.* slandered, disgraced 526/338; assend *pp.* 624/414.
ascorn *adv.* scornfully 633/705.
askest *v.* 2 *pr.* question, ask for 218/33; askeþ *pr.* 637/826; (ne)askede *pt.* 637/832; yasked *pp.* 146/286; see axi, esche.
asle *v. inf.* kill 19/15; asle *pr. subj.* 73/78; aslou(ȝ) *pt.* 264/510, 512/26; aslauwe *pp.* 3/51.
asoili *v. inf.* absolve from excommunication 673/1910, 1915; asoilede *pt.* pardoned 210/197; asoiled *pp.* released 631/656.
asommed *pp.* assessed 621/347, var. asummed A; asommeþ J.
asonke *pp.* sunk 563/404.
aspille *v. inf.* destroy, perish 130/59, 321/170; aspilþ *pr.* 674/1952.
ass *n.* ash-tree 285/171.
assame *adv.* shamefully 447/131.
assigneþ *v. pr.* allots 53/185; assigned *pp.* directed 241/71.
astiked *v. pt.* stabbed 274/280; var.

GLOSSARY

astikede H; astiked A; a stiket J. Perhaps to be read a (he) stiked.
astinte, astunte v. inf. stop, make stop 563/391, 602/285; astunte pt. 35/83; pt. pl. 387/88.
astoffe v. inf. suffocate 409/233.
astonde v. inf. pause 69/216, 81/23; see atstonde.
astoned pp. astounded 265/21, 301/292.
astrangli v. inf. strangle 230/278; astranglede pt. 565/467; astrangled pp. 48/36.
aswagi v. inf. soften, relieve 433/141, 468/136; asuaged pp. 703/176.
aswydeþ v. see following word.
aswonde pp. finished, 'done for' 391/60; aswydeþ pr. perhaps for aswyndeþ fades 576/142, var. A.
atende v. inf. kindle 459/88.
atȝeue v. pt. gave over 79/52.
athelt, athuld v. pt. withheld, retained 668/1755, 562/363; atholde pp. 355/190.
atir n. equipment of a knight 335/228.
ato, atuo adv. apart, in two 263/465, 487/113.
atroute v. inf. turn aside, escape 414/389, 456/6; see aroute.
atstonde v. inf. remain, resist 47/6, 209/146; atstode pt. pl. 58/128.
atte a. see eiȝte.
attenone adv. at once 248/53.
atter n. poison 26/53.
attorne, aturne v. inf. run away 532/523, 429/15; atorn pt. 310/215; atourne pt. pl. 588/55.
attri a. poisonous 410/252.
atwo adv. asunder 270/164; half ∼ in half 483/18.
auanced pp. promoted 505/387.
aueisure n. ? pleasure 32/7, var. auysure A; aueisure J; Iolifte Laud 108 256/5. Perhaps for OF anveisure, enveisure gaiety.
aueld adv. see veld.
auyli v. inf. dishonour, defile 238/492 var. H; auilede pt. pl. 8/82; auyled pp. 624/414.
auis n. opinion 435/21, 613/101.
auisyon n. trance 646/1107; auisions pl. 181/31.
avisseþ adv. see afischeþ.
auncre n. recluse, anchoret 648/1161; ancres pl. 191/331.
auonge v. inf. beget 693/30; aueng pt. received with ceremony 10/54.
auowede v. pt. pl. confirmed 210/49.
auowes n. pl. patron saints 680/2134.
avure adv. on fire 40/80, 401/132.

awaite, awaiti v. inf. take note 613/86, 552/48; awaited pt. 239/15.
aweiȝte v. pt. waked up 15/213; aweiȝt pp. 533/540.
awelde v. inf. control, command 518/101, 636/814; see awolde.
awend pp. departed 290/322.
aweode v. inf. go mad 271/212; awedde pt. 496/112; pt. pl. 454/162; awed pp. 659/1494.
awer adv. anywhere 16/S7, 80/64.
awinne v. inf. gain 496/102, 519/115.
awolde v. inf. control 503/338; see awelde.
axi v. inf. ask, ask for 635/784; axest 2 pr. 319/111; ax(e)de pt. 520/157, 525/295; see askest, esche.

bachouse n. a place where bread is baked 120/73.
baillie n. authority, office 414/378, 700/79.
baldeloker adv. comp. more confidently 102/481.
balled(e) a. bare of meaning, bald 131/68, 424/679.
balu a. ? deadly, deathlike 352/115 var. H.
bane n. destruction 30/172, 682/2198.
baneour n. standard-bearer 2/49, 3/51.
*baret n. strife 634/731; fraud 697/137.
barme n. lap 387/90.
baronie n. body of barons 10/71.
barwe n. stretcher 639/899.
bate v. inf. ? prosper 523/247.
battes n. pl. ? knobs 362/128.
baþ n. place for bathing 97/353; *baþ-water 46/255 var. A J.
baudestrote n. procuress 54/7.
baundone n. control 391/52.
beau douȝ frere (in address) my dear sir 604/339.
bed n. bed 29/133; bede dat. 160/35, but see Laud 108 363/35; beddes pl. 184/126; to bedde 121/85.
bede n. prayer, devotions 73/66, 122/8; beden pl. 9/20; bedes 567/37, cf. Laud 108 363/35.
bedrede a. confined to bed 518/91, 523/236.
beie a. both 17/15, 603/294; beire g. 9/30, 73/54.
bel amy (in address) good friend 257/283, 636/808.
belhous n. belfry 9/32.
belwy v. inf. roar, bellow 329/55; belwede pt. pl. 644/1053.
bem n. ray of light 43/169; piece of wood 63/46.

44 GLOSSARY

bend(e) *n.* bond, fetter 66/126, 646/1105; **bendes** *pl.* 62/40, 253/172; **benden** 254/198.
beneson *n.* benediction 355/174.
beode *v. inf.* offer 125/104; **beost** *2 pr.* 663/1622; **beot** *pr.* 664/1650; **beode** *pr. subj.* 37/147; **bode** *pt. pl.* 503/328; **bode** *pt. subj.* 611/35.
beome *n.* trumpet 80/61.
beorþene, berþene *n.* load 454/152, 393/116.
bere *n.*[1] outcry 73/66, 92/194.
bere *n.*[2] bier 15/211, 115/184; litter 639/899.
beringe *n.* child-bearing 38/34.
berkinge *a.* barking 324/277.
bern *n.*[1] man 127/8, 441/54; **berne** *pl.* 165/52.
bern, biern *n.*[2] child 693/16; 698/5.
berne *v. inf.* burn 191/340; **barnde** *pt.* 23/113; *pt. pl.* 150/54; **bernynge** *pr. p.* 29/117; **ybarnd** *pp.* 27/77.
berninge *n.* burning 459/97.
berste *v. inf.* break suddenly 159/6; **barst** *pt.* 297/163; **borste** *pt. pl.* 291/355.
bete *v.*[1] *inf.* beat, strike 65/99; **bet** *pr.* 199/565; **bet** *pt.* 49/67; **bete, beote** *pt. pl.* 76/160, 457/45; **ibete** *pp.* 49/69.
bete *v.*[2] *inf.* amend, make good 35/97; **bette** *pt.* 37/145; **ibet** *pp.* 105/568, **ibeet** 233/343.
betinge *n.* striking 26/44; of noise 196/470.
beuerege *n.* (fig.) 'dose' 155/224.
beye *n. pl.* rings 171/134.
bi *prep.* in phr. ~ *on* with even temper 489/184.
bycaste *v. inf.* cover 183/93.
biclippeþ *v. pr.* surrounds, embraces 425/715; **biclipte** *pt.* 521/188; **biclupte** *pt. pl.* 95/275; **biclupt** *pp.* 169/75.
biclupe *v. inf.* appeal, summon 630/598; **biclupie** *1 pr.* 644/1047; **biclupeþ** *pr. pl.* 643/1020; **bicluped** *pp.* accused 622/365.
bidaubed, bidoubed *pp.* bespattered 589/95, 587/34.
bidde *v. inf.* ask, pray 7/74; **bit** *pr.* 48/42; **bad, bed** *pt.* 24/142, 41/118; **bade, bede** *pt. pl.* 76/146, 90/132; **ibede** *pp.* 19/87.
bieste *n.* see **biheste**.
bifonde *pp.* established 131/83.
bigabbed *pp.* mocked 340/383.
biȝete *n.* gain 207/84, 241/89.
biȝute *v. inf.* beget, acquire 133/134; **biȝut** *pr.* 573/48; **biȝat, biȝet** *pt.* 37/7, 407/170; **biȝete, biȝite, biȝute** *pp.* 614/119, 425/698, 37/2.
bihalues *adv.* to one side 534/13.
biheste *n.* promise, command 91/173, 164/17; *lond of bieste* land of promise 193/393, 182/76.
byhofþe *n.* use, service 37/141.
bihote *v. inf.* promise 54/8; **bihat** *pr.* 20/32; **bihoteþ** *pr. pl.* 216/57; **bihet** *pt.* 33/18; **bihete** *pt. pl.* 54/13; **bihote** *pp.* 182/77.
bihoue *n.* benefit 299/223, 476/364.
bilek *v. pt.* locked up 359/37, 586/25; **biloke** *pp.* 226/176.
bileue *v. inf. intr.* remain 41/107; **bilefþ** *pr.* 427/765; **bileuede** *pt.* 76/151; *inf. tr.* abandon 160/42, 251/123; **bileuede** *pt.* 71/32; **byleued** *pp.* left 84/16.
bileue *adv.* by permission 59/9, 10.
biliȝe, biliȝhe *v. inf.* belie, deny truth of 540/236, 113/96; **bilowe, bylou** *pt.* 155/224, 291/358.
bilymed *pp.* dismembered 84/19, 628/552.
biliue *n.* sustenance 388/116, 141/128.
biluue *v. inf.* believe 67/138; **biluf** *imper.* 24/165; **biluuede** *pt. pl.* 8/86; **byluued** *pp.* 79/40.
bymelde *v. inf.* reveal 560/322.
bimene *v. inf.* lament, pity 19/12, 43/161; **bimene** *pr. subj.* 69/202; **bymende** *pt. pl.* 591/52.
binime *v. inf.* take away, deprive of 20/38, 214/93; **binom** *pt.* 218/18, 104/534; **binome** *pp.* 92/201, 100/430.
biputted *pp.* buried 471/225.
biqueþe *v. 1 pr.* assign 497/135; **biquede** *pp.* 523/246.
biradde *v. pt. pl.* advised 683/2231.
bireued *pp.* bereft 288/268, 348/214.
birod *v. pt.* rode around 478/62.
biseo *v. inf.* provide 206/60; **bisay** *pt.* 206/55; **biseye** *pt. pl.* 693/23; **biseie** *pp.* 277/105.
biset *pp.* planted 203/693.
bisext *n.* leap-year 129/8.
bisigede *v. pt.* laid siege to 513/34; **bisiged** *pp.* 469/156.
bisinge *v. inf.* charm 325/297.
bispeche (bispeke H A J**)** *v. inf.* speak for, arrange 401/114; **bispecþ** *pr.* 284/144; **byspeke** *pt.* 173/178; *pt. pl.* 15/4.
bisprengde *v. pt.* sprinkled over 271/210; **bisprengd** *pp.* 272/224.
bissint *v. pr.* shines on 415/408.
bistod *v. pt.* constrained 7/67; **bistode** *pt. pl.* ? prospered 111/28.

GLOSSARY 45

biswinke v. inf. make ready, prepare 562/364; biswonke pp. 50/103, 524/269.
biswoc v. pt. deceived 528/398.
bitake v. 1 pr. commit to, commend 90/142; bitok 1 pt. 355/183; bitoke pt. pl. 682/2195; bitake pp. 12/133, 92/205.
biteche v. 1 pr. commit, entrust 163/28; biteiȝte pt. 327/359; pt. pl. 109/690.
bitelle v. inf. defend 102/475.
bytrufleþ v. pr. befools 604/325.
biturnde v. pt. turned about 487/116; cherde Laud 108 452/115 gives correct rime.
bitweye prep. between 662/1589; probably mistake for bi weye as in H A J.
biþenche v. inf. take thought 611/43, 74/83.
byuond v. pt. instituted 161/17, 34.
biuore prep. superior to 427/769.
biwade v. inf. wade into 479/72; biwade pp. swamped 152/114.
bywepe v. inf. be lamented 337/304.
biweued pp. covered 148/338, 483/22.
biwicched pp. bewitched 588/64, 66.
biwoke v. pt. pl. kept watch over 682/2214.
bywone adv. customarily 4/13, see wone n.
bywrenche v. inf. cheat 74/84.
blandisinge n. flattery 538/165.
blanket n. woollen cloth 648/1173.
blaste v. inf. blow, puff 299/213; pt. 333/173, 343/99; in phr. com(e) blaste with a blast, blowing 100/442, 199/579.
blede v. inf. tr. make bloody, fill with blood 395/169; bledde pt. 395/171; ibled pp. 394/142, 683/2226.
blenche v. inf. flinch, draw back 91/176, 220/86.
blende v. inf. make blind, deceive 454/148, 653/1301.
bleo n. colour, complexion 376/63, 425/708.
blete v. inf. bleat 86/20, 21.
blynne v. inf. cease 57/89.
bliue adv. quickly 92/206, 351/66.
blodhond n. bloodhound 132/113.
blode see ablode.
blodrede a. red with blood 564/448.
blouman n. blackamoor 379/174; blomen pl. 456/205.
blowinge n. noise (of bellows) 196/469.
boban, bobance n. pomp 275/46, 45.
bocsomhede n. patience 442/64.

bode n. messenger 631/662.
bodieþ v. pr. pl. foretell 409/227.
boffeted(e) v. pt. pl. struck 263/459, 395/166.
boie n. fellow, rogue 256/277, 124/86; boyes pl. 613/79.
boistous a. coarse 424/667.
bold n. building 573/49, 675/1996.
bolkeþ v. pr. pl. belch 130/51, 53.
bolle n. globe, vesicle 426/731; bollen pl. 425/699, 426/730.
bone n. prayer, petition 18/61, 73/74.
bordel n. prostitution 21/51; a brothel 568/92.
borgeis n. citizen 616/164.
borȝ-ȝulde n. pledge-payer 555/153.
borȝhod n. ? pledge 573/56.
borwi v. inf. ransom, take on pledge 249/74, 560/306; borwede pt. 561/327.
boskes n. pl. bushes 111/44.
bost n. pomp 275/43; menace 509/521.
bostar n. braggart 424/683; bostares pl. 334/221.
bote n. deliverance, help 58/135, 130/59; see soule-bote.
botened v. pt. pl. grew better 279/153.
botnynge n. power to heal, cure 114/146, 609/494.
bouk n. belly, body 194/414; term of contempt: deueles ~ 55/20, unwreste ~ 56/61, wrecche ~ 57/89.
boule n. something said or done in mockery 491/245.
bounte n. value 644/1037.
bourser n. treasurer 696/114.
bowe v. inf. submit to, bend 340/16; bouȝ imper. 560/294; see abowe, buye.
braid, breid v. pt. flung, drew 260/384, 483/17; breide pt. pl. pulled 569/108.
brech n. pair of breeches 393/101, 498/163.
*brede v. inf. roast 68/170 var. A J.
breide n. twist, jerk 333/184.
brenne v. inf. burn 22/110; brende pt. 151/83; ibrend pp. 27/74; see berne.
brennynge n. action of fire 459/94.
brerde n. rim 43/158, 158/68.
brestbon n. breast 594/24.
bretfol a. brim-full 395/171.
breþ n. emanation, vapour 103/514, 419/521; see water-breþ.
breþe v. inf. respire 478/44, breþi evaporate 421/596; breþede pt. 310/231.
briȝte n. brightness 370/152.
briȝthede n. brightness 21/56.

brymme *n.* shore 196/478, 487/121.
broches *n. pl.* ornamental pins 20/22.
broken *pp. a.* ruined 275/41.
brouke *v. inf.* possess 339/367.
browen *n. pl.* eye-brows 450/48.
buffet *n.* blow 574/94.
bugge *v. inf.* atone for, buy 4/18, 44/212; boȝte *pt.* 122/25; iboȝt, ibouȝt *pp.* 3/57, 568/67.
buye, bye *v. inf.* bend, submit 128/8, 498/170; buide, byde *pt.* 680/2131, 498/171; ibud, ibuyd *pp.* 425/717, 426/721.
bulies *n. pl.* bellows 196/469.
buriels *n.* place of burial 23/134, 234/399.
buringe *n.* interment 177/302, 578/194.
busmare *n.* scorn 2/37, 31/12; see abusmare.
buttok *n.* buttock 498/166; bottocs *pl.* 426/720.

cacche *v. inf.* take, catch 1/15, 299/221; cacþ *pr. pl.* 331/97; necaȝte *pt. pl.* 387/78; icaȝt *pp.* 69/201.
calis *n.* chalice 191/314.
calwe *n.* baldpate 207/89.
camayl *n.* camel-hair 462/59.
can *v. 1 pr.* know, be able 65/84; couþe *pt.* 12/111, 139/85; *pt. pl.* 114/130; couþ *pp.* 153/167.
cancre-frete *a.* eaten away with sores 155/221.
canoun seculer *n.* member of cathedral clergy 505/385.
caruol *a.* anxious 139/76; carefulle *pl.* 506/425.
carie *v. 1 pr.* feel concern 662/1579; carede *pt.* 19/10, 82/38; see karie.
caroine *n.* corpse 308/172; caroignes *pl.* 517/82.
cartare *n.* one who draws a cart 431/75.
caste *v. inf.* reckon 129/21; *pt.* 500/226; *pt. pl.* close (of eyes) 15/210.
catel *n.* personal property, wealth 252/166, 497/135; see chateus.
caudron *n.* large kettle 179/27, 185/159; caudrons *pl.* 586/26.
ce, se *n.* bishop's see 74/98, 79/35; ce king's throne 635/771.
celer *n.* store-room 189/288.
cene *n.* Last Supper 144/228, 594/25.
chaere *n.* judgement-seat 250/116, 396/192; chaire seat 7/80.
chaynes, cheynen *n. pl.* fetters 459/101, 375/42.

change, changi *v. inf.* alter, modify 88/79, 54/14; changed *pt.* 105/564; ichanged *pp.* 57/82.
chanteor, chantor *n.* enchanter 39/55, 38/17; chief singer 369/135.
charge *n.* load 431/78.
chargeþ *v. imper. pl.* load 203/710; chargede *pt.* 187/227; icharged *pp.* 431/86; chargi *1 pr.* enjoin 561/332; icharged *pp.* commissioned 637/834.
chast *a.* pure, modest 75/120, 110/18.
chaste, chasti *v. inf.* discipline 496/124, 72/36; chastede *pt.* 699/61; ichasted *pp.* 694/55.
chastement *n.* correction 606/396.
chateus *n. pl.* possessions 628/554, 555; see catel.
cheff *n.* bishop's see 281/50; chef leader 643/1007; in ~ as direct tenant of king 676/2030.
cheffare *n.* bargaining 226/165; merchandise 568/67.
cheisil *n.* linen 29/131, 578/192.
cheitif *n.* wretch 239/38.
chele, chile *n.* cold 182/62, 122/7.
cheose, chese, chuse *v. inf.* choose 15/4, 209/139, 552/68; chesþt.78/11; chose *pt. pl.* 333/181; ichose *pp.* 10/52, icore 204/720.
cheosinge *n.* election 552/72.
chepede *v. pt.* bargained with 43/184.
chepinge *n.* market-place 66/130, 572/36; marketing 276/56, 490/215.
chepmen *n. pl.* merchants 430/49, 432/105.
chesible *n.* chasuble 211/21, 641/953.
cheson *n.* reason 128/10, 613/89.
cheste *n.* strife 43/177.
cheue *v. inf.* succeed 638/856.
cheueintein *n.* leader, chieftain 618/251, see var., cheueyntein J.
cheuese, *v. 1 pr.* get on, succeed 224/104.
cheuerchef, keuer- *n.* head-cloth 271/213, 702/127.
chide *v. inf.* rebuke, scold 15/215, 88/93; chidde *pt.* 51/109; *pt. pl.* contended 154/191.
chikene *n. pl.* in phrase deueles chikene devil's brood 156/13; note var. *deueles cunne* H, *deuelischildren* J. Probably C H J are corruptions of OE. *deofolscin* demonic illusion, phantom, glossing *daemonia* (Bosworth–Toller); var. A *deuelscine* and Laud 108 (294/13) *deuelschine* preserve the correct reading. The passage in question is a paraphrase of Ps. xcv. 5: *Omnes dii gentium*

GLOSSARY 47

daemonia (*L.A* 262); see also *O.E.D.* under **devilshine**.
child-beringe *n.* child-birth 477/28.
chile *n.* see **chele**.
chitel *n.* kettle 64/54, 68/171.
*****chyuerede** *v. pt. pl.* shivered 98/385, see var., **chiuerepe** J; see **clyueri**.
choʒen *n. pl.* choughs 498/188.
churchei *n.* churchyard 201/624, 469/179 var. J; *chirche heie* 469/179 var. A.
churche-ʒard, -ʒerd *n.* churchyard 114/141, 87/63.
chuste *n.* coffin, chest 691/34.
citacion *n.* summons 630/607.
clansi *v. inf.* purify 265/9, 379/164.
clansing(e) *a.* purifying 129/12, 13.
clef *v. pt.* cut in two 163/23; see **forclef**.
clene *a.* cleared, open (of land) 342/52.
clergeonettes *n. pl.* young clerks 40/86 var. A.
cler(e)gie *n.* learning 268/99, 434/153; **clergi** benefit of clergy 622/371.
cleriones *n. pl.* young clerks 40/86 see var., **clergeouns** J.
clerte *n.* brightness 203/698.
cleueþ *v. pr.* clings, adheres 422/621, 623; **cleuede** *pt. pl.* 371/185, 588/75.
clib *a.* eager, aggressive 410/273, 411/281; **clibbost** *superl.* 411/285.
cliʒte *v. pt.* ? clutched 45/220 var. A, probably error for **diʒte**; var. **dyʒte** J.
clymme *v. inf.* climb 695/72; **clam** *pt.* 9/35; **clomme** *pt. pl.* 9/34.
clyngge *v. 1 pr.* shrink, waste 705/223; **clonge** *pt.* 705/217; **clongge** *pt. pl.* 705/216.
clipie *v. inf.* call, summon 457/42, 479/88; **iclipied** *pp.* 479/75; see **clupie**.
clips *n.* eclipse 84/6.
clyueri *n. inf.* ? **clemeri** A J, **coueri** Laud 108 (210/352); **clyuerede**, emended in text to **chyuerede** *pt. pl.* 98/385, var. **chiuered(e)** A J, **chyuereden** Laud 108 (210/335); in this case C's reading is probably a mistake.
clomp *n.* mass, lump 468/134.
cloudy *a.* dense (of smoke) 197/497.
clot *n.* lump 693/25.
cloutmele *adv.* piecemeal 140/108.
clupie *v. inf.* call, name 17/25; **clepede** *pt.* 484/46, **clupede** 38/20; **icleped** *pp.* 481/147, **icluped** 4/12; see **clipie**.
cluppe *v. inf.* embrace 587/31; **clipte** *pt.* 521/191, **clupte** 115/176; **iclupt** *pp.* 294/82.

coeng *n.* imbecile 603/323; see **congons**.
cof *a.* prompt 122/21, var. **cofe** J.
cofre *n.* strongbox 673/1931; **coffren** *pl.* 682/2192.
cokken-crowe *n.* dawn 608/463; **cokkes-crowe** 646/1096.
coler *n.* collar (of iron) 319/131.
coluer(e) *n.* dove 16/F7, 285/189.
combes *n. pl.* combs (for dressing wool) 50/89, 541/250.
come *v. inf.* 366/44; **comist** *2 pr.* (with future sense) 109/688; **comynde** *pr. p.* 608/472; **com** *pt.+inf.*: *c. reke* came rushing 22/85, *c. pulle* 77/188, *c. smite* 279/147, *c. swie* 297/157.
comencede *v. pt.* began 690/3.
comynge *n.* probably mistake for **connynge** knowledge 436/47, var. **cominge** H, **knowynge** A, **knouyng** J.
comun *n.* community (of Christians) 15/4; people in general 18/60.
comunite *n.* whole body of people 653/1308.
conceili *v.* take counsel 628/540.
concente *v. inf.* agree 652/1298; **consenti** *1 pr.* 216/59.
condut *n.*[1] channel for water 577/165.
condut *n.*[2] convoy 656/1398, 669/1802.
confermi *v. inf.* ratify 626/481; **confermede** *pt. pl.* 212/45; **yconfermed** *pp.* 161/32; **iconfermed** confirmed 46/247.
conforti *v. inf.* encourage 344/116; **confortede** *pt.* 401/116, **comfortede** 16/S10.
confusiun *n.* ruin 56/64.
congons *n. pl.* fools 213/75; see **coeng**.
coniuri *v. 1 pr.* charge, invoke 142/162, 261/419; **coniurede** *pt.* 329/45, 686/2329.
coniuringe *n.* working of magic 329/59.
conquerede *v. pt. pl.* ? worked out 435/26; see var.
consailli, conseile *v. inf.* advise 506/441, 363/138; **conseili** plan 630/622.
conseil *n.* assembly 82/39; consultation 82/42; plan 82/50.
constables *n. pl.* officers of the law 164/8; *g.s.* 19/8.
contak, contek *n.* contention 256/278, 154/191.
contekki *v. inf.* contend, quarrel 663/1626; **contekede** *pt. pl.* 289/310, 596/82.
contekour *n.* quarrelsome person

GLOSSARY

642/982; **contéccours** *pl.* 617/198, **contéckours** 616/196 var. H.
contynuelliche *adv.* constantly 499/223.
contreie *n.* people of the district 155/208.
contreiemen *n. pl.* rural inhabitants, natives 276/56, 289/291.
cop *n.* summit, top 261/412; **coppe** 80/78.
cope *n.* priestly or clerical cloak 475/348, 641/956; **copes** *pl.* 189/270.
copyner *n.* paramour 517/58.
coppe *n.* cup 46/260, 336/257; **coupe** 562/360; **coupen** *pl.* 562/369.
corden *n. pl.* ropes 545/68.
cors *n.* dead body 116/198, 155/210.
cos *n.* kiss 112/76; **cosses** *pl.* 587/39.
cosyn *n.* cousin, relative 475/356; **cosins** *pl.* 166/58.
costnede *v. pt.* cost 407/151.
costome *n.* in phr. *bi costome* usually 161/27.
costret *n.* bottle 125/125; **costres** *pl.* 125/123.
cou *n.* cow 120/51, 286/221; **kun** pl. 39/62, 42/142.
couele *n.* cowl 684/2244.
couenant *n.* agreement 223/64.
couent *n.* community of monks 9/25, 119/36.
counti *v. inf.* give account 700/87.
couple *n.* pair 242/21.
cours *n.* in phr. *in cours* in due order 500/225.
courteors *n. pl.* attendants at court 616/196.
coust *n.* in phr. *up is coust* at his expense 301/281.
couþ *pp. a.* known 24/151, 293/65.
couwardes, couwars *n. pl.* cowards 2/31, 345/141.
crapoudes *n. pl.* toads 95/281; **crapoudes** for crope ek var. J, **crupoudes** var. A 95/274.
criant *a.* vanquished 29/128, var. crea(u)nt A J.
crie *v. inf.* proclaim, implore 176/266; **cride** *pt.* 139/80; **icryd, ycried** *pp.* 691/36, 596/83.
crips *a.* curly 376/64, 424/672; **crispore** *comp.* 376/64.
Cristendom *n.* baptism 472/270, 473/295.
croici *v. inf.* sign with cross 495/76.
croke *n.* hook 28/90; **crokes** *pl.* 102/493.
croked *a.* misshapen, bent 380/181, 426/726.
crokkes *n. pl.* pots 586/26, 587/39.

crompe *n.* cramp 61/8.
crop *n.* harvest 505/392.
crope, icrope *v.* see **kreopen**.
croserie *n.* crusade 503/319, 321.
croume *n.* bit of bread 53/182.
croune *n.* tonsure 251/137; **crounen** *pl.* 91/161.
crounement *n.* coronation 626/488.
crouni *v. inf.* crown king 113/104, 580/260; **icrouned** *pp.* tonsured 628/545.
crounynge *n.* coronation 205/23.
crowen *n. pl.* crows 498/188.
*****cruets** *n. pl.* altar vessels 191/314.
crupel *n.* cripple 120/44; **crupeles** *pl.* 115/183.
crusinge *n.* crashing 487/115.
cun, kun *n.* kindred 20/21, 24/142; **cunne, kunne** 148/3, 55/37.
cunde *n.* see **kunde**.
cundehede *n.* kindness 49/77, 92/208.
cunrede *n.* see **kunrede**.
cupe *n.* basket 151/105.
cure *n.* duty, office 637/835, 838.
curnels *n. pl.* seeds 170/88.
cusse *v. inf.* in phr. ∼ *þes* kiss the pax 145/265; **custe** *pt.* kissed 74/92; *pt. pl.* 29/135.
cuþe *n.* understanding 218/16.
cuþe *v. inf.* reveal, make known 210/177; **cust** *2 pr.* 226/155; **kuþ** *imper.* 61/20; **kuddest** *2 pt.* 9/42; **cudde** *pt.* 22/110; **ikud** *pp.* 15/219.

dai, dawe *n.* space of time, appointed time 3/66, 113/94; **dawes, dauwes** *pl.* 83/65, 161/13; *ibroȝt of dawe* deprived of life 113/94; *for þe day* because of the feast-day 639/891.
day-þat *interj.* a curse on 67/134, 380/183.
danger, donger *n.* reluctance, difficulty 82/43, 212/25.
dasche *v. inf.* fall, strike violently 504/369; **dasste** *pt.* 219/51; *pt. pl. tr.* 363/150; **idasst** *pp.* 381/232.
dawe *v. inf.* dawn 477/23; **daweþ** *pr.* 109/684, 271/198.
dawynde *n.* dawning 271/198 var. A.
deale *interj.* ? look you 490/212.
deboner(e) *a.* mild, kindly 110/17, 179/25.
debruse *v. imper.* crush 324/255; **debrusede** *pt.* 379/155; *pt. intr.* dashed to pieces 268/120.
ded-bore *a.* still-born 493/13.
dede, deþe *n.* death 175/248, 250.
dedein *n.* contempt 606/389.
dedlich *a.* mortal 258/316.
ded-strong *a.* very strong 424/667.

GLOSSARY 49

dedut n. pleasure 32/5.
defaute n. lack, failure 125/98, 223/78.
defoule, defouli v. inf. maltreat 91/182, 25/10; **defoulede** pt. dirtied 113/99; **defouled** pp. 383/292.
degre n. step 8/17.
deie n. dairy maid 43/161.
deie, dei3e v. inf. die 67/152, 23/116; **deide** pt. 8/91; **deyinge** pr. p. 353/120.
dei3erie n. dairy 42/150.
deiny v. inf. impers. condescend 260/371; **deineþ** pr. 260/370; **deinede** pt. 391/41.
deinte n. esteem 205/35, 650/1221; **deintes** pl. delicacies 649/1208.
deis n. in phr. to þe heie ~ at the high table 120/71.
del, deol n.¹ grief, distress 296/140, 23/131.
del n.² share, part 46/264; in phr. þe meste del mostly 110/21.
del, deol n.³ devil 240/42, 108/670; see **adeolwey**.
dele v. inf. share, divide 46/261, 61/21, negotiate 222/46; **delde** pt. 42/149; **ideled** pp. 424/659.
delices n. pl. delicacies 130/46.
delyuere a. free 502/293.
delue, dolue v. inf. dig 177/294, 279/146; **delueþ** imper. pl. 471/244; **dalf** pt. 147/322; **dolue** pt. pl. 235/405; **idolue** pp. 177/295.
demande n. requirement 636/815; **demaunde** question 548/173.
deme v. inf. judge 249/72, 259/342; **dempnede** 1 pt. 704/196; pt. 701/104; **idemd** pp. 300/264.
den n. dean (of canons) 72/34.
deoluol a. distressful 10/73.
deoluoliche adv. grievously 73/67, 94/255.
deope, dupe adv. deeply 67/145, 144.
deore a. expensive 44/212; scarce 126/135; **dureste** superl. least productive 461/39.
deore, dere, dure adv. at a high price 98/366, 17/34, 3/57.
deorne, durne a. dark, privy 73/65, 490/219.
deorneliche adv. secretly 288/283.
deppore a. comp. more profound 432/117.
dere n. harm 63/36.
dere v. inf. harm, trouble 66/108; **derieþ** pr. pl. 299/226, 559/274.
derkhede n. darkness 28/116, 90/147.
derst v. 2 pr. darest 66/117, **dorstou** darest thou 200/587; (ne)**dar** pr. impers. needs 313/308; (ne)**der** pr. dares 130/63; **dorre** pr. pl. 65/97;

dorre pr. pl. need 184/119; **dorre** pr. subj. 331/100; (ne)**deorste** pt. 253/176; **derste, dorste** pt. pl. 382/250, 23/132; see **þerftou**.
deruelynges n. pl. probably error for deorlinges 182/56 var. A; **derlinges** J.
desclandre n. defamation 678/2077.
desclandrest v. 2 pr. slanderest 678/2066; **desclandred** pp. 526/346, 652/1272.
deserited pp. disinherited 11/97.
desertison, diserteisoun n. disinheritance, denial of rights 672/1878, 558/230.
deseruede v. pt. earned 58/134; **deserued** pp. merited 7/62.
desordeiny, disordeiny v. inf. deprive of orders 630/613, 622/378; **desordeined** pp. 623/402, 624/415.
despupli v. inf. publish 148/344.
destance n. disagreement 652/1293.
destorbance, distorbance n. interference, trouble 139/78, 668/1758.
destorbi, desturbi v. inf. interfere with 212/36, 504/363; **destourbed** pt. 621/326; pp. 704/202.
destourbour n. troubler 646/1116.
destreini v. inf. distrain (legal) 634/740; **destreined** pp. 634/750.
destresse, distresse n. distraint (legal) 634/753, 638/855.
destruie v. inf. lay waste, overthrow 443/16; **destrude** pt. pl. 173/190; **destrud** pp. 173/168, 392/72.
deþ-prowes n. pl. death-struggle 347/192.
deþ-vuel(e) n. mortal illness 175/237, 465/59.
deuelscine n. 156/13 var. A; see **chikene**.
deuelwey see **adeolwey**.
deuys n. plan 577/160.
deuise, deuisi v. inf. plan, arrange 577/167, 638/876; **diuisede** pt. 577/166.
dich n. hole, ditch 199/576, 291/364; **diches** pl. 97/359, 276/70.
di3te v. inf. arrange, fix 25/20, 63/22; pt. 35/87, 45/220; **idi3t** pp. 427/762.
dinge n. dung 588/55.
do, done v. inf. do, perform 133/123, 4/20; **dest, dust** 2 pr. 133/135, 137; **deode, dude** pt. 338/319, 35/96; **ide** pp. 34/54; as substitute verb **do** inf 80/62; **deode** pt. 448/170; as auxil **deþ** pr. 160/42.
dobbe-dont n. ? hitter of teeth, 'dent ist' 363/151; var. **double dunt** H line om. A J.

GLOSSARY

doghede *n.* ? trick 122/17; var. text lost H; **dogheþe** J.
dom-hall *n.* judgement hall 57/93; *domes halle* 371/193.
doste, doust(e) *n.* dust 347/189; ashes 27/74, 227/182.
doubli *v. inf.* make double 200/600; **idoubled** *pp.* 190/296.
douedoppes *n. pl.* dive-dappers, dabchicks 487/128.
doune *n.* upland 290/328, 456/9.
dounor *adv. comp.* lower down 98/367.
draȝt *n.* drink 600/222; drawing (of bow) 604/338; **drauȝtes** *pl.* lines 500/228.
drawinge *n.* pulling, compulsion 570/133, 136.
drei *v. inf.* endure 61/10, **dreoye** 606/378, var. **drie** H A.
dreinte *v. pt.* drowned 350/52; *pt. pl. subj.* 308/160.
drench *n.* drink, dose 70/19, 459/100.
drinkare *n.* tippler 424/685.
driue *v. inf.* overthrow 124/74; **drof** *pt. intr.* passed (time) 611/45; **drive** *pt. pl.* forced 260/390; **droue** *pt. pl. intr.* floated 557/215; **idriue** *pp.* driven off 75/141.
droppinge *adv.* in drops 422/606.
drowe *v. inf.* dry 43/170.
drowe *a.* dry 419/521, 527.
drueri, druori *n.* devotion 562/366, 450/45.
dulfulliche *adv.* miserably 499/216, 558/238.
dunt *n.* stroke 80/61; **duntes** *pl.* 419/541.
durc, durke *a.* dark 504/357, 538/170; **dercoste** *superl.* 104/549.
dure *n.* deer 132/114.
dure, dury *v. inf.* bear, hold out 459/98, 699/50.
dut *n.* delight 181/44; see **dedut**.
dutte *v. pt.* shut, closed 228/223, 298/208; *pt. pl.* 383/276; **idut** *pp.* 299/210, 481/134.
dwele *n.* delusion 261/405, 388/109.
dwelling *n.* trance 8/18, 15/210; deception 277/107.

eche *v. inf.* increase, lengthen 49/78, 578/216.
eche *a.* eternal 160/32.
eching *n.* increase 464/44.
eddre *n.* adder 126/132; **addren, eddren** *pl.* 95/274, 5/16.
edy *a.* blessed 369/131.
efd *n.* head 270/158.
efleue *a.* see **eleuene**.
ey *a.* high 72/34; see **hei(e)**.

ey *interj.* see **hei**.
eiȝe *n.*¹ eye 45/235, 77/202; **eien, eiȝene, eiȝne** *pl.* 145/269, 84/4, 15/210.
eiȝe, eyȝe, eye *n.*² fear, awe 130/64, 592/86, 589/91; see **loue-eiȝe**.
eiȝe, ey *n.*³ egg 415/396, 134/165; **eiren** *pl.* 276/57, 60; see **nest-ey**.
eiȝte *n.* possession 507/476.
eiȝte *a.* eight 132/120, 418/492; **atte** 415/413; **heyte** 690/4.
eiȝtetene *a.* eighteen 533/5.
eiȝteþe *a.*¹ eighth 3/4, 211/203, 274/5.
eiȝteþe *a.*² eighteenth 127/167.
eileþ *v. pr.* is amiss 175/245.
eir *n.*¹ the atmosphere 348/210, 418/512; violence, commotion 185/162, 499/213; þer=þe eir 419/518.
eir *n.*² heir 148/3, 384/7; **eirs** *pl.* 432/112.
eirmangars *n. pl.* dealers in eggs 276/69.
eld(e), eolde, vlþe *n.* age 40/75, 607/433, 533/6; *in eld* ripe 170/85.
elefþe, elleueþe *a.* eleventh 626/487, 461/34.
elenge *a.* wretched, lonely 92/185; **elinge** 201/639, 297/151.
eleuene *n. pl.* elves 410/255.
eleuene *a.* and *n.* eleven 443/35; **efleue** (should read **efileue**) ? for **enlleue** 443/1; **enleue** 444/56.
elleccioun *n.* choice, election 505/409.
elles *adv.* ? for **alles** completely, finally 273/267, var. **alles** H A J; 613/73, see var., **alles** J.
elne *n.* ell (measure) 170/99.
elot *n.* fuel 430/37; var. **elet** H A J.
embe *prep.* about 156/27, 538/164.
emuorþ *adv.* even 392/88.
enchantement *n.* magic, sorcery 331/102; **enchantementȝ** *pl.* 559/274, 569/124.
enchanterie *n.* magic 325/305.
encheson *n.* cause, reason 4/23, 22/94.
enclinede *v. pt.* bowed 448/159.
encontrede *v. pt.* met in conflict 194/413.
ene *adv.* once 23/114, 106/615.
enes *adv.* once 14/172, 42/136.
eneten *n. pl.* for **emeten** ants 684/2257; see var., **ameten** J; perhaps confused with **euete** newt, see 86/12.
engendrure *n.* begetting 409/242.
engini *v. inf.* deceive 410/275.
enginne *n.* contrivance, trick 560/319.
engynous *a.* crafty 410/265; var. **enignous** H; **enuyous** J.
enioigneþ *v. pr.* imposes 464/39.

GLOSSARY

enquere, enqueri *v. inf.* investigate, seek out 621/333, 175/233; enquereþ *pr.* 655/1379; enquerede *pt.* 440/30.
enqueste *n.* investigation 621/333, 348; body of investigators 704/197.
ensenteþ *v. pr. pl.* consent, agree 155/201; ensentede *pt.* 495/84; encented(e) *pt. pl.* 61/26, 674/1944; encendede 186/197.
ensignede *v. pt. pl.* appointed 278/133; var. assignede H A.
entempri *v. inf.* moderate 425/690; entempreþ *pr.* 425/687.
entende *v. inf.* give attention, understand 500/230; entendiþ *pr.* 598/158; entende *imper.* 500/237.
entente *n.* purpose 48/46, 213/77.
ententifliche *adv.* earnestly 464/23, 625/460.
entrediti *v. inf.* place under interdict 668/1754.
entre-metie *v. inf.* intermeddle 651/1259.
entri *v. inf.* engage, take part 568/66, 631/632.
enuenimed *v. pt. pl.* poisoned 325/308; *pp.* 402/19.
enuily *v. inf.* defile 238/492; see auyli.
eode *v. pt.* went, lived 696/107; *pt. pl.* 8/4; see ȝeode.
eoly *n.* oil 157/36, 431/86; see oil(e).
eorlich *a.* earthly 129/27.
eorne, erne, *v. inf.* run 27/61, 607/425; orn *pt.* 115/175, arnde rode 607/418; arnde, ernde *pt. pl.* 111/52, 456/5, ȝorne 325/291; yorne *pp.* 32/10; see vrne.
eorþe liȝt *n.* earth's light, natural light 369/120.
er *adv.*¹ ever 193/398, var. euer J.
er *adv.*² before 98/379, 193/399.
ere *a. comp.* earlier, elder 118/260; erore former 289/290, 428/788.
erende *n.* petition 37/147.
erie *v. inf.* plow 40/126.
erlich *adv.* early 639/905.
ern *n.* eagle, symbol of St. John 441/53, 598/160.
errour *n.* mistaken opinion 212/51.
ert *v. 2 pr.* art 65/82, 66/128; erte, ertou art thou 341/41, 66/118.
escere *n.* questioner 550/219.
esche, esse *v. inf.* ask 507/461, 13/136; esseþ *pr.* 376/72; esste *pt.* 72/47, eȝste 695/75; esste *pt. pl.* 19/13, est 228/229; see askest, axi.
eseliche *adv.* comfortably 35/87, 193/396.

est *n.* east 181/35; bi este east of 114/141; in the east 511/2.
est *a.* eastern 87/63, 405/89.
est *adv.* to the east 87/64; est norþ north-east 183/108.
estor *a.* eastern 405/83; see var., estor or estore J.
ete *v. inf.* eat 81/7; et, het *pt.* 9/21, 140/101; ete *pt. pl.* 120/63, neete 129/24; (i)ȝete *pp.* 130/50, 431/61.
eþ *a.* easy 229/250.
eþe *adv.* easily 506/429, 704/192.
eþi *v. inf.* breathe 386/61.
euene *a.* exactly fitting 332/135, 464/45; well-proportioned 376/65; al ~ just enough 130/60.
euene *adv.* directly 87/64, 185/154, heuene 415/404; proportionately 332/133; exactly 129/18; ? steadily 414/395.
eueneþ *v. pr.* likens, compares 664/1637, 1638.
euesong *n.* evensong 187/215, 190/312.
euete *n.* eft, newt 86/12.

See also under V

failli *v. inf.* be wanting, fall short 190/290, 334/203; faillest *2 pr.* 536/105; faillede *pt.* 62/16; *pt. pl.* 11/85.
faillynge *n.* lack 131/78.
fayn, faine *a.* glad 505/416, 447/134.
fairhede *n.* beauty 445/63, see var., 515/9.
fale *a.* many 126/151, 431/79; fele 470/204.
falle *v. inf.* rush, crowd 479/93; folle, fulle *inf.* fall 99/412, 470/204; fel, ful *pt.* 240/68, 471/222; folle, fulle *pt. pl.* 21/76, 457/52; folde *pt. pl.* 432/106, see var., fol J.
falling-dore *n.* trap-door 481/135.
falshede *n.* deception, untruth 337/287, 520/144.
fame *n.* reputation, public report 218/27, 303/25.
fare *n.* way of acting 251/123, 508/506.
fare *v. inf.* act, go 182/67; farþ *pr.* 34/51; fareþ *pr. pl.* 472/269; ferde *pt.* 362/115.
fastyng-day *n.* day appointed for fasting 131/74.
fastnede *v. pt. pl.* took hold 454/154.
fawe *a.* glad 45/231, 359/23; see fayn.
feble *a.* weak 25/13; mean (of clothes) 303/96; feblore *comp.* 413/360.
feblesce, feblesse *n.* infirmity 519/126, 81/11.

52 GLOSSARY

febli *v. inf. intr.* weaken 510/550, 604/342.
fecche *v. inf.* fetch 570/129; **fech** *imper.* 562/375; see **fette.**
fede *v. inf.* give food to, nourish 205/26; **fedeþ** *pr.* 473/279, **fet** 661/1566; **fedde** *pt.* 472/254; **ifed** *pp.* 539/202.
feinest *v. 2 pr.* dissemblest 27/55; **feinede** *pt.* pretended, disguised 586/8, 611/42.
fel, felle *n.* skin 19/6, 110/16.
fel, felle *a.* false, crafty 517/57, 60; **fellor** *comp.* 111/40.
felde *v. pt.* experienced 267/88; tested 572/8.
fellich *adv.* treacherously 112/85.
felon, feloun *n.* criminal 633/720, 628/557.
felonie *n.* treachery, deception 283/110, 526/319.
feme *v. inf.* froth at the mouth 329/54; **femede** *pt.* 156/15.
fenestre *n.* window 191/333, 268/116.
fentise *n.* cowardice 293/34.
feor, fur *adv.* far 383/300, 479/72; **fer, fur** *comp.* 8/15, 488/156.
feorde, furde *n.* invading force 10/67, 469/156; 'national' army 483/3; **ueorde** band 58/111.
ferce, fers *a.* haughty 341/35, 287/247.
ferde *v.* see **furde.**
fer(e) *n.* companion, spouse 488/169, 540/214; **feren** *pl.* 53/195.
ferblet, fereblet *a.* ? timid 424/674, 669.
ferede *n.* beauty 445/63 var. H A; see **fairhede.**
ferine *a.* see **foreyne.**
ferst *n.* respite, delay 301/266, 639/882.
ferst *adv.* first of all 1/7; for the first time 43/164, 188/247, **feorst** 2/45.
feteres *n. pl.* see **veteres.**
fette *v. inf.* obtain, fetch 30/151, 244/76; **fette** *pt. pl.* 48/34, 531/476; **ifet** *pp.* 568/71; see **fecche.**
feueres *n. pl.* in phr. *in* ~ in attacks of fever 219/59.
figure *n.* likeness, image 449/33, 450/39; **figurs** *pl.* numerical symbols 500/226, 227.
fiȝte *v. inf.* fight 3/54; **faȝt, fauȝt** *pt.* 2/50, 476/362; **foȝte** *pt. pl.* 391/50.
fil *a.* vile 218/45; **vylore** *comp.* 612/65.
fille *n.* full amount 505/395.
fille, fulle *v. inf.* cut down, fell 573/68; 172/151; **feolde** *pt.* 57/93.
fillich *adv.* see **villich.**
finde *v. inf.* provide for 615/161; **fonde** *pt. subj.* 685/2301.
fine, fini *v. inf.* cease 39/49, 142/167; **finde** *pt.* 453/124.

firmament *n.* vault of heaven 188/244, 408/204; **firmamens** *pl.* spheres 415/413.
fisschin *n.* fishing 543/4, var. **fischinge** A; **visching** J.
fiþele *n.* violin 341/18, 574/84.
flecchi, fleichi *v. inf.* waver, flinch 3/55, 16/S12; **flecchede** *pt.* 447/124; *pt. pl. subj.* 344/116.
fleinge *n.* flight 678/2088.
fleiss, flesch, flesse *n.* flesh 4/18, 496/117, 425/710; **fleissis, flesses** *g.* of body 2/42, 4/26.
fleme *n.* and *a.* fugitive 207/101, 671/1858.
fleme *v. inf.* exile 530/459; **iflemd** *pp.* 5/H10, 167/19.
fleo *v.¹ inf.* flee 6/42, 144/212; **flucþ** *pr.* 659/1497; **flei** *pt.* 47/5, 386/59; **fleide** *pt. pl.* 3/64, **flouwe** 71/11; **yflowe** *pp.* 34/70.
fleo *v.² inf.* fly 37/151; **fliȝþ** *pr.* 473/281, **flucþ** 442/79; **fleoþ** *pr. pl.* 80/63; **fleinge** *pr. p.* 404/63; **flei** *pt.* 122/13, **fleȝ** 460/127; **flowe** *pt. pl.* 85/22; **iflowe** *pp.* 442/81.
flet *v. pt.* floated 383/282, 406/144; **flote** *pt. pl.* 195/454, 517/72.
flo *n. pl.* arrows 347/207.
flod *n.* stream 64/56, 350/48.
floweþ *v. pr.* flows (of sea) 423/647; **fleu** *pt.* (of mist) 118/246.
flum *n.* river (Jordan) 2/46, 139/90.
fneosynge *v. pr. p.* sneezing 161/28, var. **fnesing(e)** A J.
fo, uo *n.* enemy 218/34, 325/313; **fon, von** *pl.* 13/158, 71/8; *fon of werrors* ? hostile bands of invaders 450/53, see var.
fode *n.* sustenance 20/29; child, offspring 20/23, 284/143.
fol, ful *a.¹* full, sated 131/79, 496/99.
fol, fole *a.²* foolish, wanton 535/54, 21/63.
folende *v. inf.* complete 449/27, 686/2321, **fulenden** 465/74.
folfelle, folfeolle, folfulle *v. inf.* complete 409/214, 408/210, 324/266, **folveolle** 686/2320; **folueolde** *pt.* 354/160.
follich(e) *adv.¹* fully 10/57, 408/193.
follich(e) *adv.²* foolishly 12/114, 631/639.
folie *n.* lechery 21/53, 496/104.
fonde, fondi *v.¹ inf.* test, try 632/674, 54/10; **fonde, fondede** *pt.* 111/24, 297/172; **ifonded** *pp.* 524/265.
fondede *v.² pt.* built, founded 213/57; **ifonded** *pp.* 620/320.
*****fonding** *n.* temptation 122/19.

GLOSSARY

fondour n. organizer, founder 149/21.
fonge v. inf. accept 16/S 11.
forbeode v. pr. subj. prohibit, forbid 89/104; **forbed, forbeod** pt. 6/22, 200/603; **forbode** pt. pl. 401/127.
forbere v. inf. tr. spare 270/171; intr. refrain 521/187; **forbere** pt. pl. 408/202.
forberne v. inf. burn up 57/91; **forbarnt** pr. 442/80, var. **brenþ** H; **forbrenneþ** J; **forbarnd, forbrende** pt. 321/176, 401/136; **forbarnd, forbrend** pp. 68/180, 245/95.
forbite pp. bitten to pieces 260/387.
forbonde pp. closely fettered 154/174.
forbroide pp. distorted 379/173, var. **forbrode** H.
forbusne n. example, precedent 397/11, 460/13.
forclef v. pt. split 194/414.
forcliȝt pp. clutched fast 98/380, var. **uorcluȝt** A; **uer cluyt** J.
forcroked pp. misshapen 379/175, 503/339.
fordrou v. pt. pl. cramped 61/8; **fordrawe** pp. tortured 94/242.
fordronke pp. thoroughly drunk 50/106.
fordwyne v. inf. waste away 558/257; **fordwineþ** pr. pl. 410/250.
fore n. track 121/77; *fore ? course of action, event 541/241; see var.
foreyne a. outside, in phr. chambre ~, c. ferine privy 67/131, 18/79; **furrene** (land) alien 534/20, 546/121; **furrenes** pl. as n. invaders 450/53 var. H.
for(e)ward(e) n. agreement 232/321, 573/54; **uorewarde** 391/49.
forfare v. inf. perish 517/66, 527/362.
forgnowe v. pt. pl. gnawed through 95/277; **forgnawe** pp. 454/162, 518/100.
forgon v. inf. lose, avoid 40/81, 113/104.
forgulte v. pt. forfeited 106/598, 409/216.
for-ȝelde v. pr. subj. reward 146/271.
forȝete, forȝute v. inf. forget 495/75, 15/218; **forȝat, forȝet** pt. 499/219, 56/70; **forȝet** pt. pl. 113/120; **forȝute** pp. 134/166.
forȝiue v. inf. pardon 412/330; **forȝifþ** pr. 412/332; **forȝef** pt. 76/165; **forȝiue, vorȝiue** pp. 76/164, 703/168.
forhote v. inf. renounce 524/282; **forhet** pt. 495/89, var. **vorhet** A.
forles v. pt. wasted, lost 502/311; **forlore** pp. 81/8.

forlete v. inf. surrender, abandon 12/110, 520/144; **forlet** pt. 487/126; **forlete** pt. pl. 676/2003; pp. 67/132.
forme, fourme n. agreement, decree 289/311, 75/121; **forme lair** 426/718.
formede v. pt. gave instructions 75/119, 209/139; shaped 148/334; **iformed** pp. 426/740.
formowed pp. ? rotted, mouldered 154/196; var. ~ H; om. A J.
forneis n. cauldron 157/61.
foroldeþ v. pr. grows old, decays 376/70; **forolded** pp. 154/196, 169/74, **forolþed** 498/178.
forpere v. 2 pr. subj. impair, spoil 295/101.
forpined, vorpinede v. pt. wasted 351/76, 689/2403; **forpined** pp. tormented 95/285.
forsake v. inf. refuse, renounce 47/4, 543/6; **forsok, vorsok** pt. 131/93, 148/4; **forsoke** pt. pl. 382/265; **vorsake** pp. abandoned 706/240.
forserit v. pr. withers 576/142 var. J.
forswelþ v. pr. scorches 442/80, 599/166.
forswolwe v. inf. swallow up 682/2208; **forswolwyde** pt. 297/161; **forswolwe** pp. 352/98.
forswore pp. perjured 526/339, 561/352.
fortrauailed pp. fatigued 290/313.
forþer a. fore (feet) 201/641.
forþward a. pre-eminent 19/6, var. **uorþward** A; **forwarþ** J.
forþward adv. from this time 34/66.
forwelwed pp. withered 169/55.
fot n. in phr. fot wiþ ~ together 653/1326; **fet, uet** pl. footprints 405/90, 84.
foulares n. g. cloth-fuller's 647/1141.
foulhede n. foulness 379/164.
fouly v. inf. pollute 20/24.
four-heornede a. four-cornered 608/465, var. **four-hurnede** H J; **four cornerde** A.
fourteþe a. fourteenth 191/332.
framward prep. away from 181/48; ? contrary to, against 161/9.
franchise n. spiritual freedom 55/39; authority 641/950.
fredde v. pt. pl. experienced 182/62 var. A; **fred ȝe** J.
freitor n. refectory 189/276, 190/309.
freo-stone n. sandstone or limestone 290/333.
frere n. friend in phr. beu ~ 105/565; monk 190/295; friar 104/552.
frest v. pr. freezes 422/617, 621;

E

GLOSSARY

freoseþ *pr. pl.* 422/608; freose ? *pr. subj.* 422/618; ifrore *pp.* 422/609.
frete *v. inf.* devour 321/162; frete *pt. pl.* 161/22; ifrete *pp.* 454/158; see cancre-frete.
friinge *v. pr. p.* frying 28/92.
front *n.* forehead 379/171, 649/1201.
fulle *n.* fill, satisfactory amount 43/183; full measure 554/137, 555/142.
fulle *v.* fill 179/27; fulde *pt. pt. pl.* 68/171; ifuld *pp.* 98/361.
fulþhede *n.* filth 18/79; discharge 266/56.
fur *n.* fire 93/218; the element 418/511; *a fure* on fire 94/252, see avure.
furde *n.* see feorde.
furde *a.* fourth 471/236, 578/193; see veorþe.
furde *v. pt.* acted, behaved 503/331, 514/86, ferde happened 680/2147; furde *pt. pl.* 186/186 var. H A; ferde J.
fur-gleden *n. pl.* coals of fire 323/239.
furi *a.* fiery, red-hot 28/89, 95/273.
fur-ire *n.* metal for striking sparks 201/641.
furrene *a.* see foreyne.
furste *a.* first 484/38; see veorste.

gaihol *n.* prison 28/111, 56/47.
gailers *n. pl.* jailers 251/117, 458/69.
gal *n.* evil 65/84.
galou-treo *n.* gallows 337/299.
galpede *v. pt. pl.* yawned 161/29; galpinge *pr. p.* 161/28.
game *n.*[1] see gome.
game *n.*[2] joy, pleasure 26/27, 511/575; play 68/184, 119/26; games *pl.* 119/21.
gameninge *n.* sporting 551/10.
Gangdawes *n. pl.* Rogation days 161/11.
gareisoun, gerison *n.* treasure, provision 577/171, 635/788.
gaste *v. pt. reflex.* fear 343/97.
gastliche *a.* terrifying 345/147.
*gawe *v. inf.* stare 66/125, var. gawen A; gawy J.
gentrise *n.* gentility, courtesy 64/52, 705/221.
ger *n.* action 72/35.
gering *n.* ? crude fellow 34/46; gerings *pl.* 213/69, var. geringes J.
gerner *n.* granary 126/143.
gibet *n.* gallows 27/60, 438/126.
Gibolot *n.* ? giblet, 'accessory' 465/55, var. gibilot A; gibelot J. H capitalizes the word; J reads sire gibelot for here Gibolot; A condenses the passage (see var.) and substitutes gibilot for Gilbert in l. 52. Probably used as term of contempt; see *O.E.D.* giblet 1.
gydihede *n.* foolishness 534/13, 535/52.
gidiliche *adv.* wantonly 272/218.
gile *n.* trickery, deceit 111/36, 699/48.
gili *v. inf.* deceive 339/369; gileþ *pr.* 338/324.
gilour *n.* deceiver 217/13; gilours *pl.* 548/172.
gin, ginne *n.* trick, device 55/32, 36/123; gynne skill 414/392; gynnes *pl.* 151/82.
gist *n.* guest 351/83; gustes *g.s.* 120/74; gistes *pl.* 120/61, 64.
gistnynge *n.* hospitality 120/64; gustnynge 608/474, var. gisnynge J.
gywise *n.* judgement 533/10.
glad *n.* gladness 117/229.
gladful *a.* joyous 516/39.
gladi(e) *v. inf.* make glad 593/96, 649/1210; gladede *pt.* 253/176; igladed *pp.* 253/174.
glide *v. inf.* move smoothly, slide 504/367, 517/71; glide *pr. subj.* 102/476.
glose *n.* flattery 54/12.
gloue *n.* glove 355/188; glouene *pl.* 355/182.
gnawe *v. inf.* chew, gnaw 321/162; gnou(3) *pt.* 349/21, 518/88; gnowe *pt. pl.* 94/256; ignawe *pp.* 85/33.
gnawynge *n.* action of gnawing 454/164.
goday, godday *n.* good day (in greeting) 13/136, 211/200.
goder *a.* in phr. *of ~ half* ? of good sort 441/60, see var. H A; *in gode half* J. The readings of H A suggest confusion with phr. *a godes halue* in God's name.
goder-hele *n.* prosperity 216/52; *to ~* to their good fortune 531/484.
godhede *n.* goodness 472/261.
goinde *pr. p. a.* thriving 615/148.
golion *n.* '? a kind of gown or tunic', *O.E.D.* 376/67.
gome *n.* heed 41/126, 211/13; game ? for gome 47/26; see ȝeme.
go(n) *v. inf.* go 8/14, 108/656; geþ *pr.* 20/33, 106/609, goþ 108/656; goynde *pr. p.* 19/7; igone *pp.* 121/85.
goninge *n.* yawning 161/27 var. H.
gostliche *adv.* as a spirit 354/149.
goþely *v. inf.* bubble, rumble 419/532; goþeleþ *pr.* 419/530, 534.
gouern *n.* rule 669/1798.
goute *n.* podagra, gout 119/39, 468/131.

GLOSSARY 55

gracious *a.* pleasing 349/11.
gram *a.* angry 456/208, 457/41.
gramerie *n.* learning 123/45.
grece, gresse *n.* fat 28/92, 459/89.
grede *v. inf.* cry out 21/81; **gret** *pr.* 640/914; **gradde** *pt.* 48/50; *pt. pl.* 76/176.
gredil, gridil *n.* instrument of torture 347/202, 179/17; **gridils** *pl.* 96/319.
grei(e) *a.* grey (of Cistercian monks) 119/35, 660/1539.
grein *n.* granular matter (manna) 609/493; **grenes** particles *pl.* 609/489.
greipe *v. inf.* prepare 10/65; **greiped(e)** *pt.* 215/39, 401/119; **greipede** *pt. pl.* 562/372.
grene *a.* verdant 154/197, 168/47; **grenor** *comp.* 191/341.
grenne *v. inf.* bare the teeth 329/54; **grennynge** *pr. p.* 92/198; **grennede** *pt.* 156/15; *pt. pl.* 93/218.
gretnesse *n.* bulkiness 186/172.
greue, greui *v. inf.* harass, trouble 103/516, 216/63; **greueþ** *pr.* 27/55; **greuede** *pt.* 32/22; **igreued** *pp.* 278/122.
greuous *a.* severe (of disease) 566/5.
gridire *n.* gridiron, instrument of torture 347/204.
grihoundes *n. pl.* greyhounds 487/138.
grip *n.* griffin 194/429.
grislich *a.* terrifying, horrible 7/70, 36/117; **grislikere, -loker** *comp.* 504/360, 588/61; **grislikeste, -lokest** *superl.* 504/356, 325/300.
groynynge *n.* grumbling 424/668.
grom *n.* boy 124/82, 615/148.
gronde, grounde *n.* bottom 77/180; *agrond gan valle* submitted 349/12; *at is herte* ~ from the bottom of his heart 180/19; *al to* ~ completely 696/118.
grunte *v. pt.* groaned, grunted 343/99; *pt. pl.* 454/168.
gruwel *n.* liquid food 9/22.
gurd *v.* ? *pt. pl.* entwined 95/276, see var., hi gurþe J; **igurd** *pp.* girded 498/167.
gwie *v. inf.* command 33/24.

ȝar(e) *poss. a.* their 130/56, 193/378, **ȝhare** 688/2400; see hare².
ȝare *a.* ready, quick 6/30, 23/117; **ȝaru** 562/361.
ȝare, ȝore *adv.* long, for a long time 12/119, 253/195.
ȝarke, ȝarki *v. inf.* make ready 10/70, 562/360; **ȝarkede** *pt.* 404/69; (i)**ȝarked** *pp.* 146/270, 360/63.

ȝat, ȝet *n.* gate 87/65, 103/506; **ȝate, ȝete** *d.* 109/685, 103/517; **ȝetes** *pl.* 364/181.
ȝe, ȝo *pron.*¹ see heo.
ȝe *pron.*² ye 65/96; **ȝoure** *g.* 183/101; **ȝou** *d.* and *acc.* 12/125, 273/260, **ou** 65/95.
ȝef, ȝif *conj.* if 53/176, 179.
ȝelde *v. inf.* render (accounts) 65/98, give up, surrender 100/432; **ȝeld** *imper.* 606/399; *pt.* 658/1453; see ȝulde.
ȝelle *v.* see ȝolle, ȝulle.
ȝeme *n.* heed 119/9, 123/44; see gome.
ȝend *a.* in phr. *aȝend half* on the other side 36/110, 204/714.
ȝend *adv.* over there 12/127, 180/1.
ȝen-ȝeld *n.* ? one who redeems his pledge 555/153 var. A.
ȝeode, ȝude *v. pt.* went 6/43, 581/310; **ȝeode** *pt. pl.* 63/42; see eode.
ȝeord(e) *n.* branch, rod 284/165, 368/85; **ȝeorden, ȝerden** *pl.* 170/98, 104/556.
ȝeorne, ȝerne *adv.* earnestly 183/92, 85/40.
ȝep *a.* shrewd 304/33.
ȝeresday *n.* New Year's Day 3/67, 1.
ȝilpe *v. inf.* boast 241/86.
ȝiue *v. inf.* give, grant 77/196, 199/566; **gifþ** *pr.* 44/188; *pr. pl.* 213/70; **ȝaf, ȝef** *pt.* 136/48, 43/175; **ȝeue** *pt. pl.* 287/233.
ȝolke *n.* yolk 423/634.
ȝolle *v. inf.* howl, shout 197/500, **ȝelle** 196/479; **ȝollinde, ȝollinge** *pr. p.* 92/193, 177/307; **ȝal** *pt.* 207/83; **ȝolle** *pt. pl.* 93/227; see ȝulle.
ȝollinge, ȝollynde *n.* shouting 102/491, 196/490.
ȝonede *v. pt.* gaped 297/159; *pt. pl.* 93/218; **ȝonynge** *pr. p.* 92/198, 96/321.
ȝong *a.* young 21/58, 169/79; **ȝonge** *pl.* 260/389; **ȝongore** *comp.* 127/10, 434/160; **ȝengoste, ȝongoste** *superl.* 165/45, 49.
ȝonghede, ȝunghede *n.* youth 20/47, 516/42.
ȝonglich *a.* youthful 203/703.
ȝorne *v.* see eorne.
ȝote *v. pt. pl.* poured 64/55.
ȝoure *poss. a.* your 330/85, 534/22.
ȝulde *v. inf.* give up, repay 12/124; **ȝoulde** 2 *pt.* rendered 636/811; **ȝulde** *pt. pl.* 469/183; **iȝoulde, iȝulde** *pp.* 12/134, 464/40; see ȝelde.
ȝulle *v. inf.* yell 541/242; **ȝullinge** *pr. p.* 514/87; see ȝolle.
ȝus(e) *adv.* yes 55/39, 560/317.

56 GLOSSARY

habbe v. inf. have 131/89; haste 2 pr. 129/20; hadde pt. 135/26, hauede 551/23; ihaued, iheued, ihed pp. 472/249, 28/84, 663/1624.
hacche n. opening, hatch 299/222.
hale interj. hail 343/86.
half num.: see ȝend a.
halibred n. blessed bread 467/105.
halidom n. saintly relics 685/2289.
halsinge n. supplication 313/307.
halsni v. 1 pr. adjure 313/305, 467/109; halsnede pt. 686/2329 var. A.
halst v. 2 pr. salutest 324/276.
haluendel, haluondel half; n. 432/110; a. 140/101, 415/412; adv. 182/58.
hamely v. inf. break (of teeth) 84/16.
hamme n. bend of knee 119/42.
handly v. inf. touch, manipulate 21/76, 120/50; handlede pt. 276/60; ihandled pp. 131/77.
hange, honge v. inf. tr. and intr. hang, be suspended 18/80, 199/571; hongeþ pr. 199/557; honge pr. s. 199/564; heng pt. 27/64, heong 697/140; honge pt. pl. 96/315.
hanne, henne, hunne adv. hence 15/197, 82/51, 559/289.
hant n. practice, use 137/30.
hardie v. inf. strengthen 2/28.
hare poss. a.¹ her 18/56, hire 523/235, hure 19/15.
hare poss. a.² their 1/18, 194/411, her(e) 2/36, 86/30, hore 37/4, 91/163, ȝare 13/154, ȝhare 691/47.
harlede v.¹ pt. ? confused, harried 163/17.
harli v.² inf. drag 570/131; harlede pt. 188/241; harled(e) pt. pl. 97/348, 330/77; iharled pp. 659/1505.
harmi v. inf. hurt 570/142.
harmles a. unharmed 9/40, 48/56.
hasewe adv. hoarsely 96/303 var. A; aswe J.
hastelich adv. quickly 133/146, 177/291.
hasti v. inf. quicken, make haste 318/90; hastede pt. 619/272.
hastyve a. in a hurry 688/2399.
hauberk n. armour worn as penitential garment 493/30.
hauene n. inlet, harbour 184/115, 188/251.
hauly v. inf. hail 203/685.
haunti v. inf. frequent 606/383; hantede pt. practised 606/384.
hawel n. hail 422/610.
he pron. he 1/9, a 47/21; him d. and acc. 12/126, 4/27; hine acc. 106/618, ine 12/121.
hebbe v. inf. lift, raise 123/60, 484/44; haf pt. 322/197, 429/20; heue pt. pl. 117/218, houede 448/168; ihoue pp. 143/194.
hede n. attention 205/25, 275/47.
hei, ey interj. 538/137, 299/220, var. hei A J.
hey n. dry grass 185/143.
heiday n. festal day 86/18, 128/23.
hei(e) a. high, exalted 3/1, 118/257; heiȝe 109/698; heiere comp. 549/197, her(r)e 115/158, 164; heiost superl. 16/3, hecst, hext 246/1, 71/4; anhey aloud 653/1314; fram heie from above 9/43.
heie adv. high, aloft 96/310, heiȝe 7/81, hey 123/63; heȝere comp. 464/30, herre 149/38, 442/92.
heie v. inf. hasten 301/267, hie 171/115, hiȝie 541/248; hiede pt. 78/13, hiȝede 207/92; pt. pl. 30/164.
heilich adv. ceremoniously 78/219, 90/131.
heinesse n. height 143/194; heinesse majesty 372/219, heȝnisse 462/55.
heyte a. see eiȝte.
heiuol n. full (of the moon) 135/9, hey uolle 135/13.
heiuol a. at the full 417/468, 434/13.
heie-way n. main road (fig.) 589/102.
helde v. inf. take charge of 42/145; var. ȝelpe yield J; see holde.
hele n.¹ heel 493/30; helen pl. 426/720; heles 532/508.
hele n.² health, cure 61/3, 388/112; to luper ~ to bad purpose 273/255; see goder-hele.
hele v.¹ inf. heal 31/16; held pt. 429/24, hel(e)de 70/17, 71/28; iheld pp. 57/80.
hele, helie v.² inf. cover, hide 72/49, 141/148; helede pt. 20/49, iheled pp. 40/78, 290/333.
helie v.³ inf. anoint 77/209; var. elie A J.
helpe v. inf. aid 317/54; halp pt. 95/286; holpe pt. s. 102/480; pt. pl. 76/161; iholpe pp. 253/184.
helue a. half 483/20.
hende a. gentle, gracious 54/16, 132/105.
hendeliche adv. courteously 188/228, 616/167.
hendessipe, hendyssipe n. courtesy 298/189, 66/107.
hendi a. pleasing, courteous 26/50, 120/69.
hene v. inf. stone 151/108; pr. subj. 410/270; hende pt. pl. 154/180, 591/30.
hente v. inf. catch, seize 267/74, 395/170; pt. 207/80, 503/336.

GLOSSARY

heo *pron.* she 19/3, he 39/55, 134/166, ƷƷe 417/456, ʒo 222/62; hure g. 38/36, 41/108; hire d. and acc. 539/180, 535/64, hure 42/139.
heorne, hurne *n.* corner 53/175, 83/66; heornes *pl.* 379/161.
hep(e) *n.* crowd, mass 195/445, 553/89.
herbigour *n.* host 32/3.
herborwe *v. inf.* lodge 352/108; herborwedest 2 *pt.* 352/107.
her(e) *n.*¹ hair 20/48, 373/239.
here *n.*² haircloth, hair-shirt 157/42, 493/29; here(n) *pl.* 494/52, 682/2199.
herʒund *adv.* over here 577/164, 165.
herie *v.* praise 83/72; herede *pt.* 78/215; ihered *pp.* 26/40, yherd 167/4.
heriet *n.* feudal death-duty 507/468.
heriinge *n.* praising 393/118.
heste *n.* command 48/57, 430/39; promise 215/35.
hete *n.* vital heat 428/787.
hete *v. inf.* make hot 36/123; hatte, hette *pt.* 228/221, 459/94; hatte *pt. pl.* 438/123.
heþenesse *n.* state of being heathen 82/33, 435/35.
heu, hiu *n.* colour 538/150, 104/553, hiwe 376/69.
heued, efd *n.* head 8/16, 270/158; heueden *pl.* 51/133, heuedes 575/113.
heued-sunnes *n. pl.* cardinal sins 303/24.
heuegy *v. inf.* grow heavy 14/186, 343/96, heuy 510/550.
heuene *adv.* see euene.
heueneriche *n.* kingdom of heaven 568/67.
heui(e) *a.* sluggish 130/48, 56; heui of great weight 343/83; heuegore *comp.* 344/106.
heuynesse *n.* weight 418/500.
hewe *v. inf.* cut, cut to pieces 75/136, 172/151; heu *pt.* 67/154; hewe *pt. pl.* 347/189.
hi, i, y *pron.* they 3/55, 10/82; hore *g.* 9/30, ore 142/176; am *acc.* and *dat.* 65/86, ʒam 222/50, ʒham 691/35, ham 2/37, hem 2/24, hom 5/H 7, is 43/168, 170/105; amsulue *refl.* 10/72.
hiden *n. pl.* hides (of land) 116/213.
hinde *n.* female deer 385/43, 387/74.
hinder *a.*¹ back 201/640.
hinder *a.*² crafty 424/683.
hine *n.* servant, fellow 49/64, 244/85; *pl.* 52/155, 125/124.
hire see hare *poss. a.*¹
ho *n.* heel 152/118, 297/160.
ho *adv.* how 99/415, var. hou A J.

hoked *a.* hook-shaped 349/19.
hoker *n.* contempt 2/37, 31/8; hokeranswere scornful reply 213/70.
hol *n.* opening 43/169, 340/382.
hol(e) *a.* sound, unhurt 9/40, 246/133; holor, hollere *comp.* 429/24, 581/284.
holde *v. inf.* keep, uphold, esteem 76/147; halst 2 *pr.* 324/276; halt, halþ *pr.* 113/92, 574/75; held, heold, huld *pt.* 82/51, 699/58; helde, hulde *pt. pl.* 398/42, 113/119; iholde *pp.* 119/38; halt *pr. intr.* profits 45/238, 273/261.
holou *a.* hollow 332/134, *holwe 90/146, var. A J.
holour *n.* lecher 606/386.
homage *n.* acknowledgement of allegiance 222/42, omage 629/592.
hond-habbinge *a.* 'red-handed' 336/267.
hongri *a.* barren (of land) 385/31.
hontares *n. g. pl.* hunters' 646/1105.
honte, hunte *n.* hunter 387/89, 488/144; honten, hontes *pl.* 47/19, 386/55.
honte, hunti *v. inf.* seek, hunt 102/489, 477/26; hontest, huntest 2 *pr.* 260/370, 569/113; hontede *pt.* 32/7.
honteþ *n.* see anhonteþ.
honting *n.* hunting 387/73.
honurance *n.* honour 54/200, 246/136, *onorance 230/281, see var.
honuri, onury *v. inf.* pay respect to 33/37, 50/98, honure 62/42; onuryeþ *1 pr. pl.* 458/79; (h)onurede *pt.* 14/175, 221/14.
honuringe *n.* expression of honour 256/259.
hoppe *v. inf.* dance 410/254; see huppe.
hoppinge *n.* dancing 574/83.
hor(e) *a.* white with age 141/147, 200/615.
hordom *n.* adultery, prostitution 242/32, 551/27.
hordres *n. pl.* monastic rules 73/51.
hore *n.*¹ harlot 34/47, 54/7; horen *pl.* 54/8, 588/65.
hore *n.*² uncleanness 47/1, 54/2.
hore see hare *poss. a.*²
horegeþ *v. pr.* infects 57/84.
hor-forst *n.* white frost 422/617, 423/626.
horling *n.* paramour 34/50.
hors-her *n.* material made of horse-hair 498/161.
hors-knaues *n. pl.* stable-boys 536/78 var. A.
hosewif *n.* manager 310/233.
hostesse *n.* mistress of inn 352/117, ostesce 496/101.

58 GLOSSARY

hote v. inf. tr. command 62/14; **het** pt. 5/20; **hete** pt. pl. 83/61; **ihote** pp. 63/25; **hatte** 1 pr. intr. am called 156/23; **het** pt. 88/90; **hete** pt. pl. shouted 469/161; **ihote** pp. 150/67.

houe, houi v. inf. be suspended 146/296, 192/371; **houeþ** pr. 422/605; **houede** pt. 143/195; stood in doubt 233/352.

houede v.¹ pt. pl. see hebbe.

houede v.² pt. pl. shouted, in phr. *houede and cride* 447/131, see var., **hweþe** J.

houseli v. inf. give or receive communion 127/164, 405/96; **houseled** pt. 353/135; **ihouseled** pp. 147/315, 140/127.

houte v. inf. shout at 163/20; **hoting** pr. p. 336/262.

howe n. concern 490/220.

hucche n. pen, hut 481/136, see var., **wute** (l. 139 **wiuche**) J; coffer 533/547, var. **wuche** A; **whuche** J.

hude n. human skin 424/667; *bole huden* pl. bull-hides 183/94.

hude v. inf. conceal 239/13; **hudde** pt. 47/7; pt. pl. 174/222; **ihud** pp. 21/73.

hudels n. hiding-place 151/107.

hudynge n. concealment 206/53, 655/1387.

hul n. hill 58/122, 98/376, **hulle** 333/171; **hulles** pl. 406/121, 122.

hulde v.¹ inf. flay 382/243; **hult** pr. 382/244; **hulde** pt. 382/244; **ihuld** pp. 382/247, 577/183.

hulde v.² pt. pl. poured 40/88.

*****huppe** v. inf. hop, spring 276/70; **hipte** pt. 563/391, **hupte** 68/174; pt. pl. 52/155.

hure n.¹ iron 66/113, see var., **iren** J.

hure n.² fee 137/39, 206/64.

hure v.¹ inf. hear 3/59; **hurþ** pr. 440/26; **hureþ** pr. pl. 348/1; **heorde, hurde** pt. 447/151, 10/69; **heorde, hurde** pt. pl. 680/2132, 80/75; **ihurd** pp. 22/96.

hure v.² inf. hire 363/152; **hurede** pt. 648/1179; 1 pt. subj. 573/43.

hure poss. a. see hare¹.

hurst n. hillock 414/394.

hurtynge n. injury 159/6.

hutte v. pt. struck, shot 326/336, 387/92.

iambeleue adv. head first 407/177; see *Land of Cockaygne*, l. 166 (ed. Heuser, *Die Kildare-Gedichte*, Bonn, 1904).

iascony n. name of the great fish, whale 185/171.

ibarred pp. closed with bars 558/242.

ibide v. inf. endure 284/141; **ibod** pt. 348/4.

ibonde pp. bound 328/37; ? **iboned** 588/83, see var., to **boneþ** J; perhaps mistake for **ibanned** cursed.

ibroide pp. braided 498/159.

ibust pp. beaten 441/61.

icche v. inf. move 75/138, 570/132.

idaubed pp. besmeared 588/83.

ideorked pp. darkened 656/1422.

idoʒt pp. in exclam. *vuele mote hem beo* ~ may it be of no profit to them 457/47.

idreiʒt pp. troubled, distressed 533/539, 535/45.

ifele v. inf. feel 498/164; **iuelde** pt. 99/395; **yuel** inf. intr. be sensitive 427/747.

ifulled pp. baptized 473/285, 538/141.

igraued pp. carved, inscribed 56/56, 495/94.

igremed pp. angered 233/363.

iʒete pp. see ete.

ihol a. solid, complete 90/155, 455/193.

ihole pp. concealed 86/22; see hele v.²

iholed pp. hollowed 560/320.

ihure v. inf. hear, listen to 28/102, 500/240; **ihure** imper. 48/42; **ihurde** pt. 398/31.

ihurt pp. injured 387/93.

yhuwed pp. coloured 683/2222.

iknewe, iknowe v. inf. recognize, acknowledge 271/187, 376/61; **ikneu** pt. 23/112; **iknewe, iknowe** pp. 175/241, 235.

ikud pp. see cuþe.

ilaste, ileste v. inf. continue 360/66, 544/61; **ileste** pt. 546/97.

ileoue, ileue v. inf. believe 272/222, 124/81; **iluue** 2 pr. subj. 270/162; **ileoue** pr. subj. 418/497; **iluued** pt. 152/111.

ilich(e) a. similar 4/22, 82/28; *euere iliche* always the same 378/120.

iliche adv. equally 104/541, 376/70.

ilyk n. counterpart 694/66.

ille a. harmful 411/297.

ille adv. amiss 26/25.

illespyl n. hedgehog 513/47.

ilome adv. frequently 86/25, 88/67.

ilong a. depending 664/1650.

ymage n. painted likeness 702/143; **ymages** pl. idols 359/16.

imaymed pp. mutilated 46/244.

imassed pp. said mass 227/185, 475/344.

imedled pp. mingled 189/277.

GLOSSARY 59

ymete *a.* fit 172/156.
imette *v. pt. pl.* met 358/32.
ymone *n.* intercourse 4/26, 348/4.
imone *adv.* together 193/381, 460/8.
in, inne *n.* lodging, shelter 32/2, 60/37.
inliche *adv.* feelingly 658/1454, 667/1720.
inne, inni *v. inf.* give shelter, lodge 352/118, 37/144; innedest 2 *pt.* 352/118; ynnede *pt.* 523/235.
innore-more *adv.* farther in 102/481, 405/91.
inobedient *a.* not submissive 12/123.
inou, inowe *adv.* sufficiently 98/370, 95/290; of inou ? for oft inou 442/77.
insiȝt *n.* understanding 415/410, 576/134.
inwit *n.* conscience 199/563, 412/321; reason 534/28.
iogelor *n.* buffoon, jester 125/118, 341/19.
ioyned *v. pt. pl.* affixed 58/115.
ioious *a.* joyful 213/62, 275/36.
ioyuol *a.* delightful 17/19, 185/148; glad 41/116.
iolif *a.* gay 303/16.
iolifte *n.* pleasure 54/16, 602/258.
iordred *pp.* regulated 428/4.
iorneis, iourneyes *n. pl.* days' travel 181/32, 542/300.
ioutlawed, y- *pp.* exiled 596/79, 71.
ipeired *pp.* harmed 310/226.
ipiched *pp.* covered with pitch 183/95.
iquede *pp.* allotted 523/254.
irchon *n.* hedgehog 18/50.
ire *n.* iron 28/85, 94/252; ires *pl.* instruments of iron 84/16.
iredi *a.* prepared 10/71, 361/89.
irescettet *pp.* given refuge 651/1248.
iryue *pp.* pierced 97/331.
is *n.* ice 98/382, 244/61; yse *d.* 244/60.
is *pron.* see hi.
ise(o) *v. inf.* see 84/5, 254/208; isay, isey *pt.* 126/156, 16/14; iseȝe, iseie *pt. pl.* 530/471, 290/323.
isene *a.* visible 405/84.
isib, isibbe *a.* akin 445/85, 122/5.
issil *n.* exile 596/84, var. exil A; jssil J.
ysome *a.* in agreement 150/52.
istabled *pp.* established 264/488, 357/5.
iswowe *pp.* in a swoon 29/125, 308/165.
iþeined *pp.* served 587/37.
iþeo *v. inf.* thrive 49/83, 185/146; iþeȝ, iþei, iþeyȝ *pt.* 493/17, 40/73, 698/9.
ivare *v. pr. pl.* act 45/237.
yuel see ifele.

iuelynge *n.* sensation 427/746.
iugeþ *v. pr.* passes judgement on 655/1372; iugede *pt.* decreed 704/182; iuggede *pt. pl.* 22/89.
iupe *n.* tunic 490/205, 218.
iveost *pp.* see wite *v.*²
ivere *n.* companion 103/522, 353/130; yuere *pl.* 82/31.
yuere *adv.* together 17/19, 586/20, ifere 421/579 var. H.
*yuetered *pp.* fettered 214/88, see var., al ifedereþ J.
ius *n.* juice 120/52.
iwar *a.* aware 37/11, 197/520.
iweld *pp. a.* molten 64/59, 179/15.
iwelde *v. inf.* control 119/42.
iwemmed, y- *pp.* harmed, defiled 23/114, 85/4.
iwepned *pp. a.* armed 603/320.
iweue *pp.* woven 498/159.
iwynne *v. inf.* gain, find 305/67, 448/179.
iwite *v. inf.* know, recognize 134/165, 387/83.
ywon *n.* resource 170/96; see won.
iworþe *v. inf.* in phr. *let* ~ let go one's way 201/635, 401/128.

See also under C

karie *v. inf.* lament 597/100.
keie *n.* key 87/66, 263/482; keien *pl.* 247/21.
kele *v. inf.* cool 344/102.
kende *v. pt.* made known 176/278, 181/31; took the way 260/382, 348/212; *pt. pl.* 335/250.
kene *a.* sharp 23/123, 50/88; kennore *comp.* more fierce 260/375.
kenneþ *v. pr.* is conceived 425/702; *pr. pl.* 425/699; ikend *pp.* 425/716, (i)kenned 105/577, 273/253.
keouere, keueri *v. inf.* regain, recover 697/136, 266/60; ykeuered *pp.* 266/61.
kepe *v. 1 pr.* have regard, care (for) 642/1002; kepte *pt.* 206/64, 671/1847; *pt. subj.* 79/25.
kerue *v. inf.* cut, slice 84/17, 326/321; carf *pt.* 140/101, 338/341; corue *pt. subj.* 513/50.
kete *a.* powerful 423/656.
kychene *n.* kitchen 577/165, 586/25.
kinriche *n.* kingdom 533/8.
kippe *v. pr. pl. subj.* should snatch, seize 331/96; kipte *pt.* 320/157 var. H, 575/102.
knen *n. pl.* knees 225/141, 426/720, knou 224/106.
kneole, kneoli *v. inf.* kneel 145/258,

GLOSSARY

259; **kneoleþ** *pr.* 375/52; **kneolede** *pt. pl.* 628/536.
knowe *v. inf.* recognize, acknowledge 383/297; **knoweþ** *pr.* 204/718, **knouþ** understands 375/57; **kneu** *pt.* 96/324; **knewe** *pt. pl.* 86/23; **iknewe** confessed 86/24.
knowede *v. pt. pl.* kneeled 527/379.
knyt *v. pr.* nets, fastens 498/160; **knutte** *pt. pl.* 220/94; **iknyt** *pp.* 498/160.
kreopen *v. inf.* creep 496/110; **krep** *pt.* 528/397; **crope** *pt. pl.* 95/274; **icrope** *pp.* 126/133.
kun see **cou**.
kunde *n.* nature, state 4/25, 82/26, **cunde** 20/27, 49/80, **kende** 598/157.
kunde *a.* natural 1/2; well-born 291/2; **kundest** *superl.* having most right by birth 11/96, var. **kendest** J.
kunrede, cunrede *n.* family, kin 293/62, 65; **kunrede** *pl.* generations 369/131.

lac *n.* blemish 45/227.
laddes *n. pl.* fellows 481/140.
laȝinge *n.* laughing 551/10.
lampen *n. pl.* lamps 163/34, 369/114.
langages *n. pl.* national ways of speech 214/16.
langur *n.* distress 58/120.
lappe *n.* hem 566/29.
larder *n.* storeroom for provisions 287/236.
largeliche *adv.* generously 120/72, 357/22.
lasi *v. inf.* fasten 172/153, see var., **lacy** A; **laci** J.
lasse *a.* of less importance 161/33, 34; smaller 264/498.
laui *v. inf.* pour out, bail 469/166; **laueþ** *pr. pl.* 77/189, var. **lauede** A; **laueþe** J.
lauwe, lawe *n.* law 4/16, 621/346; **lawen** *pl.* 657/1431; **lawe** belief 62/18, 123/51.
lay *n.*[1] law, religion 3/3, 222/44.
lay *n.*[2] song 210/170.
leche *n.* physician 120/50, 414/371; **leches** *pl.* 347/190, 388/108; name for the fourth finger 412/309, 315.
leche? *a.*? for **lasche** slow 414/371, no var.; see Laud 108 310/371 *guod leche* (physician) *and milsful*.
ledare, ledere *n.* guide 246/126, 152/124.
lede *v. inf.* lead, conduct 27/60, 63/24; **ledeþ** *imper. pl.* 27/71; **ladde** *pt.* 81/2; *pt. pl.* 116/203; **ilad** *pp.* 155/216.
lees *a.* false 527/350.

legge *v. inf.* lay, place 8/16; **leggeþ** *pr. pl.* 134/163; **leide** *pt.* 33/38; *pt. pl.* 116/208.
legistre *n.* one skilled in law 536/97 var. J.
leie, lie *n.* flame 197/514, 198/541; **leiȝe, liȝe** 23/115, 40/80.
leiting *n.* see **liȝting**.
lene *v. inf.* lend, grant 50/99; **lenede** 1 *pt.* 635/773; **lente** *pt.* 564/433; **lende** *pt. pl.* 555/146; **ilend** *pp.* 386/66.
lene *a.* thin, scant 19/11, 42/150.
lenie *v. inf.* recline, lean 387/96; (**leine** 387/90 is a misreading of **lenie**); **lenede, lynede** *pt.* 158/68, 511/585; **lenede** *pt. pl.* 236/455.
leode *n.* people, in phr. *lond and* ~ 35/80.
leof *a.* dear, desirous 43/185, 44/202; **leoue, leue** 66/124, 17/18; **leouer, leuer** *comp.* 45/235, 64/68; **leuost** *superl.* 42/136, 44/196.
leom(e) *n.* light, brightness 104/534, 107/634, **lime** 107/632; **lemes** *pl.* rays 423/656.
leorni, lerni *v. inf.* learn, study 307/128, 122/2, **lurny** 496/116; **leornede, lurnede** *pt.* 148/12, 499/221; **ileorned** *pp.* 137/38.
leose *v. inf.* lose 42/148; **les** *pt.* 70/23; **lore** *pt. subj.* 508/481; **ilore** *pp.* 2/31.
leosnesse *n.* forgiveness 342/75, var. **lisnisse** H; **lesnesse** A J.
leoue *v. pr. subj.* grant 15/222, 215/34.
lep *v. imper.* leap 335/231; **lep** *pt.* 21/81; **ilope** *pp.* 517/77.
lepe *n.* basket 267/76.
leprous *a.* having leprosy 304/36.
lere *v. inf.* teach 64/71, 76/152; **ilered** *pp.* 615/158.
lere *a.* unoccupied, bare 9/51, 169/73.
les *n.* falsehood 255/251, 570/155.
lese *n.* pasture 130/50, 184/132.
lesinge *n.* lie, deception 3/60, 62; **lesinges** *pl.* 590/115.
leste *a.* smallest 106/604, 412/308.
lete *v. inf.* (*a*) leave, abandon 96/318; **lete** *pr. pl.* 25/24; **let** *pt.* 112/83; **lete** *pt. pl.* 87/50; **ilete** *pp.* 158/81; (*b*) allow, lest 2 *pr.* 306/101; **lete** *pr. subj.* 91/165; **let** *pt.* 177/291; (*c*) esteem, **lete** 2 *pr. subj.* 635/755.
lette *n.* hindrance 99/397.
lette *v. inf.* hinder 43/176, 469/170; **let** *pr.* 222/52; **ilet** *pp.* 233/341.
letuse *n.* lettuce 396/210.
lepegi *v. inf.* loosen 254/198, var. **liþie** H.
leue *n.* permission 41/120, 126/146;

GLOSSARY 61

nom(e) ~ bade farewell 182/69, 183/96.
leui *v. inf.* put forth leaves 285/170, 344/110; ileued *pp.* 155/202, 169/78.
lewed(e) *a.* lay 622/378, 628/565.
libbe *v. inf.* live 104/540; libbe *1 pr.* 34/67; liuest *2 pr.* 201/622; lyuede *pt.* 140/119; iliued *pp.* 106/599, ilyue 451/78.
licame *n.* body 83/90, 142/166; corpse 706/245.
lich(e) *n.* flesh, body 451/68, 618/259; like form 297/171.
liche *adv.* uniformly 204/716.
licke *v.* lick 47/10, 147/324; lickede *pt.* 260/380; likked *pt. pl.* 325/304; ilikked *pp.* 121/93.
lie *n.* see leie.
lie, liȝe *v. inf.* tell lies, deceive 100/449, 649/1189; lie *1 pr.* 123/46; luxst, luxt *2 pr.* 588/60, 233/350; lieþ, lucþ *pr.* 517/68, 272/226; lowe *pt. pl.* 101/451.
lyfles *a.* dead 86/11.
lif-lode *n.* livelihood 137/18, 518/96.
lift(e) *n.* sky 186/201, 421/573.
ligge *v. inf.* lie, rest 8/18; list *2 pr.* 24/166; liþ *pr.* 34/58; liggeþ *pr. pl.* 78/220; lai, ley *pt.* 157/45, 33/38; leiȝe *pt. pl.* 15/209; ileie, ileiȝe *pp.* 361/70, 141/146.
liȝe, liȝhe *v. inf.* laugh 26/31, 255/243; laȝinge, liȝinge *pr. p.* 510/574, 683/2223; loȝ, lou, louȝ *pt.* 511/583, 28/94, 570/152; lowe, louwe *pt. pl.* 452/109, 2/37.
liȝhinge *a.* laughing 206/72, 424/677.
*liȝnye *v. inf.* belie, deny 527/349, see var.; liȝny *1 pr.* 527/357, var. lyne A; lene J; liȝnest *2 pr.* 528/394, var. lynest A; lyest J.
liȝt *n.* light, brightness 40/84, 656/1421; pur liȝt probably mistake for purliche 450/39, see var.
liȝte *v.*[1] lighten (of lightning) 60/35; ignite 369/114; shine 656/1424; liȝte *pt.* 79/49.
liȝte *v.*[2] *pt.* dismounted 672/1903.
liȝting(e) *n.* lightning 79/53, 419/526; leiting 419/536.
liȝtliche *adv.* easily 117/217; liȝtloker *comp.* 55/31, 450/42.
liȝtore probably mistake for *liȝt tre* lightweight wood 117/218, see var., *liȝt* ... (spot in MS.) *tre* J.
lim(e) *n.*[1] limb (of body) 107/624, 143/196; *deuelles* ~ imp of Satan 20/37; *d. limes pl.* 308/20; *doorno* ~ private parts 20/43, 96/317.
lime *n.*[2] see leom(e).

lim *n.*[3] lime, mortar 316/14, 333/189.
lyme-mele *adv.* limb from limb 670/1821.
lyne *v. inf.* ? falsify 527/349 var. A; *1 pr.* 527/357 var. A; lynest *2 pr.* 528/394 var. A; see liȝnye.
linne *a.* linen 450/37.
lisse *v. inf.* ease, abate 56/69, 522/204.
list *n.* hearing 530/442.
lite *a.* small, little 412/325, 599/163, lute 468/141, 505/405.
liteman *n.* the little finger 412/308, 315.
liþ *n.* joint, limb 107/624.
liþe *a.* flexible 468/138.
liþe *v. inf.* to render mild, ease 225/123; liþede *pt.* 253/173.
liþi *a.* weak 604/340.
liuerance *n.* liberation 58/134.
lyuerede *v. pt.* relieved 7/68.
loddere *adv. comp.* more loudly 195/452.
lode *n.* in phr. *cartes* ~ cartful 28/86.
lof *n.* loaf (of bread) 140/101, 189/279; loues *pl.* 121/82, 140/105.
logge *n.* place of confinement 411/279.
lok *n.* offering 537/128.
loky *v. inf.* guard 76/148; lokede *pt.* decreed 336/267; iloked *pp.* 289/301, preserved 599/170.
lokinge *n.* judgement 7/61, 673/1917.
lolich *a.* loathsome 588/62, see var.; lolloker *comp.* 587/34, see var.
lome *n.* vessel, utensil 43/158; lomen *pl.* 28/100.
lome *adv.* often 80/68, 467/110.
londe see alonde *adv.*
lond-folk *n.* inhabitants 113/110.
lone *n.* grant 554/134; *to* ~ as a loan 508/483.
longe *a.* long 349/19, 412/316; lengore *comp.* 349/18; lengost *superl.* 93/238, 412/311.
longe *adv.* for a long time 656/1400; leng *comp.* 98/374, lengore 27/65.
longe-man *n.* the middle finger 412/311, 316.
longeþ *pr.* yearns 476/377; longede *pt.* 74/86; *impers.* 30/175, 59/12.
lore *n.* instruction, learning 83/81, 84; a science 500/227.
loreins, *n. pl.* straps of harness 120/48, 616/190.
loþ *n.* ill-will, dislike 38/13, 45/216.
loþ *a.* hateful, reluctant 188/249, 623/410.
lou, lowe *a.* low-lying, humble 98/381, 115/160; louwore *comp.* 162/35; lowoste *superl.* 418/509.
louedai *n.* day for settlement of disputes out of court 508/498.

GLOSSARY

loue-ei3e n. dread tempered by love 82/53, var. loueeie A J.
louerding n. master 380/183; **louerdinges** pl. 355/189.
louerdles a. without a leader 632/668, 670.
louerdling n. young lord 603/319.
louke v. inf. lock up, fasten 223/71; lek pt. 90/144; **iloke** pp. 87/65, 458/56; ~ *alleluye* cease singing Alleluia during Lent 128/S2, see 128/S7, 505/403.
lourede v. pt. scowled 156/16.
loute v. inf. bow 174/198, 359/16; **lotte** pt. 86/28, 429/19; pt. pl. 255/226.
louwe, lowe adv. down 1/8, 99/390; lowe meanly 115/157.
lucþ see lie v.
Lude n. name for March 118/260, 121/106.
lunatik a. moon-crazed 377/99.
lupe n. quick movement 345/148.
luste v. inf. impers. please, be desirable 107/634; pt. 15/208, 98/374; **luste** pt. pl. pers. desired 578/198.
lutles a. g. in phr. *what* ~ scraps 505/400.
luþer n. evil 187/203, 694/48.
luþer a. barren, cursed (of ground) 1/5.
luþerhede n. wickedness 282/88, 187/203 var. A.
luue, leoue v. inf. believe 154/198, 272/245; **lufþ** pr. 278/112; **liuie** 2 pr. subj. 20/34; **luueþ** pr. pl. 544/45; **lufde** pt. 593/105; **luuede** pt. pl. 5/H 6.

macche n. equal 339/364.
may n. maiden 55/26, 68/172.
may v. *1* pr. am able to, can 137/32; **mi3t** 2 pr. 137/39; **mouwe** pr. pl. 85/30, **mowe(þ)** 13/136, 85/29; **mowe** *1* pr. subj. 366/41; **mi3te** pt. 1/10, 6/24.
maidenot n. virginity 66/118, 444/31.
main n. strength 342/56, 446/111.
maine, mannie n. household, retinue 61/33, 222/34, **meine** 360/58.
maystrede v. pt. subdued 699/60.
*****make** n. mate 55/22.
make, makie v. produce, prepare, render 134/172, 79/44; **makeþ, makieþ** pr. pl. 134/3, 460/11; made, **makede** pt. 135/22, 461/38; mad, **ymaked** pp. 634/754, 473/294; ~ *þe dore* close the door 679/2102.
mande n. rites of Maundy Thursday 192/360, 361.

manere n.¹ estate 76/169; **maners** pl. 285/200.
manere n.² practice 77/193.
manfischers n. pl. 'fishers of men' 543/6.
manhede n. manliness 11/96; human nature 441/56.
mankunde n. human nature 160/30.
mankunne n. the human race 1/2; ~ *g.* 146/280.
manquellare n. executioner 68/185; **monquellare** murderer 229/244.
manrede n. homage 100/421, 286/203.
mansinge n. cursing, excommunication 219/51, 291/348.
mansla3t n. murder 172/138, 622/365.
manssipe n. honour 252/146, 304/48.
mare n. goblin causing nightmare 409/228.
marie v. inf. intr. wed 443/14.
mariner n. sailor, captain 138/42, 49; **mariners** pl. 30/163, 308/159.
mascos n. kiss of peace at Mass 669/1785.
mase n. delirium 693/14.
mased a. bewildered 184/116.
maskede a. bewildered 184/116 var. H.
mason n. worker in stone 276/58; **masons** pl. 9/33.
materas n. mattress 29/131.
matte v. see mette.
maudeflank n. 'A continuall stitch in the side; or, a Pleuresie' (Cotgrave (1611) under Flanc) 639/893.
maugrey prep. in spite of 695/77.
maumet n. idol 324/257; **maumetis** pl. 17/43, **maumes** 123/52, 305/78.
mei n. kinsman 446/103, 581/291; **meyes** g. 476/360.
mele n. basin 550/6.
mene v.¹ inf. have in mind, intend 400/98; **munte** pt. pl. 395/172; **yment, ymunt** pp. 430/56, 623/400.
mene v.² inf. complain, complain of 14/180, 233/349; **meneþ** pr. pl. 642/987, ? complain of 130/54; **mende** pt. 555/145.
meneisoun, menyson n. dysentery 566/6, 689/2403.
menge v. inf. mix 427/759; **mengi** *1* pr. deal with 223/63; **mengeþ** pr. mingles 427/762; **imengd, ymeng** pp. 425/696, 681/2163.
menging n. mingling 490/565.
merceri n. cloth wares 81/20.
merciable a. merciful 433/140.
mere n. boundary 430/44.
mes n. prepared food 120/68.

GLOSSARY 63

meseise, miseise *n.* misery 463/18, 361/80.
meseise, miseise *a.* miserable 523/242, 35/94; miseisore *comp.* 36/118.
mesel, musel *n.* leper 36/117, 199/559; meseles, museles *pl.* 46/253, 31/16.
messauntre *n.* mischance 706/242.
mest(e) *a.* greatest 103/525, 110/21, 130/46.
mester *n.* craft, profession 136/13, 221/9, myster 137/38.
mester-mon *n.* craftsman 136/13.
met *n.* measure 554/133, 555/148.
mete *n.* food, meal 77/196, 185/158; metes *pl.* 106/616, 130/46; *atte ~ at table* 77/196.
mete *v.*[1] *inf.* measure 172/152; met *pt.* 550/217; mete *pt. pl.* 172/154; ymete *pp.* 7/80.
mete *v.*[2] *inf.* encounter 102/485; *pr. pl.* 94/260; mette *pt.* 34/55, 120/48.
meteles *a.* without food 182/60, 287/240.
metinge *n.* dream, trance 409/225, 516/21.
mette *v. pt. impers.* came in dream 516/23, matte 250/88; ymet *pp.* 516/21; matte, mette *pt. tr.* dreamed 283/116, 692/8.
meue, meuy *v. inf.* stir, change 202/672, 22/104; meoueþ *pr. pl.* 128/S 5.
middelerde, myddelherde *n.* earth 39/58 var. A J.
middemost *a.* middle (finger) 412/311.
mid-ouer-non *n.* middle of the afternoon 434/11.
miȝtles *a.* powerless 381/224.
milch *a.* milk-giving 385/44; melche 42/142 var. A J.
milce *n.* mercy 14/166, 366/43.
milceful, milsfol *a.* merciful 555/167, 414/371.
milde *a.* tame 333/180.
myleward *n.* keeper of mill 698/6; milewardes *g.* 698/4.
mylþe *a.* mild 512/6.
mis *adv.* wrongly 18/59.
misanswere *v. inf.* answer unfittingly 213/81; misanswereþ *pt. pl.* 213/74.
misbileue *n.* false belief 5/H 9, 83/76; misbileoue doubt 572/9.
misbileueþ *v. pr. pl.* hold a false belief 18/59; misbiluf *imper.* 317/52; misbiluuede *pt.* 57/104; misbileoued, misbiluued *pp.* 572/14, 8/86.
misbileued, misbiluued *a.* heathen 5/H 5, 399/76; misbileuede, misbiluued unorthodox 162/2, 163/16.
misbore *v. pp.* misbehaved 651/1254.
misdo *v. inf.* injure, do amiss 376/76, 623/403; misdude *pt.* 631/634; misdo *pp.* 85/40, 88/93.
misdrawe *v. inf.* go astray 407/168.
misfaringe *a.* misbehaving 391/36, 408/180.
misfleo *v. inf.* fly off course 387/91.
misgon *v. inf.* go wrong, stray 413/360; misȝeode *pt.* strayed 430/44.
mislere *v. inf.* lead astray 54/9, 338/322.
mislike *v. inf.* displease 627/531.
mispaieþ *v. pr.* offends 677/2050.
misseist *v. 2 pr.* slanderest 678/2076; missede *pt.* 695/80; missed, misseid *pp.* 324/281, 590/11.
misset *v. pp.* wrongly placed 324/258.
misstep *v. pt.* made a false step 9/37.
misþenche *v. imper.* misjudge 86/35.
misþoȝt *n.* error 408/201.
miswene *v. inf.* think amiss 312/282.
moker *n.* hoard 467/124.
molde *n.* ground 525/290.
mone *n.*[1] fellowship, intercourse 431/85, 495/89.
mone *n.*[2] lament 367/57, 538/140.
mone *n.*[3] memory 165/36, 236/445.
mone *n.*[4] moon 415/402, 416/440.
moneie *n.* valuables, coin 138/41, 655/1394, see var., Inou J.
montance, mountance *n.* extent of time or space 439/149, 580/281.
mopiss *a.* bewildered 613/78; mopis, mophisch 184/116 var. A J.
more *n.* root, stock 1/6, 204/1; moren *pl.* 189/280; fig. 168/24.
morȝiue *n.* dowry 33/26.
morie *v. inf.* take root 1/10; ymored *pp.* 171/126.
morþry *v. inf.* kill violently 693/21; ymorþred *pp.* 115/159.
morunynge, morwenynge *n.* morning 33/41, 39/57.
mossel, musel, *n.* morsel 30/150, 86/19; mossels *pl.* 160/27.
mossel-mele *adv.* piecemeal 541/251.
mouable *a.* variable in date (feasts) 128/S 5.
mowe *v. inf.* reap 480/98.
muchel *a.* great, large 23/128, 180/16; mochele 537/120; muchel probably for melch 42/142, see var.
mulc *n.* milk 542/296.
multe *v. inf.* melt 14/188, 585/412; *multe *pt.* 347/204; ymolte *pp.* 469/171, ymult 157/63.
munde *n.* remembrance 33/18, 80/67; commemoration service 590/114.
*munegede *v. pt.* reminded 605/370, see var.
mulston *n.* millstone 421/580.

GLOSSARY

murȝþe *n*. melody 574/84.
muri(e) *a*. gay, pleasant 80/80, 185/142; murgore *comp*. 186/187, 407/178.
murie *adv*. gaily 90/151; muriere *comp*. 511/583.
musel *n*. see mesel, mossel.

naked *a*. bare, unarmed 94/250, 484/39.
nare, narȝ, naru *a*. narrow 407/157, 101/470, 407/163.
narwe *adv*. closely, carefully 74/83, 111/34.
nature *n*. natural need 113/101.
neb *n*. nose, face 450/48, 581/310.
nede, neode *adv*. necessarily 133/125, 136/44.
nedles *a*. unnecessary 665/1670.
ney wat *adv*. almost 28/86, 29/125.
nel *v*. *1 pr*. will not 20/32, inelle 12/125; nelt *2 pr*. 91/176; nel *pr*. 55/44; nost *2 pt*. 624/437; nolde *pt*. 9/19; *pt*. *pl*. 52/136.
nemne, nemny *v*. *inf*. name, mention 26/44, 57/88, nempne 693/39; nemdest, nemnedest *2 pt*. 294/75, 502/302; nemnede *pt*. *pl*. 40/88; ynemd *pp*. 85/31.
neode *n*. call of nature 7/58.
neodi *a*. necessary 131/85.
neoȝe *a*. nine 581/287, nie 171/118, 277/85.
ner *adv*. *comp*. nearer 94/245, 141/144.
neschede *v*. *pt*. *pl*. grew soft 525/290.
nesse *a*. soft, timid 12/131, 664/1629; *nessost *superl*. 29/130.
nesse *adv*. gently 29/132, 122/3, nesche 465/53.
nest-ey *n*. nest-egg 134/169, 172.
neþemost *a*. *superl*. lowest 426/731.
nie *a*. see neoȝe.
nime *v*. *inf*. take, undertake 16/S 14; nam, nom *pt*. 2/40, 24/163; neme, nome *pt*. *pl*. 546/101, 3/55; inome *pp*. 82/25, ynome 'carried away' 107/626.
niþe *a*. ninth 146/281, 630/609.
niwe, nyuwe *a*. new 1/1, 15.
nobleie *n*. splendour 87/57, 221/6; nobility of rank 253/179.
noblich *adv*. splendidly 78/220; noblikere *comp*. 578/207.
noȝt *a*. short-haired 20/47, var. nowt J.
non(e) *n*. noon, the ninth hour 139/93, 141/139; *heie non* midday 177/301; nones *g*. 415/403; anone *adv*. at the ninth hour 145/248.
none in phrase *for þe* ∼ then, on purpose 193/382, 195/452; see attenone.
norice, norise *n*. nurse 567/59, 122/3, norse 283/135.
norisschi, norissi *v*. *inf*. nurture 1/18, 205/26; norisside *pt*. 373/222; ynorissed *pp*. 17/38.
norissinge *n*. nourishment 426/733, 735.
norþ see est *adv*.
nost *v*. *2 pt*. wouldst not 642/987, var. noldest H A; see nel.
not *v*. *1 pr*. know not 152/109; nost, noste *2 pr*. 20/25, 123/41; not *pr*. 105/587; nute(þ) *pr*. *pl*. 80/62, 435/46; nuste *pt*. 7/74, 74/82; *pt*. *pl*. 32/22, 51/124.
note *n*. gain, advantage 260/388, 535/53.
noþemo *adv*. never the more 79/26, 130/45.
nouþe *adv*. now 8/5, 79/36.
nou non *adv*. ? now, riming with gon 202/651, 429/35; in address, now then 226/157, 259/369.
nuene, nyuwene *adv*. soon 509/532, 37/138.
nuye *v*. *inf*. harm, trouble 52/152; nuyede *pt*. *pl*. 617/198.
numbre *n*. arithmetical symbol 500/228.

obeie *v*. *inf*. submit to 14/169.
*odren *n*. *pl*. teats 386/45.
oelle *n*. see oil(e).
of-cale *pp*. chilled 36/126; see acale.
ofcet *pp*. beset 117/232.
ofclupie *v*. *inf*. summon 358/10.
ofdrede *v*. *1 pr*. fear 177/310; ofdrad *pp*. afraid 63/27, 485/65.
ofesse *v*. *inf*. inquire 39/55; ofeschte, ofesste *pt*. 512/27, 290/343.
offalle *pp*. crushed 57/94, 599/188.
offonge *v*. *inf*. receive 104/545.
ofgo(n) *v*. *inf*. overtake 150/76, 612/52.
ofgremed *pp*. vexed 30/167.
ofhongred *pp*. distressed by hunger 81/9; see afingred.
of-liggeþ *v*. *pr*. *pl*. overlie 409/228, 233.
of-longed *pp*. filled with desire 140/113.
ofmene *v*. see mene *v*.²
ofride *v*. *inf*. ride around 478/58.
ofsake *v*. *inf*. deny 342/60; ofsak *imper*. 650/1228; ofsoke *pt*. *pl*. 336/266.
ofscape, ofscapie *v*. *inf*. escape 319/121, 637/823; ofscapede *pt*. 267/70; *pt*. *subj*. 249/80.

GLOSSARY

ofseche *v. inf.* search out, probe 387/72, 429/22; **ofso3te** *pt.* besought 515/13.
ofsende *v. inf.* summon 65/98, 82/52; *pt.* 82/55; **ofsend** *pp.* 5/14.
ofseruy *v. inf.* deserve, earn 107/646; **ofseruede** *pt.* 119/28; **ofserued** *pp.* 89/111, 364/181.
ofssamede *v. pt. pl.* felt shame 323/242; **ofssamed** *pp.* ashamed 30/167, 86/23.
ofswinke *v. inf.* work for 430/36, 610/9; **ofswonk** *pt.* 170/96.
of-take *v. inf.* overtake 27/62, 290/324; **oftok** *pt.* 675/1972; **oftake** *pp.* 194/411.
oftriwede *v. pt.* suspected 443/26; **oftrowede** *pt. pl.* 683/2234; see **ortrowede**.
ofþenche *v. inf. impers.* grieve 138/44; **ofþincþ** *pr.* 337/308; **ofþo3te** *pt.* 116/190; **ofþencheþ** *pr. pl. pers.* regret 642/1005; **ofþo3te** *pt.* 85/33.
oignement *n.* ointment 556/171, 185; **oynemens** *pl.* 56/72.
oil(e) *n.* oil (of mercy) 167/14, 168/38, **oelle** 560/302, **oylle** 542/303; see **eoly**.
ok *v. pt.* ached 433/149; **oke** *pt. subj.* 545/66.
ok *conj.* see **ac**.
olde *a.* old, former 3/3, 152/130, hold 171/132; **eldore, eoldere** *comp.* 40/93, 127/10; **eldost, eoldoste** *superl.* 111/33, 391/39.
on in phr. *in* ~ continually 225/144; *bi* ~ ? in one mood, even-tempered 489/184.
onde *n.* envy 4/23, 75/134.
one *adv.* in phr. *no3t* ~ not only 153/141, 156/19.
ones *adv.* once 549/190.
oneiware *a.* unaware 452/110.
oneyde *a.* one-eyed 45/234.
openheued *adv.* bare-headed 272/218.
ordeini *v. inf.* arrange, ordain 134/8, 10/67; **ordeyni** *pr. pl. subj.* 212/33; **ordeinede** *pt.* 428/6; **iordeined** *pp.* 206/56.
ordeinour, *n.* director 617/211, 206/45.
ordinal *n.* service-book 161/16.
ore *n.* grace 14/166, **hore** 66/114.
orf *n.* cattle 49/80, 83.
orn, ourne *v.* see **vrne**.
ortrowede *v. pt. pl.* suspected 114/129, 289/292; see **oftriwede**.
ospital *n.* hostel 613/84.
ospring *n.* progeny 4/21, 182/66.
ost(e) *n.*[1] body of soldiers 2/24, 80/65.

oste *n.*[2] inn-keeper, host 649/1194, 650/1214.
ostiler *n.* host (in monastery) 120/61.
oþer *a.* additional 323/240, 393/122; in phr. ~ *half 3er* one and a half years 610/11.
ou *pron.* see **3e**.
ou *interj.* 89/103.
ouemoste *a. superl.* uppermost 415/414.
ouercast *v. pr.* covers 656/1424; **ouercaste** *pt.* 471/222, 504/357; **ouercast** *pp.* 79/47, 656/1421.
oure *poss. a.* our 65/101, 329/52; **vure** 626/476.
ouerful *v. pt.* fell upon 487/119.
ouergult *pp.* gilded 538/159.
ouerspradde *v. pt.* extended over 107/621, 580/279.
ouertok *v. pt.* caught up with 406/143.
oules *n. pl.* hooks 50/88, 93/220, **houles** 95/298.
out *adv.* probably for *ou3t* in any way 387/84, var. *om.* H A J.
outlich(e) *adv.* completely 44/187, 621/329.
outrage *n.* extreme injury 150/57, 282/95.
outso3te *v. pt.* examined 398/24.
out-trie *v. inf.* select 316/19.
owe *v. inf.* accept as debt 270/184.
ower *adv.* anywhere 161/25; see **awer**.

pain *n.* pagan 174/204, 434/1; **pains** *pl.* 267/95, 268/103.
paynime *n.* heathendom 37/4, 268/102.
pays see **apays**.
pak *n.* bundle 134/158.
pal, palle *n.* rich cloth 405/92, 29/131; **palles** *pl.* coverings 575/125.
palm *n.* pallium 618/248, 255, see var.
palsie *n.* palsy, paralysis 331/114, 371/186.
pameri *n.* ferule 499/211, 212.
panes *n. pl.* pence 139/95, 217/8.
panne-uol *n.* panful 323/240.
panter *n.* snare 409/220.
parais *n.* paradise 105/572, 185/148.
parye *v. inf.* pare (of fruit) 705/236.
parisse *n.* parish 41/102.
parissens *n. pl.* parishioners 672/1887.
parlement *n.* consultation 6/46, 626/487.
parti *v.*[1] *inf.* share 35/77, 142/180; **partede** *pt.* 583/365; *pt. pl.* 54/200.
parti *v.*[2] *inf.* depart 34/74, 144/232; **partede** *pt. pl.* 146/282; **iparted** *pp.* 525/312.
partie *n.* piece 390/11; **partis** *pl.* 194/414; **partie disputant** 629/569.

66 GLOSSARY

partiner *n.* sharer 575/130.
pas *n.* step, movement 196/491; *pl.* 431/75.
pasken *v. inf.* dabble 543/8, var. **pasky** J.
passi *v. inf. tr.* cross, go beyond 182/59; **ipassed** *pp.* 342/52; **passi** *inf. intr.* come to trial 705/212; **passede** *pt.* gave judgement (of inquest) 705/206.
pate *n.* head 695/83.
pauement *n.* paved floor 139/83, 681/2162.
paume *n.* palm (of hand) 500/235.
peinte *v. inf.* draw in colour 449/33; **peint** *pr.* 681/2167; **ipeint** *pp.* 138/66, 681/2168.
peinto(u)r *n.* artist in colour 449/35, 450/40.
penancer *n.* one appointed to hear confession 546/123.
peer, per *n.* equal 39/58, 540/213.
pelrynage, pilrenage *n.* pilgrimage 515/99, 311/239.
per *a.* equal 52/148.
perche *n.* staff 343/80; clothes-pole 43/171; fuller's rod 166/87; measuring-rod 576/159.
perilous *a.* dangerous 35/82, 89/120.
perseþ *v. pr.* penetrates 419/536.
perssede *v. pt. subj.* come to an end 61/18; **yperissed** *pp.* 1/20.
pich *n.* pitch 96/314, 459/89.
piche *v. imper.* fix, set 344/109; **piȝte** *pt.* 157/54.
picher *n.* jug 472/250.
pikes *n. pl.* spikes 93/220; spines (of hedgehog) 513/47.
pile *n.* spine (of hedgehog) 18/50.
pine *n.* torment 16/16, 91/179; **pines** *pl.* 108/650; sufferings 615/134.
pini *v.* suffer, torment 95/287, 253/186; **pinede** *pt.* 108/670, 477/30; **ipined** 96/299.
piteisliche *adv.* pitiably 200/592; **pitousliche** devoutly 500/251.
plai *n.* suit at law 628/551, 629/568, **ple** 629/593; **plee** debate 524/260.
plaide, plaidi *v. inf.* dispute, argue 328/14, 15; **pleidieþ** *pr. pl.* 525/288; **plaidede** *pt.* 5/H 7.
plaidinge *n.* argument 131/68, 70; **pleidinge** lawsuit 630/603.
plaidors *n. pl.* disputants 453/132.
plaine *v. inf.* make complaint 587/53; **playnede** *pt.* 582/334.
plainte *v. inf.* complain 587/51, see var., **painte** A, **playne** J.
plastre *n.* medicinal application 120/54, 57 (**plestre** incorrect).

plat *adv.* flat 63/41, 83/70.
platen *n. pl.* sheets of metal 362/123, 459/91.
plawe *n.* trick 113/108.
ple *n.* see **plai**.
plei *n.* amusement 445/73; **pleies** *pl.* 445/68.
pleyfere *n.* playfellow 494/67.
pleinde *pr. p. a.* indulging in play 605/354.
pleiinge *n.* romping 119/14, 551/10.
plener *a.* plenary 506/439, 661/1543.
plenerliche *adv.* in full number 661/1544.
plente *n.* abundance 193/398, 215/32.
pliȝte *v. inf.* pledge 330/66, 334/205; *pt. pl.* 334/205; **ipliȝt(e)** *pp.* 334/209, 630/604.
podagre *n.* gout 468/132.
poer(e) *n.* armed force 10/65; authority 82/35, 171/114.
poffe *v. inf.* breathe in gasps 409/234; **poffeþ** *pr. pl.* 130/54.
point *n.* in phr. *upe þe* ~ just about 77/179.
pol, polle *n.* head 297/177, 412/323; crown of head 251/137.
polled(e) *pp. a.* close-cropped 124/82, 86.
polles *n. pl.* staves 50/107.
porchacy *v. inf.* contrive 629/574.
porche *n.* covered entrance 405/83, 577/162.
porpos *n.* aim, object 105/563, 159/8.
porreie *n.* broth 9/22.
porsiwede, *v. pt.* followed, hunted down 679/2117; **porsuwede** *pt. pl. subj.* 645/1075; **porsuede** *pt. pl.* 640/937.
port-dogge *n.* town-dog 410/267.
port-hond *n.* town-dog 410/274.
portoun *n.* market-town 410/267.
porture *n.* behaviour 54/3, 275/25.
porueie *v. inf.* supply, provide for 385/34, 658/1463; **porueide** *pt.* 35/91; **purueid** *pp.* 119/22.
pose *n.* cold in the head 207/92.
poste, pouste *n.* authority 653/1329, 556/173.
posterne *n.* back gate or door 57/100.
poudre *n.* dust 500/228.
poune *v. inf.* beat, crush 260/389; *imper.* 120/53.
powe *v. inf.* ? lean, be supported 426/726; var. with rime-words: **birue: pue** H, **abuye: puye** J, text om. A. See **püen** Stratmann–Bradley.
prece *n.* crowd, crowding 263/458, 597/114, **presse** 566/30.
preche, prechi *v. inf. intr.* proclaim,

GLOSSARY

preach 31/6, 25/8, *tr.* 70/14; preching *pr. p.* 86/27; prechede *pt.* 70/16; ipreched *pp.* 79/45.
prechinge *n.* delivery of a sermon, preaching 76/170, 400/96.
prechor *n.* preacher 81/3; prechors *g.s.* 264/493.
preciouse *a. pl.* valuable 181/42, preciouses 545/76.
predicacion *n.* preaching 77/184, 675/1975.
preie *n.* catch, quarry 329/49, 387/78.
preiudice *n.* detriment 667/1741.
preoui, proui *v. inf.* put to test, demonstrate 536/100, 254/206; preouede *pt.* 534/31; preuede *pt. pl.* 54/201; ypreoued *pp.* 633/720; proui *inf. intr.* turn out 49/81.
presant *n.* gift 62/12; presentation 126/127.
presenti *v. inf.* offer as gift 377/110; ipresented *pp.* introduced 618/231.
prestore *a. comp.* more ready 679/2112, 2113.
pri3te *v. pt.* pricked 159/12; ipri3t *pp.* 159/16.
prikie *v. inf.* spur on 570/131, 607/425; ipriked *pp.* 441/61.
prikke *n.* goad, spike 265/27; pricken *pl.* 295/118.
principals *a. pl.* chief 280/15.
priso(u)ns *n. pl.* prisoners 229/254, 477/9; prisones *g.* 477/11.
procuracies *n. pl.* provision for entertainment of ecclesiastical visitor 503/323.
procuratour *n.* official host 192/353, 202/681, prokereatour 202/667.
procuri *v. inf.* effect 652/1284.
profound *a.* deeply learned 500/224.
propherede *v. pt.* offered 151/87.
prou *n.* profit 215/47, 502/314.
prouendre *n.* prebend, revenue 505/386.
prute *n.* pride, display 67/140, 377/111.
pulle *v. inf.* in phr. *com* ~ *up* came drawing or drawn up 77/188.
pultatorie *n.* purgatory 87/48, 56, see var., purgatorie J. Probably should be read pulcatorie; see pulcatorry E.E.T.S. o.s. 25, p. 31.
pulte *v. inf.* push, thrust 11/99; *pt.* 138/63; *pt. pl.* 362/123; ipult *pp.* 571/160.
pur *a.* ? very 408/191, see var., om. J.
purblind *a.* wholly blind 300/41.
purgi *v. inf.* clear of charge 622/371, 373.

purliche *adv.* completely 573/60, 61.
purueance *n.* foresightedness 523/253.
put *n.* pit, grave 87/46, 147/319; puttes *pl.* 97/359.
pute *v. inf.* thrust, drive 95/294, 414/369; putte *pt.* 169/63; iput *pp.* 96/315.

quake, quakie *v. inf.* tremble 57/92, 230/273; quakynge *pr. p.* 230/274; quakede *pt.* 98/380.
qualite *n.* disposition 416/433, 435.
qualm *n.* death 158/91.
quarels *n. pl.* bolts 18/48.
quarteron *n.* a fourth part 263/479, var. quarter H J, quartron A.
quarters *n. pl.* measures (of grain) 554/128, 555/140.
quaþ *v. pt.* said 346/181; quaþ, queþe *pt. pl.* 493/39, 27/66; iquede *pp.* decreed 523/254.
qued(e) *n.* evil 222/33, 523/246; quedes *g.* devil's 286/205.
qued(e) *a.* bad 110/6, 409/226.
quede *adv.* evilly 400/92.
queinte, quointe *a.* ingenious 136/13, 218/32; queinte well-wrought 90/156; queintore *comp.* 137/14; queynteste *superl.* 577/170.
queinte *v. pt.* ceased to burn 58/130, 93/223, quente 23/119.
queinteliche *adv.* skilfully, cleverly 172/151, 218/32.
queintise, quointise *n.* ingenuity, device 30/160, 339/356; quoyntises *pl.* 699/54, var. queyntise H.
quellare *n.* executioner 68/190, 69/205.
quelle *v.* kill 22/108, 57/88; quelþ *pr.* 133/144, 420/566; quelle *pr. subj.* 175/241; *pr. pl. subj.* 430/38.
queme *v. inf.* please 123/43.
quenchinge *n.* extinction 420/556.
quene *n.*[1] in phr. *vnder þe* ~ besides or in disregard of the queen 698/5; misread querne in Furnivall, *Early Eng. Poems* (Berlin, 1862), p. 111, and so quoted in *O.E.D.*
quene *n.*[2] harlot 54/7, 475/345.
queor, quer *n.* body of choristers 506/440; part of church 15/214, 78/212.
querne *n.* mill 540/234.
queste *n.* official group of inquirers, inquest 705/206.
quilten *n. pl.* bed-coverings 29/131.
quit(e) *a.* free, clear 91/177, 540/209; qui3t 637/835.
quite *v. inf.* pay back, release 42/155; quit *pp.* 636/804, see quit(e) *a.*

GLOSSARY

quiture *n.* pus, discharge 24/156, 498/162.
qwinsames *n. pl.* the fifteen gradual psalms, cxx–cxxxiv 78/214, var. quinȝe saumes A, quinse psalmes J.

raketeye *n.* chain 66/112; **raketeien, raketeies** *pl.* 249/78, 362/105; **rakeie** probably mistake 96/312, var. raketeie(n) A J.
rakynge *v. pr. p.* rushing 679/2107 var. A; see **reke**.
rank *n.* row 435/40; see **areng**.
rasours *n. pl.* sharp-bladed instruments 67/142, 362/103.
raþe *adv.* soon, early 76/156, 130/44; **raþer(e)** *comp.* 81/9, 466/95.
rau *a.* uncooked 320/160, 407/152.
rebors *n.* antagonism 453/128.
recche *v. inf. impers.* concern 623/405; **roȝte** *pt.* 64/58; **(ne)recþ** *pr. pers.* cares 253/194.
reche *v. inf.* attain, reach 271/202; **reiȝte** *pt.* 163/22; *pt. pl.* 546/95.
reche *a.* rich, costly 491/230.
recheles *a.* imprudent 110/19.
redare *n.* one appointed to read aloud 645/1074.
red(e) *n.* plan, counsel 13/161, 74/110.
red(e) *a.* red 14/196, 405/92.
rede *v.*[1] *inf.* advise, guide 12/116, 17/26; **redeþ** *pr. pl.* 100/421; **radde** *pt.* 38/35, 110/7; **irad** *pp.* 194/433.
rede *v.*[2] *inf.* read, lecture 81/12; **rat, ret** *pr.* 246/138, 301/276; **rede** *pr. pl.* 80/58; **radde** *pt.* 121/95, 499/222; **irad** *pp.* 314/314.
redde *v. pt.* ? made ready, 'laid out' 496/111, var. **sped** ... (rest cut off) J.
redinge *n.* interpreting 500/249.
reime *v. inf.* count 44/213, var. **reymy** A J.
reinde *v.* see **rine**.
reke *v. inf.* hurry 335/245; in phr. com(e) ~ came rushing 22/85, 679/2107.
rekene, rekeni *v. inf.* enumerate, count 416/440, 70/17; **rekeni** *pr. pl. subj.* 416/442; **rekenede** *pt.* recounted 311/245; **rikenede** *pt.* calculated 693/17.
renable *a.* fluent, eloquent 25/8, 349/11.
reneide *v. pt.* renounced 244/72.
reng, renk see **areng, arenk**.
renne *v. inf.* run 286/225; **ronne** *pt. pl.* flowed 43/170, 157/34; see **eorne, urne**.

rente *n.* revenue, tax 334/194, 621/344.
rente *v. inf.* tear 157/56; **rende, rente** *pt.* 112/84, 86.
repenty *v. inf.* repent, regret 128/S 12, 183/102; **repentede** *pt.* 116/201; *pt. pl.* 13/151.
rere *v. inf.* initiate 128/S 2; **(ne)rere** *2 pr. subj.* 624/422.
rerewarde *n.* rearguard 2/29, 3/54.
respit *n.* extension of time 361/76, 630/623.
reue *n.* overseer 612/49.
reue *v.*[1] *inf.* ? go mad, rave 446/97, see var., **gan reue** A J.
reue *v.*[2] *inf.* plunder, steal 229/247; **reuede** *pt. pl.* 469/159.
reuestede *v. pt. pl.* arrayed 279/141; **reuested** *pp.* 103/522, 189/270.
reulich *a.* pitiable 371/189; **ruloker** *comp.* 94/245.
reulikere *adv. comp.* more pitifully 528/396.
reume *n.* kingdom 641/948, 667/1748.
reuþe, ruþe *n.* pity 64/67, 636/800.
rewe *n.*[1] row 15/214; streak (of blood) 683/2217; **arewe** one after the other 413/365; **bi reuwe** in order 3/66.
rewe *n.*[2] sympathy 644/1057.
rewe, riwe *v.*[1] *inf.* grieve, distress 253/180, 55/42; **reuweþ** *pr.* 224/116; **riweþ** *pr. pl.* 138/69; **riu** *pt.* 54/4.
rewe *v.*[2] *pt. pl.* rowed 183/105, 185/152, **rue** 557/198.
ribaudie *n.* scurrility 156/30.
riche *n.* kingdom 160/34, 415/415.
ridynge *n.* going on horseback 275/45, see var., om. J.
riȝte *v. pt.* set in order, adjusted 527/367; *pt. pl.* 513/43.
riȝtes *n. pl.* last rites 14/190, 211/201.
rimes *n. pl.* verses 81/13.
rim-forst *n.* hoar-frost 422/622, 423/626.
rine *v. inf.* rain 60/35, 390/23; *pr. subj.* 422/606; **reinde** *pt.* 598/140.
ringinge *n.* bell-ringing 275/45 var. H A.
ryue *a.* prevalent 494/55.
riue *adv.* abundantly 383/285.
robberie *n.* plundering 557/219, 682/2192.
robby *v.*[1] rob 150/72; **robbedde** *pt.* 229/255; **robbede** *pt. pl.* 151/91; **irobbed** *pp.* 229/250.
robby *v.*[2] rub 157/46.
roch(e) *n.* rock, cliff 58/125, 706/255; **roches** *pl.* 185/155.
rochet *n.* smock-like garment 21/70, 71.

GLOSSARY

rodde *n.* staff 343/92, 344/125.
roddede, ruddede *v. pt.* rubbed 451/68, 498/175; rodde *pt. pl.* 157/42, var. ruddede H, rodded A, roddeþe J.
rode *n.* cross 84/1, 167/1; *g.* rode loue 397/225; roden *pl.* 177/295.
rode *a.* probably for rede ruddy 428/786, see var.
rof *n.* in phr. *in þe* ~ on high 28/105.
rollede *v. pt. intr.* tossed 706/253.
rond, round *a.* plump, spherical 287/231, 415/407; ronde *pl.* circular 139/95.
rondel *n.* circular shape 416/452.
rore *v. inf.* shout 73/67, 541/242.
rosti *v. inf.* cook 347/203; rostede *pt.* 364/165; yrosted *pp.* 96/319.
roters *n. pl.* robbers 456/5.
roteþ *v. pr.* decays 309/180; rotede *pt.* 689/2422; iroted *pp.* 337/300.
rotynge *n.* decay 373/232.
Rouisons *n. pl.* Rogation days 136/57, 161/33; Roueisouns 503/351.
roume *adv.* fully 413/353, var. rombe H, roume A J.
round *n.* halo 681/2168.
round *adv.* in a circle 681/2165, 2166.
rounede *v. pt.* whispered 649/1206.
rousteþ *v. pr.* grows rusty 378/120.
route *n.* crowd 100/442; herd 386/56.
route *v.*[1] *inf.* cry out 362/108.
route *v.*[2] *inf.* stir 706/244; see **vour**.
rug, rugge *n.* back 192/364, 343/81.
ruþeren *n. pl.* cattle 402/11, 13.

For words beginning with sch- see also ss-

sac, sak *n.* bag, sackful 498/189, 502/291; sackes *pl.* 431/88.
sacrede *v. pt. pl.* consecrated 553/82; ysacred *pp.* 74/102, 149/44.
sacringe *n.* eucharistic elements 83/90; consecration of elements 238/489, 618/245.
sage *n.*: smal sage probably for small ache or smallage watery parsley 120/52, var. smalache A, smal ache J.
saisi, seisi *v. inf.* take possession, put in possession 285/200, 667/1735; seisede *pt.* 667/1748.
sak-uol *n. pl.* sackfuls 126/144.
sale *n.* in phr. *to* ~ for sale 431/80.
sanfaille *adv.* doubtless 92/206, 222/51.
sauf *a.* saved, cured 467/118, 478/51; saue intact in phr. ~ oure riȝte 624/434, 444.
sauour *n.* taste 501/265.

sawy *v. inf.* cut with a saw 487/113.
scars *a.* scanty 554/133; scarces *superl.* 461/39 var. A.
scarse *adv.* frugally 619/274.
schake *v. inf. intr.* depart 487/136; schok *pt. tr.* shook 488/166, 207/85 var. A.
schede *v. inf.* pour out, spill 545/69; schadde *pt.* 561/340, ssadde 1/16; ischad *pp.* 557/222, issad 43/162.
schende, ssende *v. inf.* dishonour 18/52, 20/43; schend *pr.* 642/977.
scheoue *v. inf.* push, thrust 459/104; ssef *pt.* 194/408; schoue, ssoue *pt. pl.* 569/105, 684/2257.
Schereþoresday, Ssere- *n.* Thursday in Holy Week 192/356, 594/25.
scherte, sserte *n.* shirt 498/163, 393/101, sseorte 619/260.
schete, ssete *v. inf.* shoot 17/47, 387/91, sseote 604/330; schet *pr.* 706/257, sset 419/529; schet *pt.* 706/257, sset 48/35; schote *pt. pl.* 513/44, ssote 347/207; ischote *pp.* 535/54, issote 48/36.
scheuwe, schewe *v. inf.* show, reveal 2/26, 491/233; schewede *pt.* 561/342; scewede *pt. subj.* 550/230.
schindnisse *n.* see ssennesse.
schyninge *n.* brightness 580/278.
schour *n.* conflict 320/148 var. A.
schowe, ssowe *v. inf.* show, reveal 547/126, 141/138; ssowedest 2 *pt.* 380/205; schewede *pt.* 479/76; issowed *pp.* 137/35.
schriffader *n.* confessor 495/85.
schrinke *v. inf.* shrivel 518/99; ssronke *pt. pl.* 119/42.
schulden, ssulde *v. inf.* protect 516/33, 199/556; schulde *inf. intr.* shelter 502/301; schilde *pr. subj.* 465/51, ssulde 44/210; ssuld *imper.* 93/222; issulde *pp.* 654/1355.
schutere *n.* archer 470/186.
sclauyn *n.* pilgrim's cloak 462/59.
scolle *n.* head, skull 141/148, 681/2161.
scorn *see* ascorn.
scorne *v. inf.* deride 368/104; scornede *pt. pl.* 613/80.
scrippe *n.* bag 336/258.
se *n.* see ce.
sed *n.* seed, sperm 1/7, 425/695.
sege, sige *n.* seat, seating 77/194, 544/53; segen *pl.* 191/316.
segge, sigge *v. inf.* say 15/206, 469/180; segge *1 pr.* 67/136; seiþ *pr.* 40/99; segge *pr. pl.* 67/136; sede *pt.* 84/13; *pt. pl.* 109/679; ised *pp.* 42/154.
seygnurye *n.* mastery 619/262.

F

GLOSSARY

seily v. inf. glide 261/421.
sel n. seal (of document) 630/619.
selde, selþe adv. seldom 81/11, 496/98.
seme a. seemly 614/116.
semlable a. similar 672/1900; see var., **semblabe** J.
semlant n. expression, demeanour 33/36, 112/75; **semblant** 506/428, 613/91.
senche v. pr. pl. subj. sink 553/98; see **sinke**.
sentence n. excommunication 640/924, 669/1806.
seo v. inf. see 13/149; **sicþ, sucþ, suk** pr. 410/254, 259/365, 692/70; **seoþ** pr. pl. 12/119; say, **sei** pt. 147/305, 84/5; **seȝen, seie** pt. pl. 480/97, 88/69; **iseȝe, iseie, isene** pp. 574/78, 21/74, 46/250; **sei** pt. probably mistake for **swie** 33/43, see var. and **swie** v.¹
seoþinge a. boiling 180/28.
sere a. worn, brittle 480/120.
sergant, seriant n. servant, follower 48/44, 457/50; **sergans, seriauns** pl. 219/74, 691/23.
seruage n. servitude 634/726, 677/2039.
seruede v. pt. deserved 476/373; **serued** pp. 198/536.
sette v. inf. put, place 83/84; **set** pr. 411/283; **sette** pr. subj. should plant 87/43; **sette** pt. pl. 189/276; **isete** pp. 189/277.
seþ v. pt. boiled 180/29; **sode** pt. pl. 185/159; **isode** pp. 49/74; **seoþinge, seþinge** pr. p. 300/247, 251.
seue, soue a. seven 79/42, 532/512.
seueniȝt, soueniȝt n. week 14/189, 532/518.
seueþe, soueþe a. seventh 424/660, 532/521.
sextein n. sexton 355/183.
si haut si bas now up, now down 223/84.
siche v. inf. sigh 119/15, 200/616; **siȝte** pt. 59/28, 88/96; see **sike**.
sid a. flowing (of beard) 376/66, 592/64.
side adv. far 395/181.
siȝt(e) n. trance 245/106, 405/110; eyesight 218/18.
sike v. inf. sigh 119/25, 541/267; **sikinge** pr. p. 29/125; see **siche**.
siker a. sure, safe 122/9; **sikeror(e)** comp. 302/318, 592/87.
siker adv. certainly 89/112, **sikere** 466/81; **sicker** 91/174; **sikeror** comp. 652/1278.
siker v. imper. assure 92/209.
sikerliche adv. safely 108/652.

sikernesse n. guarantee 226/174, 636/793.
sikinges n. pl. sighs 180/9.
sympelliche adv. weakly 25/15; **sympleliche** without concern 109/704.
sinfonye n. various musical instruments 574/84.
sinke v. inf. go down, sink 77/180, 30/162; **sonk** pt. 350/53; **sonke** pt. pl. 50/104; see **senche**.
synueu n. sinew 26/48; **sinuen** pl. 120/58, **synues** 503/338.
sitte v. inf. sit 7/74; **sit** pr. 326/338; **sat** pt. 7/78; **sete** pt. pl. 7/79; **isete** pp. 640/936; **sede** pt. pl. ? for **sete** 26/32, var. **sede** A; **sete** J.
siþe n. pl. times 312/285, 417/483.
*****siutour** n. haunter 606/384.
siwi v. inf. follow, track 365/7; **syuwestou** 2 pr. 32/12; **siwede** pt. 31/20, **suede** 514/87.
sker(e) a. clear 9/43; cleared 432/100, 468/144.
skere v. inf. clear, excuse 87/38, 231/286.
skynne n. bark 169/75.
*****slab** n. flat piece (of metal) 419/531, var. **slab** H, **sclaþ** J.
slade n. boggy land 152/113.
slake a. slow 269/154.
sle v. inf. strike down, kill 18/66; **slecst** 2 pr. 319/118; **sloȝ, slou** pt. 471/223, 10/74; **sloȝe, slowe** pt. pl. 512/11, 2/38; **islawe** pp. 319/120.
sleȝliche adv. cunningly 560/322.
sley a. skilful 252/161, 450/42.
sleue n. sleeve 124/82; **sleuen** pl. 491/227, **sleues** 490/224.
slidde n. ? smooth or level space 308/173; **slidde** H A J.
slide v. pr. subj. should slip 102/473.
slider a. slippery 102/475.
slim n. filth 266/56; **slyme** mud 532/517.
sliper a. slippery 470/201.
slo n. slough 152/115.
slou a. sluggish 424/672; lingering (of fever) 14/187.
smalache n. smallage, water parsley 120/52 var. A J.
smallore a. comp. narrower 101/459; lesser 264/494.
smart a. sharp (of wind) 95/295.
smere adv. scornfully 26/31, 452/103.
smerte v. inf. feel pain 428/776; **smerte, smurte** pt. impers. hurt 94/267, 574/94.
smertore adv. more forcefully 604/335; see **smart**.
smeþe a. smooth 102/471.

GLOSSARY

smyrie, smure v. inf. anoint 539/184, 168/38; smurede pt. 159/18; smyreden pt. pl. 560/304, smurede 50/96.
smite v. inf. strike, cut off 16/17; smist 2 pr. 269/140; smit pr. 80/66; smot pt. 12/130; smite pt. pl. 10/83; ismite pp. 124/88; smot pt. shifted 206/74; intr. in phr. com ~ came rushing (of wind, odour) 100/435, 279/147.
smiþþe n. blacksmith's shop 206/60; smiþes pl. 196/468.
smul n. smell, scent 103/512, 132/114.
smulle v. inf. give out odour, smell 279/150; smulde pt. 104/537; pt. pl. 279/148.
snytte v. pt. blew (nose) 207/85 var. H; ysnut pp. 207/91.
snyueleþ v. pr. sniffles 474/304; snyuelinge pr. p. a. 424/673.
sniwe v. inf. snow 60/35; ysnywed pp. 121/77.
soile v. imper. pollute, stain 317/67; isoilled pp. 324/280, 493/10.
soiourny v. inf. stay for a time 477/26, 510/552; soiornede pt. 207/104.
solaci v. inf. comfort 47/10, 604/346; solacy inf. intr. take one's ease 650/1215.
soler n. upper room 290/340.
somens, somonce n. command to appear 634/748, 175/232.
somer-lese n. summer-pasture 287/236.
somni v. inf. command to appear 11/99; somnede pt. 672/1887; somned pt. pl. 278/135; isomned pp. 11/103, 634/749.
son, soun n. sound 219/52, 38/22.
sonde n. present 62/14, 123/47; dispensation 4/24; mission, embassy 83/81, 214/8.
sond(e) a. unhurt, cured 9/40, 278/111.
sope n. sip 46/254.
soper n. evening meal 131/76, 187/217.
sor, sore n. disease, suffering 480/113, 48/44; sores pl. blemishes 24/169.
sor, soure a. sorrowful 59/19, var. sori A J; 320/148.
sore adv. grievously 26/33; sorere, sorore comp. 480/109, 17/42.
sori a. sad, grieved 59/17, 60/51; soriore comp. 696/105.
sorinesse n. sorrow 82/34, 131/92.
sotele a. clever 5/21.
sotylte n. ingonuity 577/168.
soþe n. truth 125/117; soþes as adv. truly 123/39, 125/99.

soþnisse n. truth 381/219, 664/1635.
souke n. mother's milk 308/155.
souke v. inf. suck 454/161; soukynge pr. p. 659/1502; soke 2 pt. 56/63; sek pt. 310/220.
soule-bote n. help of soul 142/179, 528/386.
soulement adv. only 186/198, 245/95.
soupe v. inf. eat supper 632/689.
sourmonte v. inf. surpass 37/10.
soutare n. shoemaker 159/11, 19.
souwinge, sowinge n. sewing 137/18, 518/97.
souwe, sowe v. inf. plant 1/7, 385/35; seu pt. 540/230; seuwe, sewe pt. subj. 1/9, 87/43; ysouwe pp. 1/4.
sowe n. female pig 48/49, 51.
sowi v. inf. sew 520/160; isued pp. 494/52; hy ssowede probably for yssowed pp. 671/1846, see var., y soweþ J.
speche-tyme n. time appointed for audience 635/767.
specials n. pl. intimate friends 210/194.
spede v. inf. succeed 282/102; spedde pt. pl. 196/485; isped pp. 659/1493; spede inf. impers. fare, go, 454/148; spede pr. subj. 124/65; spedde pt. 29/140, 55/28.
speke v. inf. talk, say 40/95; spekestou 2 pr. 25/15, spexst, spext 57/83, 156/27; specþ, spekeþ pr. 364/177, 191/320; spak pt. 9/21; speke pt. pl. 204/9; ispeke pr. 125/100.
spelde n. pl. sparks 96/310, spelden 99/411, 379/179.
spelie v. inf. scrimp 130/47.
spelle n. mere talk 522/212.
spence, spense n. pl. supplies 612/60, 493/33.
spene v. inf. spend, employ 568/80, 655/1395; ispend pp. 568/82.
spille v. inf. destroy, waste 18/69, 386/68; spillest 2 pr. 56/53; spille 2 pr. subj. 453/121; spilleþ pr. pl. 63/37.
spitede v. pt. impaled 459/105.
spites n. pl. spits, spikes 96/320, 459/103.
spoken n. pl. spokes (of wheel) 97/328.
spone n. splinter 18/62.
spotele n. spittle 159/17.
spousbruche n. adultery 37/2, 242/32.
spouse, spousi v. inf. marry 614/106, 443/11; ispoused pp. 37/3, 62/10.
spoushod n. marriage 293/50.
sprangling n. crackling 28/102.
sprede v. inf. intr. extend, scatter 18/76, 103/512; spradde pt. pl. 111/52;

GLOSSARY

ysprad *pp. tr.* laid (of table) 121/81, 184/123.
sprengde *v. pt.* sprinkled, spattered 1/11, 28/105; **sprenge** *pt. pl.* 89/129, var. **sprende** A, **sperng** J; **isprengd** *pp.* ? engendered 425/695.
springe *v. inf.* sprout, spread 1/1, 5; **sprong** *pt.* 24/151, 32/25; **spronge** *pt. subj.* 170/90; **sprong̃e** *pp.* 652/1293.
***spronke** *n.* spark 93/223.
spurne *v. inf.* trip, stub 526/320; **sperne** *pr. subj. pl.* 79/27.
ssab *n.* diseased skin 24/156.
ssade *n.* shadow, shape 141/142.
ssake *v. inf.* shake 230/273; **sok, ssok** *pt.* 371/187, 207/81.
ssame *n.* disgrace 4/11, 30/169; see **assame**.
ssamie *v. inf.* be or make ashamed 322/223; **ssamede** *pt. pl.* 219/48; see **ofssamede**.
ssarpe *a.* angular (of face) 379/175.
ssedinge *n.* outpouring (of blood) 113/107.
ssef *v.* see **scheoue**.
ssel *v. I pr.* shall 7/66, **ichelle** 29/129; **sselt** *2 pr.* 20/38; **schel, ssel** *pr.* 18/74, 20/36; **scholleþ, ssolleþ** *pr. pl.* 30/160, 34/48; **ssoldest, ssost** *2 pt.* 419/542, 419/541; **scholde, ssolde** *pt.* 2/28, 30/175; **ssolde** *pt. pl.* 21/53.
ssenfol, ssenfdol *a.* disgraceful 152/128, 219/47, **ssunfol** 295/114; **ssendfol** embarrassing (of disease) 24/154.
ssenfoliche *adv.* ignominiously 371/180.
ssennesse, ssunnes *n.* harm, shame 231/296, 56/62, **schindnisse** 530/464.
ssep-hurde *n.* shepherd 680/2150.
ssere *n.* groin 426/722.
ssere *a.* ? straight (of wind) used ironically 403/25, var. **scher** H, line om. A J; see *O.E.D.* under **sheer**: '? Blowing steadily in one direction.'
ssere *v. inf.* shave, shear 323/239; **schere** *imper.* 149/32; **ssere** *pt. pl.* 251/137; **yssore** *pp.* 91/161.
sserp *adv.* piercingly (of wind) 93/234.
ssewe, ssewy *v. inf.* show, point out 18/68, 80/66; **sseueþ** *pr.* 71/39; **sseweþ** *pr. pl.* 79/57; **ssewede** *pt.* 84/92; *pt. pl.* 103/531; see **scheuwe, schowe**.
ssilchene *n.* see **ssulchene**.
ssine *v. inf.* shine 38/39; **ssinnynge** *pr. p.* 450/36; **schon** *pt.* 20/26, **sson** 43/169, **ssinde** 36/132; ? **ssine** *pr. subj.* 417/456, see var.

ssire *n.* shire 280/33; **ssiren(e)** *pl.* men of the shire 290/315, 317.
ssonde *n.* disgrace 30/169.
ssoneþ *v. pr.* avoids 416/445.
ssop *v. pt.* created 104/546, 222/49; **yssape** *pp.* destined 34/52.
ssortliche *adv.* soon 175/229.
ssouele *n.* shovel 177/293, var. **schoule** H; **schole** A; 608/466, var. **schoules** H.
ssrapede *v. pt.* scratched 148/332.
ssrenche *v. inf.* cause to shrivel 421/589.
ssrewe *n.* evil creature 209/151; **ssrewen(e)** *pl.* 94/261, 219/48.
ssrewe *a.* evil 286/202; *a ~ treo* probably mistake for *asshen t.* 154/196, see var., **aschene** J.
ssrewede *n.* wickedness 358/4, 659/1508; **ssrewehede** 229/244, 396/195.
ssryned *v. pt.* enshrined 620/322; **issrined** *pp.* 15/220, 118/251.
ssulchene *n.* handmaid 55/40, 145/268, **ssilchene** 55/36.
stable *a.* steadfast 63/45, 91/175.
stableliche, stabliche *adv.* constantly 109/699, 122/8.
stak *n.* stick of wood 87/55, var. **staf** A J.
stamin *n.* undergarment of coarse cloth 684/2244.
standed(e) *a.* lifeless 21/76, 161/26.
stape *n.* step 343/99; **stappes** *pl.* footprints 169/52, 170/92.
staringe *v. pr. p.* with fixed look 428/791.
stat *n.* condition, mode of existence 107/631, 501/267; consciousness 525/295.
status *n.* statute 632/695; *pl.* 631/658, 652/1275.
steke *v. inf.* fasten 632/681.
stele *v. inf. tr.* steal 19/82; **stelþ** *pr.* 44/187; **istole** *pp.* 86/15; *~ inf. intr.* move secretly 174/199; **stal** *pt.* 122/4; **stele** *pt. pl.* 220/101; **stole** *? pt.* (text corrupt) 529/421.
stemne *n.* tune 210/179, 185.
steorne, sturne *a.* fierce, cruel 29/146, 269/147.
steorneliche, sturneliche *adv.* fiercely 380/209, 150/68.
stepel *n.* tower 419/539.
steppe *v. inf.* advance, tread 313/299, 589/93; **stap** *pt.* 343/82; **stepte** *pt. pl.* 168/50.
stiche *n.* stitch (of sewing) 159/12.
stie *v. inf.* ascend, climb 309/205; **stei** *pt.* 310/214, 436/56, **steȝ** 546/94; **ystye** *pp.* 70/5.

GLOSSARY

stif *a.* rigid, firm 503/337, 630/629; strong (of wind) 195/461; stiue *pl.* 371/186, var. steue A; stif J; 372/201, var. steue A; stiuore *comp.* 604/348 var. A.
stike *v. inf.* remain fixed, bristle 95/292; stikede *pt.* 513/48; ystiked *pp.* 67/142.
stille *a.* continual 424/668.
stinge *v. inf.* pierce, sting 84/2, 325/299; stinginge *pr. p.* 379/179; stonge *pt. pl.* 95/280, 325/308.
stinkinge *v. pr. p.* smelling foully 97/333; stank, stonk *pt.* 98/382, 99/399.
stinte, stunte *v. pt.* halted 579/245, 647/1132; stente *pt. pl.* 487/142.
stiues *n. pl.* bagpipes 574/84 var. J.
stomak *n.* in phr. *meneþ hore* ~ ? complain of indigestion 130/54.
stonde *n.* time, moment 8/18, 81/23, stounde 110/716, 156/5.
stonde *v. inf.* stand 97/349; stonstou 2 *pr.* 100/446; stont *pr.* 11/90; stod *pt.* 138/62; stode(n) *pt. pl.* 99/407, 555/157; istonde *pp.* 7/75, 100/441.
stordi *a.* aggressive 131/69, 326/333.
stoupe *v. inf.* bend, lean over 562/376; stopinge *pr. p.* 523/242; stoupede *pt.* 112/77.
strang(e), strong *a.*[1] powerful 100/435, 101/457, 340/2; severe (of disease) 31/17; straunger, strengore *comp.* more difficult 549/196; strengere mightier 504/364; strengost *superl.* 36/117, 412/314.
strange, strong *a.*[2] foreign, unknown 32/2, 189/288.
strangli *v. inf.* choke 430/46.
strapeles *n. pl.* leg-coverings 659/1485.
strau *n.* straw (as worthless) 407/151, stre, streo 17/44, 131/80.
stre *n.*[1] 'The germinal vesicle in the yolk of an egg', *O.E.D.* under strain 415/396, var. streon H.
stre, streo *n.*[2] see strau.
strecche *v. inf.* straighten out, extend 116/187; strei3te *pt.* 503/348; (i)strei3t *pp.* 376/65, 659/1485.
streit *a.* narrow, tight 188/251, 659/1484; strict 83/60, 619/275.
stremede *v. pt.* in phr. ~ *ablode* ran with blood 50/93, 64/48.
strengþe *n.* violence 653/1302.
streon *n.* see stre *n.*[1]
striue, striui *v. inf.* contend 46/261, 256/279; striuede *1 pt.* 662/1584.
striuinge *n.* contention 336/283, 628/565.
stroc *n.* blow 528/397.

strok *v. pt.* rubbed 207/85.
stronge *a.* as *n.* name of the thumb 412/317.
struyde *v. pt.* destroyed 704/197.
strupe *v. inf.* unclothe 20/42; strupte *pt.* 122/23; *pt. pl.* 295/116.
stude, steode *n.* place 6/25, 117/224; studes *pl.* 193/386; positions in time 134/5, 135/20.
studie *n.* concentration of mind 499/220, 501/279; steodie perplexity 649/1205.
studie *v. inf.* put one's mind on a subject 501/282; studede *pt.* 260/395, 433/119.
sturde *v.*[1] *pt.* ruled, steered 483/4.
sturede *v.*[2] *pt.* bestirred 286/211.
sturte *v. pt.* moved quickly 260/384, starte 310/217, sterte 323/235; sturte *pt. pl.* 195/453, 250/110.
sucþ, suk *v.* see seo.
suelle *v. inf.* become bloated 273/262.
sulle *v. inf.* sell 38/12; sul *imper.* 475/359; solde *pt.* 39/50; isold *pp.* 568/77.
sulte *v. inf.* sprinkle with salt 157/46; sulte *pt. pl.* 157/41, 179/20.
sunegi, sungy *v. inf.* do wrong 136/8, 138/50, synewi 507/454; sunegede *pt.* 409/215; isuneget *pp.* 224/116, isuneged 338/335.
sunne *n.* sin 6/41; sunnen, sunnes *pl.* 131/84, 139/82; sunnes perhaps for ssunnes shame 144/212, see var., schamnesse J.
surance *n.* guarantee 673/1916.
suspendi *v. inf.* deprive (of office) 668/1753; *wy suspendest 2 pr.* probably mistake for *we suspendieþ* put aside 638/848, see var., *we suspendeþ* J.
suspetion *n.* mistrust 17/29.
susteini, susteny *v. inf.* support, maintain 661/1547, 479/94; susteined *pt. pl.* 661/1551; ysusteined *pp.* 18/61.
sustenance *n.* supply of food 312/282, 445/70.
suyþe *adv.* persistently 515/13; swuþe very 98/376; þe swuþþore *comp.* the more 28/93.
sute *n.* pursuit 336/262.
suþþe *adv.* afterward 2/22
swagi *v. inf.* abate, mitigate 55/44, 658/1460.
sweng(e) *n.* swing 407/173, 408/179.
swenge *v. inf.* in phr. *com* ~ came sweeping 407/177.
sweore, swere *n.* neck 331/110, 98/365, swure 96/313.

GLOSSARY

sweriare *n.* one who curses 424/684.
swete *v. inf.* sweat 421/596; **swatte** *pt.* 142/178; *pt. pl.* 529/430.
swie *v.*¹ *inf.* ? breathe regularly as in sleep 33/43 var. A, **sweye** J.
swie *v.*² *inf.* go, glide 246/124, 255/245.
swike *n.* deceiver 528/398.
swike *v. inf.* deceive 297/172.
swikedom *n.* deception 334/214, 557/202.
swinch(e) *n.* toil 201/621, 225/123.
swinke *v. inf.* labour 168/33; **swonk** *pt.* 35/93.
swoddringe, swoudring(e) *n.* slumber 83/71, var. **swoldrynge** A; **suoddring** J; 501/261, 502/286, see var.
swolewe *v. inf.* swallow 487/128, 514/69; **swolwe** *pt.* 397/217; **iswolwe** *pp.* engulfed 137/24.
swon *n.* swineherd 48/52, var. **suon** J.
swopeþ *v. imper. pl.* sweep 347/184.
swote *a.* fragrant 99/416, 170/106.
swote *adv.* fragrantly 104/537, 279/150.
swotnesse *n.* fragrance 132/116, 171/120.
swoudri *v. inf.* drowse 501/260.

table *n.* inscribed tablet 58/114, 118.
taborer *n.* drummer 574/92 var. J.
tabours *n. pl.* drums 574/84; **tapres** probably mistake for **tabours** 672/1893, see var., **tapres** H J.
*tade *n.* toad 27/66, see var., t- rest bound in J.
tailage, talage *n.* tax 621/343, 348.
taille *n.* cut, fashion 104/551.
tailles *a.* without a tail 86/12.
tannare *n.* one who tans hides 248/56.
taper *n.*¹ candle 205/12; **tapres** *pl.* 191/334, 672/1890.
tapres *n.*² 672/1893, see **tabours**.
targede *v. pt.* delayed 285/179.
tarieþ *v. pr.* provokes 411/285 var. A.
taste *v. inf.* feel 412/310.
techare *n.* pointer, the index finger 412/312, 316.
teche *v. inf.* instruct, point out 85/2, 412/316; **tekþ** points 325/306; **taȝte** *pt.* 59/6, **teiȝte** directed 163/21; **itaȝt** *pp.* 519/132.
tei-dogge *n.* tied watch-dog 411/280, 299.
teie *n.* cord, leash 411/299; restraint 539/172 var. A J.
teie *v. inf.* fasten, hitch 160/38, 570/130; **teide** *pt.* 260/376; **tyde** *pt. pl.* 569/107; **iteyd** *pp.* 197/523.
tellinde, tellinge *v. pr. p.* talking 341/47, 574/79.

temde *v. pt.* engendered 243/33.
temes *n. pl.* teams (of oxen) 570/129.
temie *v. inf.* tame 333/170.
tempest *n.* storm 193/403, 706/243.
tende *v. inf.* light, take fire 93/218, 419/523; **tent** *pr.* 190/303; **tende** *pt.* 191/334; *pt. pl.* 163/34; **itend** *pp.* 419/533, illumined 598/146.
tendrost *a. superl.* most solicitous 283/136.
tenebres *n. pl.* obscurity 434/9.
teo *v. inf. intr.* go 144/236, 186/185, *tr.* draw 569/112.
teone *n.* anger, distress 44/197, 167/16.
teorne *v.* see **turne**.
teoþingge, teþinge *n.*¹ a tenth part 696/119, 129/9; offering of a tenth 128/L 3, 275/40.
teoþinge, teþinge, tiþinge *n.*² see **tidinge**.
tere *v. pt. pl.* lacerated 50/89.
teseþ *v. pr.* combs (of cloth) 166/87.
tete *n.* teat 96/317.
teþe *n.* tenth part 129/21.
teþe *a.* tenth 14/195.
teþegi *v. pr. pl.* take a tenth (of time) 128/L 5.
tice *v. inf.* incite 325/305, see var., **tece** J.
tyde *n.* canonical hour 187/222; **tiden** *pl.* 313/286.
tidinge *n.* report, news 650/1238, **teoþinge** 572/35, **teþinge** 567/58, **tiþinge** 49/72.
tilie *v. inf.* cultivate 385/35; get treatment 207/92.
tilleþ *v. pr. pl.* reach, extend 423/640; **tilde** *pt.* 20/49, 170/80.
tirans *n. pl.* oppressors 270/171, 634/745.
tit *v. pr. impers.* betides, befalls 92/214; *pers.* awaits 20/22, 490/214.
to, two *n.* toe 79/27, 404/68; ***ton** *pl.* 98/380, see var., **ton** J.
toberste *v. inf.* break in pieces 95/276; **tobarst** *pt.* 346/162; **toburste** *pt. pl.* 480/120; **toborste** *pt. subj.* 92/191.
tobet *v. pt.* thrashed 694/53.
tobrak *v. pt.* shattered 157/58; **tobreke** *pt. pl.* 153/164; **tobroke** *pp.* 276/66.
tobrusede *v. pt.* crushed 157/58, 561/338.
toclef *v. pt.* divided 23/112, 706/256.
to-comynge *v. pr. p.* about to be, in the future 188/232; **to-comynge** 436/48, reading of C H is corrupt, see var. A; *Ac in þisse worle þat is to comene* J; cf. *L.A.* 683: *sed*

GLOSSARY 75

[*Deus verus*] *nobis est incognitus et nobis ignotus et saeculo venturo futurus et in perpetuum regnaturus.*

todaschte, todasste *v. pt.* split apart 561/339, 318/92; **todaʒste** *pt. intr.* 695/84.

to-drawe *v. inf.* rend, pull apart 29/143; **todrou** *pt.* 85/21; **todrowe** *pt. pl.* 93/220; **todrawe** *pp.* stretched out 95/272.

tognouʒ *v. pt.* gnawed away 518/86; **tognowe** *pt. pl.* lacerated 541/249.

toʒen *prep.* against 17/30.

toʒte *a.* taut, binding 481/128.

tohacki *v. inf.* cut to pieces 267/74.

tohewe *v. pt. pl.* hacked to pieces 358/36, 456/210; *pp.* 413/367.

toknyng *n.* sign, indication 117/216, 248/51.

tollare *n.* tax-gatherer 397/6; **tollares** *g.* 397/6.

*tolle, **tolli** *v. inf.* entice, beckon 412/324, 302; **tolleþ** *pr.* 412/304; **tollede** *pt.* 228/232.

tollinge *n.* enticing 414/379.

tombe *n.* burial monument, grave 117/217, 272/230, **tumbe** 486/82.

tombede *v. pt. pl.* danced 244/65, var. **tumbede** H, om. A J.

tonge *n.*[1] tongue 94/256, 95/279; voice 195/441, 631/637.

tonge *n.*[2] pair of tongs 207/77; **tongen** *pl.* 196/477.

tongen, tounge *n.*[3] *pl.* strips, thongs 199/571, 197/523.

tonne-voll *n.* tunful 595/53.

to-parti *v. inf.* separate 263/464.

topounede *v. pt. pl.* pounded to pieces 333/178.

toppede *v. pt. pl.* fought 698/15.

torende *v. inf.* tear apart 296/132; *pt.* 98/383; **torend** *pp.* 513/58.

toret *n.* summit 402/15, 402/18 var. H J.

torment *n.* suffering 95/285; **tormentis** *pl.* 20/40, **tormens** 623/382.

tormenti, turmenti *v. inf.* torture 20/36, 457/22; **tormentede** *pt.* 433/132; *pt. pl.* 2/38; **itormented** *pp.* 49/64.

tormentynge *n.* torturing 180/33.

tormentors, turmentours *n. pl.* torturers 26/29, 513/41.

torn *n.* see **valling-torn**.

torueþ *v. pr.* pelts 411/285 var. H.

tosprede *v. inf.* scatter, spread out 244/74, 680/2150; **tospradde** *pt. pl.* 383/290; **tooprad** *pp.* 211/80.

toswelleþ *v. pr. pl.* swell up 410/249; **toswal** *pt.* 119/41.

totere *v. inf.* tear apart 270/172; *pr. s.* 3/65; **to-tar** *pt.* 606/410.

to-tokne *v.* ? for **to-toknede** 283/133, see var.

touche, tuochi *v. inf.* come in contact with, touch 102/494, 498/183; **touched(e)** *pt.* 23/114, 328/36.

tour *n.*[1] tower 316/14, 390/14.

tour *n.*[2] summit 402/18, see var., **tour** J.

towaile *n.* towel 77/195.

toward *a.* promising 336/277, 699/39.

towonded *pp.* deeply wounded 564/442.

traceours *n. pl.* see **trassours**.

traie *v. inf.* trouble 339/355.

traison *n.* treachery 10/61, 178/324.

traitour *n.* traitor 633/698; **traitors** *g.* betrayer's 371/178; betrayers *pl.* 332/143.

transcrit *n.* copy 628/539, 631/633.

trassours *n. pl.* bands for the hair 63/46; **traceours** 518/84.

trauail *n.* hardship, labour 36/103, 188/232; ∼ *of childe* pains of childbirth 301/243.

trauaille *v. inf.* toil, exert oneself 73 75; **trauailest** *2 pr.* 284/163; **trauaillestou** *tr.* harassest 488/160; **itrauiled** *pp.* journeyed 216/61.

trecherie *n.* see **tricherie**.

treye *n.* affliction 539/172.

tresches *n. pl.* dances 445/67.

trespas *n.* offence 13/152, 210/196; transgression of law 624/418.

tricherie *n.* betrayal, treachery 10/77, 700/80, **trecherie** 557/228.

trichor, trichour *n.* deceiver 260/377, 233/347; **trichors** *pl.* 261/415.

trichour *a.* deceitful 397/7.

trie *v.* see **out-trie**.

tripet *n.* trick 44/190.

triste *v. inf.* rely on 475/357; **trist** *pr.* 283/108; **triste** *pt.* 10/80.

tristi *a.* confident 132/97.

triwelokest *adv. superl.* most faithfully 247/10.

triwenesse, trunisse *n.* truth, loyalty 334/214, 516/52.

triwes *n.* respite 443/23.

trompours *n. pl.* trumpeters 2/26.

trowede *v. pt.* supposed 143/200.

truage *n.* tribute 698/23, 26.

trufle *n.* nonsense, frivolity 253/185, 604/347.

truflinge *adv.* idly 206/74.

trupe *n.* plighted word 495/95, 630/605.

tuicche *v. inf.* tug 570/131.

tuynnes *n. pl.* twins 515/5.

76   GLOSSARY

tuo-name n. nickname 571/4, var. to name A J.
turne v. inf. change direction, turn 216/54; teorne inf. transform 602/276; turnde pt. 196/474, converted 274/10; pt. pl. 325/307; iturnd pp. 146/299, transferred 616/185.
twengde v. pt. tweaked 207/81.

þait probably error for þat 86/29, see var., A crois þer J.
þanneward adv. thence 354/163, 487/136.
þar adv. there 106/593.
þas pron. g. of it 278/124.
þe def. art. the 1/1; þan(e) acc. 72/17, 75/140; þen(e) 70/15, 122/22.
þef, þeof n. thief, villain 27/83, 86/23, þuf 239/25; þeoues, þeues pl. 406/115, 244/86.
þei n. thigh 119/43; þie, þies pl. 61/9, 459/104.
þenche v.¹ inf. impers. seem, appear 7/66; þencheþ pr. 178/325, þincþ 99/415, þingþ 204/714; þenche pr. subj. 182/68; þoȝte pt. 283/117.
þenche v.² inf. think, consider 80/68; þencstou 2 pr. 177/309, þengst 82/50; þencheþ pr. pl. 185/169; þench imper. 20/35; þoȝte pt. 283/123; iþoȝt pp. 398/38.
þeo v. inf. thrive 37/9; þeoinge pr. p. a. 524/268, 615/149.
þeodom n. prosperity 398/48 var. H, line om. A J.
þeofliche adv. thievishly 189/286.
þeos, þis dem. adj. this 304/46, 226/155, þisse 226/152; þisne acc. 121/79, 126/142; þeos(e) pl. 41/127, 116/190.
þer contraction the air 419/518, see var., þeir H.
þerftou v. 2 pr. darest thou 521/193, þerst 558/250; þer pr. needs 507/461; (ne)þer pr. impers. needs 567/48; þore pr. pl. dare 493/38, need 553/105; (ne)þerfte pt. dared 517/65; pt. pl. 512/28; see derst.
þeu, þiwe a. bond 631/640, 617/221.
þewe v. discipline 699/57.
þicke a. stout 340/3; dense (of mist) 422/620.
þicke, þikke adv. in a crowd 91/170, 579/237.
þickeþ v. pr. becomes thick 425/709.
þinne a. see þunne.
þiu n. bondwoman 658/1469.
þiwe a. see þeu.
þo adv. and conj. then, when 1/15, 5/T 8.

þole, þolie v. inf. endure, allow 267/91, 54/17; þoleþ pr. 86/10; þolede pt. 16/22; iþoled pp. 12/112.
þondri v. inf. thunder 60/35; þondrede probably mistake for þondre n. 265/22; þondred pt. 79/49.
þondringe n. noise like thunder 390/18.
þonk n. expression of gratitude 92/204; is þonkes g. as adv. willingly 97/351.
þonke, þonki v. inf. give thanks to 177/306, 479/79; þonki 1 pr. 60/48; þonkede pt. 52/161; iþonked pp. 73/58.
þor prep. through 663/1627; þoru 185/147, 616/194; see þurf.
þoume n. thumb 412/314, 317.
þral n. bondservant 55/40, 573/42.
þred n. thread, least part 588/74.
þresuold n. threshold 39/67.
þrete v. inf. menace 558/260, 587/46; þreteþ pr. 80/62.
þreting(e) n. menacing 20/38, 93/216.
þretny v. inf. make threats 80/65; þretenede pt. 306/95, þretnede 25/11.
þretteþe a. thirtieth 559/292.
þreu n. distance thrown 386/63.
þrie adv. thrice 125/111, 131/93.
þrift n. in phr. luþer ~ bad luck 242/22, 340/386.
þritteþe a. thirteenth 191/331.
þrou, þrowe n. coffin 116/215, 332/135.
þrouweþ v. pr. pelts 411/285; þreu pt. hurled 23/111, 350/35; þrewe pt. pl. 591/45.
þrowe n. space of time 423/647, 502/295.
þrowes n. see deþ-þrowes.
þruȝt n. thrust, throw (of a stone) 313/299, var. þreuȝt H, þreut A J.
þruste v. pt. pushed 521/192; pt. pl. 591/31.
þrustel-cok n. male song-thrush 122/12.
þufþe n. theft 606/389, 623/401.
þulke dem. a. that, that same 3/2, 197/516; ulke pl. 620/308.
þunne a. sparse, slight 111/44, 605/363; þinne narrow 459/107.
þurf prep. through, throughout 458/80, 461/33.
þwonge n. strip of leather 457/44.

See also under F

vacant a. unoccupied 9/51; vacans pl. 629/586.
vad a. wan 424/667.
vain adv. gladly 342/55.

GLOSSARY

vair *a.* bright (of weather), pleasing 60/34, 111/42; **vairor(e)** *comp.* 21/74, 81/22; **vairoste** *superl.* 90/150, 152.
vale *a.* many 47/17, 123/51; **uele** 98/378.
valeie, valeiȝe *n.* valley 47/16, 6 (read ȝ for z); **faleye** 498/187.
valle *v. inf.* drop, befall 48/38, 152/128; **vallet** *pr.* 422/606, **valt** 455/192, **valþ** 3/66; **vel** *pt.* 85/38, **veol** 695/84; **volle** *pt. pl.* 155/204.
valling-torn *n.* a trick of falling in wrestling 407/176.
valshede *n.* deception 397/7, 704/201.
vant *n.* baptismal font 113/101.
vare *v. inf.* act, fare 19/13, 130/54; **varþ** *pr.* 417/459; **vareþ** *pr. pl.* 132/113; **verde** *pt.* 42/157, 286/211; *pt. pl.* 611/20.
vast *a.* tenacious 424/669.
vaste *adv.* firmly 183/94, 197/523.
vaste *v. inf.* eat sparingly 123/38, 130/36, **veste** 692/71; **vasteþ** *pr. pl.* 128/L 2, 130/41; **vaste** *pt.* 129/22, 29; **iuast** *pp.* 134/175.
vastyng-eue *n.* eve or day appointed for fasting 131/71.
vat *n.* large vessel 46/255.
vatte *a.* fertile 130/50.
vauni *v. inf.* fawn, act playfully 431/69, var. **faweny** H, **vawene** A, **vawyny** J; **vaunede** *pt.* 260/379, var. **vaȝnede** H, **uawynde** A, berginde (g doubtful, ? **berkinde**) J.
vawe, vauwe *adv.* gladly 12/122, 50/102.
veage, viage *n.* journey by water 183/92, 185/150.
vecche, veche *v. inf.* fetch, obtain 14/189, 81/90; **vette** *pt.* 120/72; *pt. pl.* 438/112; **iuet** *pp.* 395/181; see **fecche, fette**.
vede *v. inf.* give food to, nourish 121/84; **vet** *pr.* 106/615; **vedeþ** *pr. pl.* 314/317; **vedde** *pt. pl. intr.* 5/E 10; **ived** *pp.* 107/640, 121/84.
veie *v. inf. impers.* fit 426/719; **veiþ** *pr.* is suitable 631/650.
veine-glory *n.* boasting 440/17.
veines *n. pl.* water channels 423/638, 639.
veirss, verss *a.* unsalted, fresh 179/18, 422/597.
veld *n.* open or cultivated land 17/46, **feld** 94/249; **veldes** *pl.* 161/12; **aueld(e)** *adv.* in, into the field 43/165, 119/31.
velde *v. pt.* felt, experienced 14/186, 84/3, **velede** 693/18; **velde** *pt. pl.* 107/628.
vele *a.* see **vale**.
velien *n. pl.* fellies, rim of wheel 67/142.
ven, venne *n.* marshy ground 318/98, 94.
veolle *v. inf.* cause to fall 166/77.
veorne *a.* distant 216/61, var. **furrene** H, **verrone** A, **ferrene** J.
veorste, verste *a.* first, foremost 2/27, 3/67; ~ **uader** 106/598.
ver *adv.* far 17/16, 93/230; **veor** *comp.* 97/352, 648/1178.
vere *n.* companion 34/58, 35/76; *pl.* 53/192, 82/36, **veren** 138/65; see **yuere**.
verhede *n.* company 372/217, 447/145.
verlich *a.* stern 606/380.
verlich *adv.* suddenly 155/220, 161/24.
verss *a.* see **veirss**.
verss *adv.* afresh 26/38.
verst *n.* respite 301/267, 361/72.
verst *adv.* first of all 1/17, 3/67.
verþing-worþ *n.* small amount 131/70.
veste *v.* see **vaste**.
vestes *n. pl.* fists 426/722.
vestemens *n. pl.* ecclesiastical garments 91/160, 211/18.
vestiarie *n.* vestry 490/217.
veteres *n. pl.* shackles 480/105, 611/15, **feteres** 479/79.
vetles *n.* receptacle 383/275, 396/205, **veteles** 298/207.
veu, vewe *a.* few 75/141, 111/51.
vifteþe *a.* fifteenth 89/124.
vil(e) *a.* base 18/80, 624/413; **vil** worthless 173/183.
vilenie *n.* indecorum 582/339.
vyly *v. inf.* degrade 173/183; **vileþ** *pr.* revile 31/9.
ville *n.* ? leaf, as type of the worthless, in *a.* and *adv.* phr. **worþ a uille** 18/70, 296/146.
villich(e) *adv.* basely 18/77, 112/90, **fillich** 395/166; **vyloker** *comp.* 692/59.
vilte *n.* baseness 238/499, 635/761.
vinde *v. inf.* find 76/159; **vinst** 2 *pr.* 406/117; **vint** *pr.* provides 388/116; **vyndeþ** *pr. pl.* 65/100; **vond** *pt.* 6/26; **vonde** *pt. pl.* 77/189; **ivonde** *pp.* 71/35.
vynegre *n.* vinegar 459/99.
vingres-ende *n.* finger-tip 95/294.
vinlyng *n.* foundling 694/56.
visc, viss *n.* fish 185/170, 159; **visses** *pl.* 195/450.
vissare *n.* fisher 246/3; **vissares** *g.* 264/494; **visssares** *pl.* 246/5.
viþele *n.* fiddle 186/186.

GLOSSARY

vleiss, vless *n.* flesh 109/701, 67/145; *vleisses mod* bodily desire 133/133.
vleo *v.*[1] *inf.* flee, depart 72/17, 79/50; *pr. subj.* 22/84; **vlei** *pt.* 124/86.
vleo *v.*[2] *inf.* fly 60/59; **vleoþ** *pr. pl.* 80/64; **vley** *pt.* 186/185.
vleote *v. inf.* float 173/179, 383/280; **vleotinge** *pr. p.* 173/180.
ulke 620/308 see **þulke**.
vlore *n.* floor 121/78.
vlþe *n.* age 533/6; see **elde**.
vlþere *a. comp.* elder 497/153, 515/4; see **olde**.
vnarmede *v. pt.* disarmed 607/439; **vnyarmed** *pp.* without armour 484/42.
vnbarnd *pp.* unburned 220/100.
vnbend *v. inf.* relax (tension of bow) 604/334; **vnbende** *pt.* 604/333; **vnbend** *pp.* 604/343.
vnbinde *v. inf.* undo, set free 46/250, 330/92; **vnbind** *pr.* 328/37; **vnbunde** *pt. pl.* 262/435; **vnbonde, vnbunde** *pp.* 329/40, 43.
vnbliþe *a.* unhappy 126/152.
vnbocsom *a.* disobedient 143/189.
vnbured *pp.* unburied 18/52, 541/252.
vnchargi *v. inf.* unload 134/157.
vnclene *a.* foul 50/99.
*****vnconnynge** *n.* ignorance 643/1030.
vncouþ(e) *a.* strange, foreign 482/157, 518/109.
vnder *prep.* in phr. ~ þe quene besides, or in disregard of, the queen 698/5.
vnderfange, -fonge *v. inf.* receive, accept 216/64, 432/96; **underfeng, -veng** *pt.* 215/31, 8/9; **underfonge, -uonge** *pp.* 33/34, 12/114.
vnderȝite *v. inf.* learn of, understand 242/4; **vnderȝat, -ȝet** *pt.* 568/69, 37/8; **vnderȝite** *pt. pl.* 73/61; *pp.* 216/60.
vnderne *n.* the third hour, tierce 187/221, 193/379; *hei vndern* mid-morning 608/464.
vndo *v. inf.* open, release 250/103, 328/30; *is mouþ* ~ speak 105/561; **vndo** *pr. subj.* 592/73; **vndude** *pt.* 354/166; **vndo** *pp.* 46/248.
vndut *pp.* opened 325/293.
vnesy *a.* uncomfortable 659/1488.
vneseliche *adv.* uncomfortably 498/164.
vneþe, vnneþe *adv.* scarcely 136/3, 1/6.
vngod *a.* evil 693/22.
vngreiþid *pp.* unprepared 683/2240.
vngurd *pp.* ungirdled 688/2377.
vnȝete *pp.* not eaten 190/297, var. **vnyete** H, **vn ete** A J.

vnȝoulde *pp.* unrewarded 231/294.
vnhende *a.* ill-mannered 125/125.
vniuele *a.* ? many; probably mistake for **unuele** wicked 451/62, see var., (þe Giwes om.) **vn uele** J.
vniknowe *pp.* unknown 435/31, 41.
vniliche *adv.* beyond comparison 184/141.
vninome *pp.* uncaptured 688/2394.
vnypyned *pp.* untormented 498/176.
vniseie *pp.* invisible 404/66.
vnywar *a.* unwary 487/130.
vnkunde *a.* ungrateful 92/206; unpleasant 420/560.
vnlawe *n.* injustice 629/594.
vnlek *v. pt.* unlocked 90/133, 586/28; **vnloke** *pp.* 109/694.
vnmiȝte *n.* weakness 657/1450.
vnmilde *a.* harsh 659/1502, 693/16.
vnpared *pp.* unpeeled 705/234.
vnriȝt *n.* wrong, injustice 11/88, 186/197.
vnseliliche *adv.* wretchedly 684/2251.
*****vnsowed** *pp.* unsewed 703/170.
vnssore *pp.* not shaved 251/139.
vnssriue, vnyschryue *pp.* unshriven 131/91, 465/54.
vnstable *a.* changeable 6/36, 704/184.
vnteid *pp.* unleashed 260/381.
vntold *pp.* unconfessed 134/167.
vntriwe *a.* faithless 10/79; **vntruere** *comp.* 496/98.
vnþonkes *n. g.* as *adv.* unwillingly 101/466, 507/460; *myn* ~ 695/102.
unuele *a.* wicked 451/62 var. A J, see **vniuele**.
vnwasse *pp.* unwashed 587/33.
vnworþ(e) *a.* undeserving, unesteemed 12/121, 31/7; **vnworþer** *comp.* 624/419.
vnworþi *a.* undeserving 578/204.
vnwreo *v. inf.* uncover 686/2316.
vnwreste *a.* wicked 56/61, 320/159.
vode *n.*[1] sustenance 162/40.
vode *n.*[2] *pl.* creatures 409/217.
voiss *n.* choice 212/35.
vol *a.* full 94/249, 96/310.
vol, vulle *adv.* fully 2/45, 610/11.
volleþ *v. pr.* baptizes 40/90.
voluelle, voluulle *v. inf.* complete 354/145, 696/122; **uolueold** *pp.* 167/13.
volwede *v. pt.* ? followed out 39/52; probably for **volvelde**, see var. A, **folfelþe** J.
vom *n.* spume 194/405.
vonde, vondi *v. inf.* test, try 122/28, 30; **vondede** *pt.* 78/19; **yvonded** *pp.* 140/112.
vont *n.* ? 450/48 var. H A, **front** J;

GLOSSARY

vorbere v. inf. put up with 695/80.
vorcroked pp. misshapen 115/183.
vordwyne v. inf. waste away 705/216.
vorlete pp. a. abandoned 305/68.
vorlore pp. lost 91/168.
vorpinede v. pt. wasted away 689/2403.
vorscronke pp. dried up 50/105 var. A.
vorswarted pp. blackened 705/228, 230.
vorswolwe v. inf. swallow up 352/96.
vortop n. topknot 422/624.
vorþ-ward adv. forward 116/199.
vot n. foot's length 47/12; vet pl. 9/36; footprints 405/84; auote adv. on foot 387/98, 648/1170.
voulares n. g. cloth-fuller's 166/87.
voule a. detestable 86/6, 257/287.
voule adv. horribly 93/218.
vour ? adv. or ? prefix 706/244; perhaps mistake for vorþ, or for vore- with route stir abroad; see var.
vourteþe a. fourteenth 172/144.
vowe v. inf. take a vow of 400/83.
vpbreid v. pt. reproached 669/1790, 694/56.
up(e) see coust and point.
vpriȝt adv. face-up, outstretched 95/271, 272.
vp-risinge n. resurrection 130/37; oprisinge 608/456.
vrete v. inf. irritate 28/101.
Vriniȝt n. Friday night 592/61.
vrinnge n. hearing, report 354/170.
vrne v. inf. run, flow 48/55; vrneþ pr. 542/303; vrnynge pr. p. 84/94; ourne, vrne pt. pl. 27/78, 456/7; see eorne.
vrnynge a. running 240/55.
vrogge n. frog 273/267.
vrþe n. in phr. ibroȝt an ∼ buried 511/598.
vrþlich a. of this world 472/263.
vseþ, vsieþ v. pr. pl. practise, make use of 83/83, 470/185; vsede(n) pt. pl. 494/47, 49; yused pp. 495/81.
vtaues n. pl. eighth day after a festival 4/9.
vuel n. disease, injury 24/155, 48/42.
vuel(e) adv. unsuitably, badly 383/279, 457/47.
vuely v. inf. fall ill 227/193; vuelede pt. 334/207.
vulle v. inf. fill, satisfy 697/129; velde pt. 171/120, vulde completed 9/29; veolde pt. pl. 323/228.
vure n. see avure.
vury a. red-hot 95/278, 191/333.
vurst adv. in the first place 12/113.

probably mistake for front face; cf. L.A. 707 longum vultum.

wade v. inf. penetrate, advance 28/94, 158/66; wod pt. 343/88; wode pt. pl. 67/144; iwade pp. 157/40.
wader n. father 337/289.
waine n. wagon 333/167.
wake v. inf. be awake, keep watch 59/6, 81/14; wakieþ pl. imper. 351/86; wakinde, wakinge pr. p. 352/92, 552/56; woke pt. pl. 15/206; iwaked pp. 552/55.
wakes n. pl. festivals 606/383.
wakiare n. a wakeful person 425/686.
walkare n. fuller of cloth 397/6 var.
walkyng n. fulling of cloth 397/6 var.
walle v. inf. boil, well out 459/89, 560/302; walde pt. pl. 96/322, 570/143; iwalled pp. a. molten 64/54; see wellinde.
walli v. inf. provide with a wall 478/63; iwalled pp. 87/65.
walwede v. pt. intr. floundered 251/125, 587/33; weluede pt. tr. tossed 481/144.
walke v. 1 pr. wander 524/272.
wandri v. inf. roam 125/96.
wane a. lacking 608/449.
wanhope n. despair 131/87, 132/102.
wanie v. inf. decrease 361/88, 555/147; waneþ pr. 107/643; waineþ, waneþ pr. pl. 106/613, 191/338.
war(e) adv. and conj. where 7/74, 107/626.
warant n. protector 387/76.
waranti v. inf. guarantee 306/114, 115.
ward(e) n. keeping, guardianship 177/310, 617/209; guarded area 458/63.
wardein n. guardian, keeper 282/105; wardeins pl. 153/146, 482/175.
warderobe, warderop n. privy 7/68, 58.
wardi v. inf. defend 78/20, 217/88; ywarded pp. guarded 243/42.
ware v. inf. reflex. guard 124/70.
ware a. watchful 27/73.
ware conj. whether 109/686, 152/109; see were.
waritreo n. gallows 683/2232.
warliche adv. cautiously 471/244.
was contraction who is or what is 222/35; see var.
wasse v. inf. wash, cleanse 50/100, wasche 474/317, wosse 77/195; wess pt. 35/88, weȝs 696/125, woiss 192/360, woss 304/37; wesse pt. pl. 15/203, wosse 432/102; iwasse pp. 327/357.
wate, whate n. fate, chance 34/31, 523/254.
water-breþ n. vapour 423/628.

GLOSSARY

watloker, whatlokere *adv. comp.* more quickly 172/142, 563/402; **watlocst** *superl.* 309/200.
watte *v. pt.* wet, moistened 145/257, 159/17, **wette** 84/4.
wawe *n.* wave 517/73; **wawes** *pl.* 198/527.
wawe, wawi *v. inf.* move, stir 13/142, 427/745; **wawede** *pt.* 143/196.
wawinge *n.* motion 428/788.
we *pron. nom.* 65/99; **oure** *g.* 329/47; us *dat.* and *acc.* 65/104, 336/273; **oure** *poss. a.* 65/94, **vure** 626/476.
wed *n.* pledge 560/307.
wed, wedded *pp. a.* pledged, married 334/204, 133/130.
wede *n.* clothing 125/120, 142/164, **weode** 140/113.
weg *n.* lump 551/31, 36.
weie *v. inf.* move 414/395, proceed 235/405, see var. and cf. *L.A.* 221: *radicem lilii de ore defuncti procedere repererunt*.
weiȝte *v. pt. subj.* should arouse 195/448.
wel, weol *n.* wheel 97/328, 67/141; **weoles** *pl.* 38/22, 362/103.
welcomye *v. inf.* make welcome 596/89; **wolcomede** *pt.* 105/562, 429/18; *pt. pl.* 103/529, 671/1854.
welde *v. inf.* manage, subdue 42/143, 570/138; **weld** *pt.* 372/201.
wele *n.* wealth 140/125; well-being 388/110.
wele *interj.* 457/41, 563/406.
welle-spreng *n.* spring 289/293.
wellinde, wellinge *v. pr. p. a.* boiling 158/66; *pr. p.* 106/608; **welde** *pp. a.* 158/72; see **walle**.
welp *n.* puppy 273/270.
wel-to-louie *a. phr.* worthy to be loved 393/112.
wem, wemme *n.* blemish 278/126, 118.
wemed *a.* choleric 424/685.
wenclen *n. pl.* children 446/98.
wende *v. inf.* grow, turn 2/29, 147/322; **wenst** 2 *pr.* 35/76; **went** *pr.* 427/768; **wendeþ** *pr. pl.* 88/76; **wende** *pt.* 546/98; **iwend** *pp.* 82/47.
wene *v.* 1 *pr.* suppose, think 78/6; **weneþ** *pr.* 412/331; *pr. pl.* 132/117; **wende** *pt.* 6/47; *pt. pl.* 121/96; **wene** *pr. s.* 25/19.
wenne *n.* blemish 115/173.
weod *n.* weed, wild growth 140/110, 312/280; **weodes** *pl.* 168/33; **weodes** 422/623 perhaps for **wodes**, see var.
weop *n.* weeping 146/282.
weope, wepe *v. inf.* weep 119/25, 13; **weopeþ** *pr. pl.* 368/107; **wepinge** *pr. p.* 139/80; **weop** *pt.* 142/167, **wep** 88/96; **wope** *pt. pl.* 23/132; **iwope** *pp.* 360/40.
weorne, werne *v. inf.* refuse, forbid 60/44, 120/65, **worne** 487/118; **wernde** *pt.* 447/127, **wernede** 637/821, **wornde** 477/6.
wepne *n.* implement 470/185.
werche, wirche *v. inf.* do, perform, make 119/21, 573/55, **worche** 428/5, **wurche** 567/32; **wircheþ** *pr.* 573/46; **wercheþ** *pl. imper.* 527/360; **wroȝte** *pt.* 31/13, 128/23; *pt. pl.* 129/6; **iwroȝt** *pp.* 78/221.
were *conj.* whether 18/65, 45/237.
weri *a.* exhausted 26/32, 146/290.
weri ? *adv.* wearily 7/75, 141/154.
werie *v. inf.* wear 580/259, 261; **werede** *pt.* 493/29, 497/157; *pt. pl.* 104/551.
werinesse *n.* fatigue 83/71, 290/318.
werre, worre *n.* strife, war 117/232, 10/73.
werri, worri *v. inf.* make war on, harass 266/42, 443/22; **worrede** *pt.* 173/194; **werrede** *pt. pl.* 591/55; **iwerred** *pp.* 71/8, **iworred** 265/26; **werry** *inf.* 113/114 probably for **worþ**, see var., **worþ** J.
werrors *n. pl.* fighters 450/53, see var., **werreors** A, **worreours** J.
werþ *v.* see **worst**.
west *a.* barren 93/230.
wete *n.* wheat 120/144.
wete-flour *n.* wheat-flour 120/52.
wette *v.*¹ *pt.* see **watte**.
wette *v.*² *pt. pl.* sharpened 158/84; **iwette** *pp.* 67/144.
weþer *n.* ram 258/321; **weþeres** *g.* 258/323.
weue *v.*¹ *inf. tr.* remove 641/953, *intr.* pass 679/2093; **iweued** *pp.* 532/533.
weue *v.*² *inf.* cover 308/176, 463/7.
weued *n.* altar 79/51, 87/64; **weuedes** *pl.* 405/91, 645/1086.
wexe, wuxe *v. inf.* grow, increase 361/88, 417/467, **wyxe** 49/78; **wax, wex** *pt.* 171/133, 343/97; **woxe, voxe** *pt. pl.* 171/130. 698/15; **iwexe** *pp.* 497/146, (y)**woxe** 2/42, 169/78.
wexinge, wuxinge *n.* growth 426/735, 734.
whyne *v.* cry plaintively 518/86.
wicche *n.* witch 21/82, 55/29; **wicchen** *pl.* 588/76, wizards 398/19.
wicchinge *n.* witchcraft 18/74, 68/182.
wiȝt *n.*¹ meaning 598/149, var. **wit** A J.
wiȝt *n.*² demon 366/44; **wiȝtes** *pl.* 85/27, 97/357.

GLOSSARY

wiȝt *n.*³ 'white' food, dairy produce 42/150, 43/159, wit(e) 42/145, 156; wite white of egg 423/634.
wiȝt *a.* white 91/160; wit(e) 23/124, 376/63; wiþ 428/786; whyttere *comp.* 538/150, wittore 24/141.
wike *n.* week 9/19, 135/18; *pl.* 129/15.
wikke *a.* evil 91/169; severe 414/384.
wilde *a. pl.* rash 110/19.
wilfol *a.* self-willed 653/1317.
wille *n.*¹ time, period, in exclam. *alas þulke sori wille* 177/312; in phr. *a wille* once 5/H 11; *þe wile, conj.* while 118/3.
wille *n.*² desire 81/8, 16, 137/17.
willede *v. pt.* wished 110/11.
wyllyngge *pr. p. a.* desirous 696/110.
wilny *v. 1 pr.* desire 168/36; wilneþ *pr.* 3/61; wilnede *pt.* 41/115.
wincy *v. inf.* kick 265/27.
wynde *v. inf. intr.* turn 486/105; *tr.* twist, wrap 56/60, 148/337; wond *pt. intr.* flew apart 46/263.
wyndowe *n.* opening 551/33.
winne *n.* gain, possessions 137/15, 479/82.
winne *v. inf.* gain, conquer 60/38, 73/70; wan *pt.* 174/217; iwonne *pp.* 75/130, 484/49.
wirled *v. pt.* spun around 100/437.
wis *adv.* surely 17/34, 336/274.
wis *contraction* with this, with his 260/383, see var., *touward þe* J.
wise *v. inf.* guide 357/8; see wisse(n).
wislich(e) *adv.* certainly 225/135, 351/63.
wisse(n) *v. inf.* instruct, guide 17/26, 416/448, wissi 64/65; wissede *pt.* 493/24.
wissinge *n.* guidance 164/29, 275/39.
wit, wite *n.* see wiȝt *n.*³
wite, wute *v.*¹ *inf.* know, understand 4/17, 696/111; wot *1 pr.* 13/164; wost *2 pr.* 35/78; wot *pr.* 134/169; witeþ *pr. pl.* 132/96, weteþ 410/245; weste *pt.* 68/188, weoste 612/66, wuste 617/208; iwest *pp.* 66/109.
wite, witie *v.*² *inf.* protect, preserve 15/217, 416/436; wit *pr.* 296/145; weste *pt.* 9/25, wiste 562/366, wuste 395/179; iveost *pp.* 105/566, iweost 57/104, iwest 87/57.
witles *a.* out of one's mind 100/439, 381/234.
witty *a.* having reason 286/217, 219.
wiþ *a.* see wiȝt.
wiþdrawe *v. inf.* withhold, retract 131/81; *pr. subj.* 550/262; wiþdrou *pt.* receded 107/629; wiþdrowe *pt. subj.* 89/118.

wiþerwine *n.* foe 241/92, 661/1547; wiþerewynes *pl.* 557/214, 571/157.
wiþsegge *v. inf.* deny, oppose 341/28; wiþseist *2 pr.* 7/62; wiþsede *pt.* 11/93, 628/542.
wiþpin *n. pl.* twists of willow 56/59.
wlak *a.* tepid 425/690.
wo *pron. interrog.* and *rel.* who 7/64, 98/386; was *g.* 274/283, whas 695/76; wam *acc.* 13/135, wan 1/3, 415/414; was *contr.* who or what is 222/35.
wo *adv.* woefully 94/242.
wod *a.* beside oneself, mad 20/36, 85/26; wode *pl.* 85/24; ∼ *wroþe* furious 22/107.
wode *n.* firewood 431/66, 70; ∼ *vur* wood fire 28/88.
wol *v. 1 pr.* will 654/1335; wolt *2 pr.* 90/135, woltou 43/185; wol(e) *pr.* 26/28, 40/99; wolleþ *pr. pl.* 29/141; wolle *2 pr. subj.* 35/75; wole *pr. subj.* 34/74; wost *2 pt.* 91/166, wostou 20/24; wolde *pt.* 9/22; *pt. pl.* 19/82.
wolchede *v. pt.* rolled, wallowed 194/406; var. om. H, wolched A, wolcheþe J.
wolde *n.* control 29/127; see var., wolde A, (to) wolþe J.
wolkene *n.* sky 352/114.
wombe-ioye *n.* belly-cheer 462/44.
won *n.* choice, resource 55/20, 144/234; *god* ∼ abundance 201/642; *luþer* ∼ bad luck, lack of favour 308/154, 643/1028.
wond *pp.* accustomed 4/20, iwond 311/254, (i)woned 33/40, 125/110.
wondri *v. inf. impers.* cause wonder 32/15, 583/345; wondrede *pt.* 588/62.
wone *n.* custom, practice 86/25, 110/14; *adv.* bywone customarily 4/13.
wonie *v. inf.* dwell 17/19; wonieþ *pr. pl.* 421/573; wonede *pt.* 19/5.
wonyinge *n.* dwelling-place 216/69, 342/75, wonynge, wonnynge 99/417, 373/230.
wop *n.* weeping 23/131, 94/244.
wori *a.* turbid 188/256, 189/275.
wors(e) *a. comp.* less well 70/22; more wicked 154/193; worst(e) *superl.* most sinful 88/94; most grievous 146/285.
worssipe *n.* in phr. *to þe worssipe of* in honour of 48/45.
worst *v. 2 pr.* becomest 19/20, 91/174, worste becomest thou 413/349; worþ *pr.* 80/68; worþe *pr. pl.* 642/

1000, **worþeþ** 527/360; **werþ** *pt.* 19/11, mounted 116/191.
worþ(e) *a.* deserving 13/162, 88/95.
wou, wowe *n.*¹ wall 318/81, 474/304; **wowes** *pl.* 556/188.
wou, wowe *n.*² harm, evil 55/34, 91/171; wrong, error 24/144, 62/43.
wou *a.* wrong 87/58, 132/100.
wowede *v. pt.* courted 400/85.
wraþþe, wraþþi *v. inf.* anger, become angry 325/310, 641/971; **wraþþede** *pt.* 642/976; **iwraþþed** *pp.* 261/403.
wraxli *v. inf.* wrestle 276/70.
wrecche *n.* miserable creature 142/182; **wrecches** *pl.* 95/284.
wrecche *a. pl.* miserable 94/253, 95/285; **wrecchedore** *comp.* 198/528, 689/2433.
wreche *n.* vengeance 7/71, 113/113.
wrechede *n.* misery 97/342, 101/466; vileness 219/48.
wrechfol *a.* vengeful 412/331.
wreide *v. pt. subj.* should expose, betray 650/1232; **iwreid** *pp.* 17/23.

wrekest *v. 2 pr. reflex.* avengest 575/108.
wrench(e) *n.* trick 283/109, 517/57, **wrenches** *pl.* 468/150.
wrickede *v. pt.* jerked 207/82.
wringe *v. inf.* twist (hands) 119/13; **wrang** *pt.* 518/85, **wrong** 139/84.
writ *n.* written statement 147/305, 287/254; **writes** *pl.* 682/2194; *in write* in writing 407/156.
wrongfol *a.* unlawful 664/1632.
wrottes *n. pl.* snouts 95/282.
wroþ(e) *a.* angry 22/88, 207/98; **wroþer, wroþore** *comp.* 32/14, 244/79.
wroþere-hele *n.* misfortune, disadvantage, in phr. *to wroþere hele* 471/221, 526/326; see **goder-hele**.
wroþer-hele *adv.* disastrously 402/140.
wroþliche *adv.* angrily 359/26.
wuch *pron.* which 106/614; **wuch(e)** *a.* 10/62, 19/84.
wuche, wute *n.* see **hucche**.

EARLY ENGLISH TEXT SOCIETY

OFFICERS AND COUNCIL

Honorary Director
Professor NORMAN DAVIS, Merton College, Oxford

Professor J. A. W. BENNETT
R. W. BURCHFIELD
Professor BRUCE DICKINS, F.B.A.
Professor E. J. DOBSON
A. I. DOYLE
Professor P. HODGSON
Professor G. KANE

Miss P. M. KEAN
N. R. KER, F.B.A.
Professor J. R. R. TOLKIEN
Professor D. WHITELOCK, F.B.A.
Professor R. M. WILSON
Professor C. L. WRENN

Editorial Secretary
Dr. P. O. E. GRADON, St. Hugh's College, Oxford

Executive Secretary
Dr. A. M. HUDSON, Lady Margaret Hall, Oxford

Bankers
THE NATIONAL PROVINCIAL BANK LTD., Cornmarket Street, Oxford

THE Subscription to the Society, which constitutes full membership for private members and libraries, is £3. 3s. (U.S. and Canadian members $9.00) a year for the annual publications, due in advance on the 1st of JANUARY, and should be paid by Cheque, Postal Order, or Money Order made out to 'The Early English Text Society', to Dr. A. M. Hudson, Executive Secretary, Early English Text Society, Lady Margaret Hall, Oxford.

The payment of the annual subscription is the only prerequisite of membership.

Private members of the Society (but not libraries) may select other volumes of the Society's publications instead of those for the current year. The value of texts allowed against one annual subscription is 100s. (U.S. members 110s.), and all such transactions must be made through the Executive Secretary.

Members of the Society (including institutional members) may also, through the Executive Secretary, purchase copies of past E.E.T.S. publications and reprints for their own use at a discount of 4d. in the shilling.

The Society's texts are also available to non-members at listed prices through any bookseller.

The Society's texts are published by the Oxford University Press.

The Early English Text Society was founded in 1864 by Frederick James Furnivall, with the help of Richard Morris, Walter Skeat, and others, to bring the mass of unprinted Early English literature within the reach of students and provide sound texts from which the New English Dictionary could quote. In 1867 an Extra Series was started of texts already printed but not in satisfactory or readily obtainable editions.

In 1921 the Extra Series was discontinued and all the publications of 1921 and subsequent years have since been listed and numbered as part of the Original Series. Since 1921 just over a hundred new volumes have been issued; and since 1957 alone more than a hundred and thirty volumes have been reprinted at a cost of £65,000.

In this prospectus the Original Series and Extra Series for the years 1867-1920 are amalgamated, so as to show all the publications of the Society in a single list.

From 1 April 1969, since many of the old prices had become uneconomic in modern publishing conditions, a new price structure was introduced and the new prices are shown in this list. From the same date the discount allowed to members was increased from 2d. in the shilling to 4d. in the shilling.

LIST OF PUBLICATIONS
Original Series, 1864–1969. Extra Series, 1867–1920

O.S. 1. Early English Alliterative Poems, ed. R. Morris. (*Reprinted* 1965.) 54s.
2. Arthur, ed. F. J. Furnivall. (*Reprinted* 1965.) 10s.
3. Lauder on the Dewtie of Kyngis, &c., 1556, ed. F. Hall. (*Reprinted* 1965.) 18s.
4. Sir Gawayne and the Green Knight, ed. R. Morris. (*Out of print, see* O.S. 210.)
5. Hume's Orthographie and Congruitie of the Britan Tongue, ed. H. B. Wheatley. (*Reprinted* 1965.) 18s.
6. Lancelot of the Laik, ed. W. W. Skeat. (*Reprinted* 1965.) 42s.
7. Genesis & Exodus, ed. R. Morris. (*Out of print*.)
8. Morte Arthure, ed. E. Brock. (*Reprinted* 1967.) 25s.
9. Thynne on Speght's ed. of Chaucer, A.D. 1599, ed. G. Kingsley and F. J. Furnivall. (*Reprinted* 1965.) 55s.
10. Merlin, Part I, ed. H. B. Wheatley. (*Out of print*.)
11. Lyndesay's Monarche, &c., ed. J. Small. Part I. (*Out of print*.)
12. The Wright's Chaste Wife, ed. F. J. Furnivall. (*Reprinted* 1965.) 10s.
13. Seinte Marherete, ed. O. Cockayne. (*Out of print, see* O.S. 193.)
14. King Horn, Floriz and Blauncheflur, &c., ed. J. R. Lumby, re-ed. G. H. McKnight. (*Reprinted* 1962.) 50s.
15. Political, Religious, and Love Poems, ed. F. J. Furnivall. (*Reprinted* 1965.) 63s.
16. The Book of Quinte Essence, ed. F. J. Furnivall. (*Reprinted* 1965.) 10s.
17. Parallel Extracts from 45 MSS. of Piers the Plowman, ed. W. W. Skeat. (*Out of print*.)
18. Hali Meidenhad, ed. O. Cockayne, re-ed. F. J. Furnivall. (*Out of print*.)
19. Lyndesay's Monarche, &c., ed. J. Small. Part II. (*Out of print*.)
20. Richard Rolle de Hampole, English Prose Treatises of, ed. G. G. Perry. (*Out of print*.)
21. Merlin, ed. H. B. Wheatley. Part II. (*Out of print*.)
22. Partenay or Lusignen, ed. W. W. Skeat. (*Out of print*.)
23. Dan Michel's Ayenbite of Inwyt, ed. R. Morris and P. Gradon. Vol. I, Text. (*Reissued* 1965.) 54s.
24. Hymns to the Virgin and Christ; The Parliament of Devils, &c., ed. F. J. Furnivall. (*Out of print*.)
25. The Stacions of Rome, the Pilgrims' Sea-voyage, with Clene Maydenhod, ed. F. J. Furnivall. (*Out of print*.)
26. Religious Pieces in Prose and Verse, from R. Thornton's MS., ed. G. G. Perry. (*See under* 1913.) (*Out of print*.)
27. Levins' Manipulus Vocabulorum, a rhyming Dictionary, ed. H. B. Wheatley. (*Out of print*.)
28. William's Vision of Piers the Plowman, ed. W. W. Skeat. A-Text. (*Reprinted* 1968.) 35s.
29. Old English Homilies (1220–30), ed. R. Morris. Series I, Part I. (*Out of print*.)
30. Pierce the Ploughmans Crede, ed. W. W. Skeat. (*Out of print*.)
E.S. 1. William of Palerne or William and the Werwolf, re-ed. W. W. Skeat. (*Out of print*.)
2. Early English Pronunciation, by A. J. Ellis. Part I. (*Out of print*.)
O.S. 31. Myrc's Duties of a Parish Priest, in Verse, ed. E. Peacock. (*Out of print*.)
32. Early English Meals and Manners: the Boke of Norture of John Russell, the Bokes of Keruynge, Curtasye, and Demeanor, the Babees Book, Urbanitatis, &c., ed. F. J. Furnivall. (*Out of print*.)
33. The Book of the Knight of La Tour-Landry, ed. T. Wright. (*Out of print*.)
34. Old English Homilies (before 1300), ed. R. Morris. Series I, Part II. (*Out of print*.)
35. Lyndesay's Works, Part III: The Historie and Testament of Squyer Meldrum, ed. F. Hall. (*Reprinted* 1965.) 18s.
E.S. 3. Caxton's Book of Curtesye, in Three Versions, ed. F. J. Furnivall. (*Out of print*.)
4. Havelok the Dane, re-ed. W. W. Skeat. (*Out of print*.)
5. Chaucer's Boethius, ed. R. Morris. (*Reprinted* 1969.) 40s.
6. Chevelere Assigne, re-ed. Lord Aldenham. (*Out of print*.)
O.S. 36. Merlin, ed. H. B. Wheatley. Part III. On Arthurian Localities, by J. S. Stuart Glennie. (*Out of print*.)
37. Sir David Lyndesay's Works, Part IV, Ane Satyre of the thrie Estaits, ed. F. Hall. (*Out of print*.)
38. William's Vision of Piers the Plowman, ed. W. W. Skeat. Part II. Text B. (*Reprinted* 1964.) 42s.
39, 56. The Gest Hystoriale of the Destruction of Troy, ed. D. Donaldson and G. A. Panton. Parts I and II. (*Reprinted as one volume* 1968.) 110s.
E.S. 7. Early English Pronunciation, by A. J. Ellis. Part II. (*Out of print*.)
8. Queene Elizabethes Achademy, &c., ed. F. J. Furnivall. Essays on early Italian and German Books of Courtesy, by W. M. Rossetti and E. Oswald. (*Out of print*.)
9. Awdeley's Fraternitye of Vacabondes, Harman's Caveat, &c., ed. E. Viles and F. J. Furnivall. (*Out of print*.)
O.S. 40. English Gilds, their Statutes and Customs, A.D. 1389, ed. Toulmin Smith and Lucy T. Smith, with an Essay on Gilds and Trades-Unions, by L. Brentano. (*Reprinted* 1963.) 100s.
41. William Lauder's Minor Poems, ed. F. J. Furnivall. (*Out of print*.)
42. Bernardus De Cura Rei Familiaris, Early Scottish Prophecies, &c., ed. J. R. Lumby. (*Reprinted* 1965.) 18s.
43. Ratis Raving, and other Moral and Religious Pieces, ed. J. R. Lumby. (*Out of print*.)
E.S. 10. Andrew Boorde's Introduction of Knowledge, 1547, Dyetary of Helth, 1542, Barnes in Defence of the Berde, 1542–3, ed. F. J. Furnivall. (*Out of print*.)
11, 55. Barbour's Bruce, ed. W. W. Skeat. Parts I and IV. (*Reprinted as Volume I* 1968.) 63s.
O.S. 44. The Alliterative Romance of Joseph of Arimathie, or The Holy Grail: from the Vernon MS.; with W. de Worde's and Pynson's Lives of Joseph; ed. W. W. Skeat. (*Out of print*.)

O.S. 45.	King Alfred's West-Saxon Version of Gregory's Pastoral Care, ed., with an English translation, by Henry Sweet. Part I. *(Reprinted 1958.)* 55s.	1871
46.	Legends of the Holy Rood, Symbols of the Passion and Cross Poems, ed. R. Morris. *(Out of print.)*	,,
47.	Sir David Lyndesay's Works, ed. J. A. H. Murray. Part V. *(Out of print.)*	,,
48.	The Times' Whistle, and other Poems, by R. C., 1616; ed. J. M. Cowper. *(Out of print.)*	,,
E.S. 12.	England in Henry VIII's Time: a Dialogue between Cardinal Pole and Lupset, by Thom. Starkey, Chaplain to Henry VIII, ed. J. M. Cowper. Part II. *(Out of print,* Part I is E.S. 32, 1878.)	,,
13.	A Supplicacyon of the Beggers, by Simon Fish, A.D. 1528–9, ed. F. J. Furnivall, with A Supplication to our Moste Soueraigne Lorde, A Supplication of the Poore Commons, and The Decaye of England by the Great Multitude of Sheep, ed. J. M. Cowper. *(Out of print.)*	,,
14.	Early English Pronunciation, by A. J. Ellis. Part III. *(Out of print.)*	,,
O.S. 49.	An Old English Miscellany, containing a Bestiary, Kentish Sermons, Proverbs of Alfred, and Religious Poems of the 13th cent., ed. R. Morris. *(Out of print.)*	1872
50.	King Alfred's West-Saxon Version of Gregory's Pastoral Care, ed. H. Sweet. Part II. *(Reprinted 1958.)* 50s.	,,
51.	Þe Liflade of St. Juliana, 2 versions, with translations, ed. O. Cockayne and E. Brock. *(Reprinted 1957.)* 38s.	,,
52.	Palladius on Husbondrie, englisht, ed. Barton Lodge. Part I. *(Out of print.)*	,,
E.S. 15.	Robert Crowley's Thirty-One Epigrams, Voyce of the Last Trumpet, Way to Wealth, &c., ed. J. M. Cowper. *(Out of print.)*	,,
16.	Chaucer's Treatise on the Astrolabe, ed. W. W. Skeat. *(Reprinted 1969.)* 40s.	,,
17.	The Complaynt of Scotlande, with 4 Tracts, ed. J. A. H. Murray. Part I. *(Out of print.)*	,,
O.S. 53.	Old-English Homilies, Series II, and three Hymns to the Virgin and God, 13th-century, with the music to two of them, in old and modern notation, ed. R. Morris. *(Out of print.)*	1873
54.	The Vision of Piers Plowman, ed. W. W. Skeat. Part III. Text C. *(Reprinted 1959.)* 55s.	,,
55.	Generydes, a Romance, ed. W. Aldis Wright. Part I. *(Out of print.)*	,,
E.S. 18.	The Complaynt of Scotlande, ed. J. A. H. Murray. Part II. *(Out of print.)*	,,
19.	The Myroure of oure Ladye, ed. J. H. Blunt. *(Out of print.)*	,,
O.S. 56.	The Gest Hystoriale of the Destruction of Troy, in alliterative verse, ed. D. Donaldson and G. A. Panton. Part II. *(See O.S. 39.)*	1874
57.	Cursor Mundi, in four Texts, ed. R. Morris. Part I. *(Reprinted 1961.)* 40s.	,,
58, 63, 73.	The Blickling Homilies, ed. R. Morris. Parts I, II, and III. *(Reprinted as one volume 1967.)* 70s.	,,
E.S. 20.	Lovelich's History of the Holy Grail, ed. F. J. Furnivall. Part I. *(Out of print.)*	,,
21, 29.	Barbour's Bruce, ed. W. W. Skeat. Parts II and III. *(Reprinted as Volume II 1968.)* 90s.	,,
22.	Henry Brinklow's Complaynt of Roderyck Mors and The Lamentacyon of a Christen Agaynst the Cytye of London, made by Roderigo Mors, ed. J. M. Cowper. *(Out of print.)*	,,
23.	Early English Pronunciation, by A. J. Ellis. Part IV. *(Out of print.)*	,,
O.S. 59.	Cursor Mundi, in four Texts, ed. R. Morris. Part II. *(Reprinted 1966.)* 50s.	1875
60.	Meditacyuns on the Soper of our Lorde, by Robert of Brunne, ed. J. M. Cowper. *(Out of print.)*	,,
61.	The Romance and Prophecies of Thomas of Erceldoune, ed. J. A. H. Murray. *(Out of print.)*	,,
E.S. 24.	Lovelich's History of the Holy Grail, ed. F. J. Furnivall. Part II. *(Out of print.)*	,,
25, 26.	Guy of Warwick, 15th-century Version, ed. J. Zupitza. Pts. I and II. *(Reprinted as one volume 1966.)* 75s.	,,
O.S. 62.	Cursor Mundi, in four Texts, ed. R. Morris. Part III. *(Reprinted 1966.)* 40s.	1876
63.	The Blickling Homilies, ed. R. Morris. Part II. *(See O.S. 58.)*	,,
64.	Francis Thynne's Embleames and Epigrams, ed. F. J. Furnivall. *(Out of print.)*	,,
65.	Be Domes Dæge (Bede's *De Die Judicii*), &c., ed. J. R. Lumby. *(Reprinted 1964.)* 30s.	,,
E.S. 26.	Guy of Warwick, 15th-century Version, ed. J. Zupitza. Part II. *(See E.S. 25)*	,,
27.	The English Works of John Fisher, ed. J. E. B. Mayor. Part I. *(Out of print.)*	,,
O.S. 66.	Cursor Mundi, in four Texts, ed. R. Morris. Part IV. *(Reprinted 1966.)* 40s.	1877
67.	Notes on Piers Plowman, by W. W. Skeat. Part I. *(Out of print.)*	,,
E.S. 28.	Lovelich's Holy Grail, ed. F. J. Furnivall. Part III. *(Out of print.)*	,,
29.	Barbour's Bruce, ed. W. W. Skeat. Part III. *(See E.S. 21.)*	,,
O.S. 68.	Cursor Mundi, in 4 Texts, ed. R. Morris. Part V. *(Reprinted 1966.)* 40s.	1878
69.	Adam Davie's 5 Dreams about Edward II, &c., ed. F. J. Furnivall. 30s.	,,
70.	Generydes, a Romance, ed. W. Aldis Wright. Part II. *(Out of print.)*	,,
E.S. 30.	Lovelich's Holy Grail, ed. F. J. Furnivall. Part IV. *(Out of print.)*	,,
31.	The Alliterative Romance of Alexander and Dindimus, ed. W. W. Skeat. *(Out of print.)*	,,
32.	Starkey's England in Henry VIII's Time. Part I. Starkey's Life and Letters, ed. S. J. Herrtage. *(Out of print.)*	,,
O.S. 71.	The Lay Folks Mass-Book, four texts, ed. T. F. Simmons. *(Reprinted 1968.)* 90s.	1879
72.	Palladius on Husbondrie, englisht, ed. S. J. Herrtage. Part II. 42s.	,,
E.S. 33.	Gesta Romanorum, ed. S. J. Herrtage. *(Reprinted 1962.)* 100s.	,,
34.	The Charlemagne Romances: 1. Sir Ferumbras, from Ashm. MS. 33, ed. S. J. Herrtage. *(Reprinted 1966.)* 54s.	,,
O.S. 73.	The Blickling Homilies, ed. R. Morris. Part III. *(See O.S. 58.)*	1880
74.	English Works of Wyclif, hitherto unprinted, ed. F. D. Matthew. *(Out of print.)*	,,
E.S. 35.	Charlemagne Romances: 2. The Sege of Melayne, Sir Otuell, &c., ed. S. J. Herrtage. *(Out of print.)*	,,
37.	Charlemagne Romances: 3 and 4. Lyf of Charles the Grete, ed. S. J. Herrtage. Parts I and II. *(Reprinted as one volume 1967.)* 54s.	,,
O.S. 75.	Catholicon Anglicum, an English-Latin Wordbook, from Lord Monson's MS., A.D. 1483, ed., with Introduction and Notes, by S. J. Herrtage and Preface by H. B. Wheatley. *(Out of print.)*	1881
76, 82.	Ælfric's Lives of Saints, in MS. Cott. Jul. E VII, ed. W. W. Skeat. Parts I and II. *(Reprinted as Volume I 1966.)* 60s.	,,

3

E.S. 37. Charlemagne Romances: 4. Lyf of Charles the Grete, ed. S. J. Herrtage. Part II. (*See* E.S. 36.) 1881
38. Charlemagne Romances: 5. The Sowdone of Babylone, ed. E. Hausknecht. (*Out of print*.) ,,
O.S. 77. Beowulf, the unique MS. autotyped and transliterated, ed. J. Zupitza. (*Re-issued as* No. 245. See under 1958.) 1882
78. The Fifty Earliest English Wills, in the Court of Probate, 1387–1439, ed. F. J. Furnivall. (*Reprinted* 1964.) 50s. ,,
E.S. 39. Charlemagne Romances: 6. Rauf Coilyear, Roland, Otuel, &c., ed. S. J. Herrtage. (*Out of print*.) ,,
40. Charlemagne Romances: 7. Huon of Burdeux, by Lord Berners, ed. S. L. Lee. Part I. (*Out of print*.) ,,
O.S. 79. King Alfred's Orosius, from Lord Tollemache's 9th-century MS., ed. H. Sweet. Part I. (*Reprinted* 1959.) 55s. 1883
79 b. Extra Volume. Facsimile of the Epinal Glossary, ed. H. Sweet. (*Out of print*.) ,,
E.S. 41. Charlemagne Romances: 8. Huon of Burdeux, by Lord Berners, ed. S. L. Lee. Part II. (*Out of print*.) ,,
42, 49, 59. Guy of Warwick: 2 texts (Auchinleck MS. and Caius MS.), ed. J. Zupitza. Parts I, II, and III. (*Reprinted as one volume* 1966.) 110s. ,,
O.S. 80. The Life of St. Katherine, B.M. Royal MS. 17 A. xxvii, &c., and its Latin Original, ed. E. Einenkel. (*Out of print*.) 1884
81. Piers Plowman: Glossary, &c., ed. W. W. Skeat. Part IV, completing the work. (*Out of print*.) ,,
E.S. 43. Charlemagne Romances: 9. Huon of Burdeux, by Lord Berners, ed. S. L. Lee. Part III. (*Out of print*.) ,,
44. Charlemagne Romances: 10. The Foure Sonnes of Aymon, ed. Octavia Richardson. Part I. (*Out of print*.) ,,
O.S. 82. Ælfric's Lives of Saints, MS. Cott. Jul. E vii ed. W. W. Skeat. Part II. (*See* O.S. 76.) 1885
83. The Oldest English Texts, Charters, &c., ed. H. Sweet. (*Reprinted* 1966.) 110s. ,,
E.S. 45. Charlemagne Romances: 11. The Foure Sonnes of Aymon, ed. O. Richardson. Part II. (*Out of print*.) ,,
46. Sir Beves of Hamtoun, ed. E. Kölbing. Part I. (*Out of print*.) ,,
O.S. 84. Additional Analogs to 'The Wright's Chaste Wife', O.S. 12, by W. A. Clouston. (*Out of print*.) 1886
85. The Three Kings of Cologne, ed. C. Horstmann. (*Out of print*.) ,,
86. Prose Lives of Women Saints, ed. C. Horstmann. (*Out of print*.) ,,
E.S. 47. The Wars of Alexander, ed. W. W. Skeat. (*Out of print*.) ,,
48. Sir Beves of Hamtoun, ed. E. Kölbing. Part II. (*Out of print*.) ,,
O.S. 87. The Early South-English Legendary, Laud MS. 108, ed. C. Hortsmann. (*Out of print*.) 1887
88. Hy. Bradshaw's Life of St. Werburghe (Pynson, 1521), ed. C. Horstmann. (*Out of print*.) ,,
E.S. 49. Guy of Warwick, 2 texts (Auchinleck and Caius MSS.), ed. J. Zupitza. Part II. (*See* E.S. 42.) ,,
50. Charlemagne Romances: 12. Huon of Burdeux, by Lord Berners, ed. S. L. Lee. Part IV. (*Out of print*.) ,,
51. Torrent of Portyngale, ed. E. Adam. (*Out of print*.) ,,
O.S. 89. Vices and Virtues, ed. F. Holthausen. Part I. (*Reprinted* 1967.) 40s. 1888
90. Anglo-Saxon and Latin Rule of St. Benet, interlinear Glosses, ed. H. Logeman. (*Out of print*.) ,,
91. Two Fifteenth-Century Cookery-Books, ed. T. Austin. (*Reprinted* 1964.) 42s. ,,
E.S. 52. Bullein's Dialogue against the Feuer Pestilence, 1578, ed. M. and A. H. Bullen. (*Out of print*.) ,,
53. Vicary's Anatomie of the Body of Man, 1548, ed. 1577, ed. F. J. and Percy Furnivall. Part I. (*Out of print*.) ,,
54. The Curial made by maystere Alain Charretier, translated by William Caxton, 1484, ed. F. J. Furnivall and P. Meyer. (*Reprinted* 1965.) 13s. ,,
O.S. 92. Eadwine's Canterbury Psalter, from the Trin. Cambr. MS., ed. F. Harsley, Part II. (*Out of print*.) 188
93. Defensor's Liber Scintillarum, ed. E. Rhodes. (*Out of print*.) ,,
E.S. 55. Barbour's Bruce, ed. W. W. Skeat. Part IV. (*See* E.S. 11.) ,,
56. Early English Pronunciation, by A. J. Ellis. Part V, the present English Dialects. (*Out of print*.) ,,
O.S. 94, 114. Ælfric's Lives of Saints, MS. Cott. Jul. E vii, ed. W. W. Skeat. Parts III and IV. (*Reprinted as Volume II* 1966.) 60s. 189
95. The Old-English Version of Bede's Ecclesiastical History, re-ed. T. Miller. Part I, 1. (*Reprinted* 1959.) 54s. ,,
E.S. 57. Caxton's Eneydos, ed. W. T. Culley and F. J. Furnivall. (*Reprinted* 1962.) 50s. ,,
58. Caxton's Blanchardyn and Eglantine, c. 1489, ed. L. Kellner. (*Reprinted* 1962.) 63s. ,,
O.S. 96. The Old-English Version of Bede's Ecclesiastical History, re-ed. T. Miller. Part I, 2. (*Reprinted* 1959.) 54s. 189
97. The Earliest English Prose Psalter, ed. K. D. Buelbring. Part I. (*Out of print*.) ,,
E.S. 59. Guy of Warwick, 2 texts (Auchinleck and Caius MSS.), ed. J. Zupitza. Part III. (*See* E.S. 42.) ,,
60. Lydgate's Temple of Glas, re-ed. J. Schick. (*Out of print*.) ,,
O.S. 98. Minor Poems of the Vernon MS., ed. C. Horstmann. Part I. (*Out of print*.) 189
99. Cursor Mundi. Preface, Notes, and Glossary, Part VI, ed. R. Morris. (*Reprinted* 1962.) 35s. ,,
E.S. 61. Hoccleve's Minor Poems, I, from the Phillipps and Durham MSS., ed. F. J. Furnivall. (*Out of print*.) ,,
62. The Chester Plays, re-ed. H. Deimling. Part I. (*Reprinted* 1967.) 38s. ,,
O.S. 100. Capgrave's Life of St. Katharine, ed. C. Horstmann, with Forewords by F. J. Furnivall. (*Out of print*.) 189
O.S. 101. Cursor Mundi. Essay on the MSS., their Dialects, &c., by H. Hupe. Part VII. (*Reprinted* 1962.) 35s. ,,
E.S. 63. Thomas à Kempis's De Imitatione Christi, ed. J. K. Ingram. (*Out of print*.) ,,
64. Caxton's Godeffroy of Boloyne, or The Siege and Conquest of Jerusalem, 1481, ed. Mary N. Colvin. (*Out of print*.) ,,
O.S. 102. Lanfranc's Science of Cirurgie, ed. R. von Fleischhacker. Part I. (*Out of print*.) 189

O.S. 103.	The Legend of the Cross, &c., ed. A. S. Napier. (*Out of print.*)	1894
E.S. 65.	Sir Beves of Hamtoun, ed. E. Kölbing. Part III. (*Out of print.*)	,,
66.	Lydgate's and Burgh's Secrees of Philisoffres ('Governance of Kings and Princes'), ed. R. Steele. (*Out of print.*)	,,
O.S. 104.	The Exeter Book (Anglo-Saxon Poems), re-ed. I. Gollancz. Part I. (*Reprinted 1958.*) 55s.	1895
105.	The Prymer or Lay Folks' Prayer Book, Camb. Univ. MS., ed. H. Littlehales. Part I. (*Out of print.*)	,,
E.S. 67.	The Three Kings' Sons, a Romance, ed. F. J. Furnivall. Part I, the Text. (*Out of print.*)	,,
68.	Melusine, the prose Romance, ed. A. K. Donald. Part I, the Text. (*Out of print.*)	,,
O.S. 106.	R. Misyn's Fire of Love and Mending of Life (Hampole), ed. R. Harvey. (*Out of print.*)	1896
107.	The English Conquest of Ireland, A.D. 1166–1185, 2 Texts, ed. F. J. Furnivall. Part I. (*Out of print.*)	,,
E.S. 69.	Lydgate's Assembly of the Gods, ed. O. L. Triggs. (*Reprinted 1957.*) 42s.	,,
70.	The Digby Plays, ed. F. J. Furnivall. (*Reprinted 1967.*) 30s.	,,
O.S. 108.	Child-Marriages and -Divorces, Trothplights, &c. Chester Depositions, 1561–6, ed. F. J. Furnivall. (*Out of print.*)	1897
109.	The Prymer or Lay Folks' Prayer Book, ed. H. Littlehales. Part II. (*Out of print.*)	,,
E.S. 71.	The Towneley Plays, ed. G. England and A. W. Pollard. (*Reprinted 1966.*) 45s.	,,
72.	Hoccleve's Regement of Princes, and 14 Poems, ed. F. J. Furnivall. (*Out of print.*)	,,
73.	Hoccleve's Minor Poems, II, from the Ashburnham MS., ed. I. Gollancz. (*Out of print.*)	,,
O.S. 110.	The Old-English Version of Bede's Ecclesiastical History, ed. T. Miller. Part II, 1. (*Reprinted 1963.*) 55s.	1898
111.	The Old-English Version of Bede's Ecclesiastical History, ed. T. Miller. Part II, 2. (*Reprinted 1963.*) 55s.	,,
E.S. 74.	Secreta Secretorum, 3 prose Englishings, one by Jas. Yonge, 1428, ed. R. Steele. Part I. 55s.	,,
75.	Speculum Guidonis de Warwyk, ed. G. L. Morrill. (*Out of print.*)	,,
O.S. 112.	Merlin. Part IV. Outlines of the Legend of Merlin, by W. E. Mead. (*Out of print.*)	1899
113.	Queen Elizabeth's Englishings of Boethius, Plutarch, &c., ed. C. Pemberton. (*Out of print.*)	,,
E.S. 76.	George Ashby's Poems, &c., ed. Mary Bateson. (*Reprinted 1965.*) 30s.	,,
77.	Lydgate's DeGuilleville's Pilgrimage of the Life of Man, ed. F. J. Furnivall. Part I. (*Out of print.*)	,,
78.	The Life and Death of Mary Magdalene, by T. Robinson, c. 1620, ed. H. O. Sommer. 30s.	,,
O.S. 114.	Ælfric's Lives of Saints, ed. W. W. Skeat. Part IV and last. (*See O.S. 94.*)	1900
115.	Jacob's Well, ed. A. Brandeis. Part I. (*Out of print.*)	,,
116.	An Old-English Martyrology, re-ed. G. Herzfeld. (*Out of print.*)	,,
E.S. 79.	Caxton's Dialogues, English and French, ed. H. Bradley. (*Out of print.*)	,,
80.	Lydgate's Two Nightingale Poems, ed. O. Glauning. (*Out of print.*)	,,
80A.	Selections from Barbour's Bruce (Books I–X), ed. W. W. Skeat. (*Out of print.*)	,,
81.	The English Works of John Gower, ed. G. C. Macaulay. Part I. (*Reprinted 1957.*) 60s.	,,
O.S. 117.	Minor Poems of the Vernon MS., ed. F. J. Furnivall. Part II. (*Out of print.*)	1901
118.	The Lay Folks' Catechism, ed. T. F. Simmons and H. E. Nolloth. (*Out of print.*)	,,
119.	Robert of Brunne's Handlyng Synne, and its French original, re-ed. F. J. Furnivall. Part I. (*Out of print.*)	,,
E.S. 82.	The English Works of John Gower, ed. G. C. Macaulay. Part II. (*Reprinted 1957.*) 60s.	,,
83.	Lydgate's DeGuilleville's Pilgrimage of the Life of Man, ed. F. J. Furnivall. Part II. (*Out of print.*)	,,
84.	Lydgate's Reson and Sensuallyte, ed. E. Sieper. Vol. I. (*Reprinted 1965.*) 50s.	,,
O.S. 120.	The Rule of St. Benet in Northern Prose and Verse, and Caxton's Summary, ed. E. A. Kock. (*Out of print.*)	1902
121.	The Laud MS. Troy-Book, ed. J. E. Wülfing. Part I. (*Out of print.*)	,,
E.S. 85.	Alexander Scott's Poems, 1568, ed. A. K. Donald. (*Out of print.*)	,,
86.	William of Shoreham's Poems, re-ed. M. Konrath. Part I. (*Out of print.*)	,,
87.	Two Coventry Corpus Christi Plays, re-ed. H. Craig. (*See under 1952.*)	,,
O.S. 122.	The Laud MS. Troy-Book, ed. J. E. Wülfing. Part II. (*Out of print.*)	1903
123.	Robert of Brunne's Handlyng Synne, and its French original, re-ed. F. J. Furnivall. Part II. (*Out of print.*)	,,
E.S. 88.	Le Morte Arthur, re-ed. J. D. Bruce. (*Reprinted 1959.*) 45s.	,,
89.	Lydgate's Reson and Sensuallyte, ed. E. Sieper. Vol. II. (*Reprinted 1965.*) 35s.	,,
90.	English Fragments from Latin Medieval Service-Books, ed. H. Littlehales. (*Out of print.*)	,,
O.S. 124.	Twenty-six Political and other Poems from Digby MS. 102, &c., ed. J. Kail. Part I. 50s.	1904
125.	Medieval Records of a London City Church, ed. H. Littlehales. Part I. (*Out of print.*)	,,
126.	An Alphabet of Tales, in Northern English, from the Latin, ed. M. M. Banks. Part I. (*Out of print.*)	,,
E.S. 91.	The Macro Plays, ed. F. J. Furnivall and A. W. Pollard. (*Out of print; see 262.*)	,,
92.	Lydgate's DeGuilleville's Pilgrimage of the Life of Man, ed. Katherine B. Locock. Part III. (*Out of print.*)	,,
93.	Lovelich's Romance of Merlin, from the unique MS., ed. E. A. Kock. Part I. (*Out of print.*)	,,
O.S. 127.	An Alphabet of Tales, in Northern English, from the Latin, ed. M. M. Banks. Part II. (*Out of print.*)	1905
128.	Medieval Records of a London City Church, ed. H. Littlehales. Part II. (*Out of print.*)	,,
129.	The English Register of Godstow Nunnery, ed. A. Clark. Part I. 63s.	,,
E.S. 94.	Respublica, a Play on a Social England, ed. L. A. Magnus. (*Out of print. See under 1946.*)	,,
95.	Lovelich's History of the Holy Grail. Part V. The Legend of the Holy Grail, ed. Dorothy Kempe. (*Out of print.*)	,,
96.	Mirk's Festial, ed. T. Erbe. Part I. (*Out of print.*)	,,
O.S. 130.	The English Register of Godstow Nunnery, ed. A. Clark. Part II. 55s.	1906
131.	The Brut, or The Chronicle of England, ed. F. Brie. Part I. (*Reprinted 1960.*) 55s.	,,
132.	John Metham's Works, ed. H. Craig. 50s.	,,
E.S. 97.	Lydgate's Troy Book, ed. H. Bergen. Part I, Books I and II. (*Out of print.*)	,,

E.S. 98.	Skelton's Magnyfycence, ed. R. L. Ramsay. (Reprinted 1958.) 55s.	1906
99.	The Romance of Emaré, re-ed. Edith Rickert. (Reprinted 1958.) 30s.	,,
O.S. 133.	The English Register of Oseney Abbey, by Oxford, ed. A. Clark. Part I. 50s.	1907
134.	The Coventry Leet Book, ed. M. Dormer Harris. Part I. (Out of print.)	,,
E.S. 100.	The Harrowing of Hell, and The Gospel of Nicodemus, re-ed. W. H. Hulme. (Reprinted 1961.) 50s.	,,
101.	Songs, Carols, &c., from Richard Hill's Balliol MS., ed. R. Dyboski. (Out of print.)	,,
O.S. 135.	The Coventry Leet Book, ed. M. Dormer Harris. Part II. (Out of print.)	1908
135 b.	Extra Issue. Prof. Manly's Piers Plowman and its Sequence, urging the fivefold authorship of the Vision. (Out of print.)	,,
136.	The Brut, or The Chronicle of England, ed. F. Brie. Part II. (Out of print.)	,,
E.S. 102.	Promptorium Parvulorum, the 1st English-Latin Dictionary, ed. A. L. Mayhew. (Out of print.)	,,
103.	Lydgate's Troy Book, ed. H. Bergen. Part II, Book III. (Out of print.)	,,
O.S. 137.	Twelfth-Century Homilies in MS. Bodley 343, ed. A. O. Belfour. Part I, the Text. (Reprinted 1962.) 28s.	1909
138.	The Coventry Leet Book, ed. M. Dormer Harris. Part III. (Out of print.)	,,
E.S. 104.	The Non-Cycle Mystery Plays, re-ed. O. Waterhouse. (See end-note, p. 8.)	,,
105.	The Tale of Beryn, with the Pardoner and Tapster, ed. F. J. Furnivall and W. G. Stone. (Out of print.)	,,
O.S. 139.	John Arderne's Treatises of Fistula in Ano, &c., ed. D'Arcy Power. (Reprinted 1969.) 45s.	1910
139 b, c, d, e, f,	Extra Issue. The Piers Plowman Controversy: b. Dr. Jusserand's 1st Reply to Prof. Manly; c. Prof. Manly's Answer to Dr. Jusserand; d. Dr. Jusserand's 2nd Reply to Prof. Manly; e. Mr. R. W. Chambers's Article; f. Dr. Henry Bradley's Rejoinder to Mr. R. W. Chambers. (Out of print.)	,,
140.	Capgrave's Lives of St. Augustine and St. Gilbert of Sempringham, ed. J. Munro. (Out of print.)	,,
E.S. 106.	Lydgate's Troy Book, ed. H. Bergen. Part III. (Out of print.)	,,
107.	Lydgate's Minor Poems, ed. H. N. MacCracken. Part I. Religious Poems. (Reprinted 1961.) 70s.	,,
O.S. 141.	Erthe upon Erthe, all the known texts, ed. Hilda Murray. (Reprinted 1964.) 30s.	1911
142.	The English Register of Godstow Nunnery, ed. A. Clark. Part III. 42s.	,,
143.	The Prose Life of Alexander, Thornton MS., ed. J. S. Westlake. (Out of print.)	,,
E.S. 108.	Lydgate's Siege of Thebes, re-ed. A. Erdmann. Part I, the Text. (Reprinted 1960.) 50s.	,,
109.	Partonope, re-ed. A. T. Bödtker. The Texts. (Out of print.)	,,
O.S. 144.	The English Register of Oseney Abbey, by Oxford, ed. A. Clark. Part II. 20s.	1912
145.	The Northern Passion, ed. F. A. Foster. Part I, the four parallel texts. (Out of print.)	,,
E.S. 110.	Caxton's Mirrour of the World, with all the woodcuts, ed. O. H. Prior. (Reprinted 1966.) 50s.	,,
111.	Caxton's History of Jason, the Text, Part I, ed. J. Munro. (Out of print.)	,,
O.S. 146.	The Coventry Leet Book, ed. M. Dormer Harris. Introduction, Indexes, &c. Part IV. (Out of print.)	1913
147.	The Northern Passion, ed. F. A. Foster, Introduction, French Text, Variants and Fragments, Glossary. Part II. (Out of print.)	,,
	[An enlarged reprint of O.S. 26, Religious Pieces in Prose and Verse, from the Thornton MS., ed. G. G. Perry. (Out of print.)	,,
E.S. 112.	Lovelich's Romance of Merlin, ed. E. A. Kock. Part II. (Reprinted 1961.) 45s.	,,
113.	Poems by Sir John Salusbury, Robert Chester, and others, from Christ Church MS. 184, &c., ed. Carleton Brown. (Out of print.)	,,
O.S. 148.	A Fifteenth-Century Courtesy Book and Two Franciscan Rules, ed. R. W. Chambers and W. W. Seton. (Reprinted 1963.) 30s.	1914
149.	Lincoln Diocese Documents, 1450–1544, ed. Andrew Clark. (Out of print.)	,,
150.	The Old-English Rule of Bp. Chrodegang, and the Capitula of Bp. Theodulf, ed. A. S. Napier. (Out of print.)	,,
E.S. 114.	The Gild of St. Mary, Lichfield, ed. F. J. Furnivall. 27s.	,,
115.	The Chester Plays, re-ed. J. Matthews. Part II. (Reprinted 1967.) 38s.	,,
O.S. 151.	The Lanterne of Light, ed. Lilian M. Swinburn. (Out of print.)	1915
152.	Early English Homilies, from Cott. Vesp. D. xiv, ed. Rubie Warner. Part I, Text. (Out of print.)	,,
E.S. 116.	The Pauline Epistles, ed. M. J. Powell. (Out of print.)	,,
117.	Bp. Fisher's English Works, ed. R. Bayne. Part II. (Out of print.)	,,
O.S. 153.	Mandeville's Travels, ed. P. Hamelius. Part I, Text. (Reprinted 1960.) 40s.	1916
154.	Mandeville's Travels, ed. P. Hamelius. Part II, Notes and Introduction. (Reprinted 1961.) 40s.	,,
E.S. 118.	The Earliest Arithmetics in English, ed. R. Steele. (Out of print.)	,,
119.	The Owl and the Nightingale, 2 Texts parallel, ed. G. F. H. Sykes and J. H. G. Grattan. (Out of print.)	,,
O.S. 155.	The Wheatley MS., ed. Mabel Day. 54s.	1917
E.S. 120.	Ludus Coventriae, ed. K. S. Block. (Reprinted 1961.) 60s.	,,
O.S. 156.	Reginald Pecock's Donet, from Bodl. MS. 916, ed. Elsie V. Hitchcock. 63s.	1918
E.S. 121.	Lydgate's Fall of Princes, ed. H. Bergen. Part I. (Reprinted 1967.) 63s.	,,
122.	Lydgate's Fall of Princes, ed. H. Bergen. Part II. (Reprinted 1967.) 63s.	,,
O.S. 157.	Harmony of the Life of Christ, from MS. Pepys 2498, ed. Margery Goates. (Out of print.)	1919
158.	Meditations on the Life and Passion of Christ, from MS. Add., 11307, ed. Charlotte D'Evelyn. (Out of print.)	,,
E.S. 123.	Lydgate's Fall of Princes, ed. H. Bergen. Part III. (Reprinted 1967.) 63s.	,,
124.	Lydgate's Fall of Princes, ed. H. Bergen. Part IV. (Reprinted 1967.) 90s.	,,
O.S. 159.	Vices and Virtues, ed. F. Holthausen. Part II. (Reprinted 1967.) 28s.	1920
	[A re-edition of O.S. 18, Hali Meidenhad, ed. O. Cockayne, with a variant MS., Bodl. 34, hitherto unprinted, ed. F. J. Furnivall. (Out of print.)	,,
E.S. 125.	Lydgate's Siege of Thebes, ed. A. Erdmann and E. Ekwall. Part II. (Out of print.)	,,

E.S.	126. Lydgate's Troy Book, ed. H. Bergen. Part IV. *(Out of print.)*	1920
O.S.	160. The Old English Heptateuch, MS. Cott. Claud. B. IV, ed. S. J. Crawford. *(Reprinted 1969.)* 75s.	1921
	161. Three O.E. Prose Texts, MS. Cott. Vit. A. xv, ed. S. Rypins. *(Out of print.)*	,,
	162. Facsimile of MS. Cotton Nero A. x (Pearl, Cleanness, Patience and Sir Gawain), Introduction by I. Gollancz. *(Reprinted 1955.)* 200s.	1922
	163. Book of the Foundation of St. Bartholomew's Church in London, ed. N. Moore. *(Out of print.)*	1923
	164. Pecock's Folewer to the Donet, ed. Elsie V. Hitchcock. *(Out of print.)*	,,
	165. Middleton's Chinon of England, with Leland's Assertio Arturii and Robinson's translation, ed. W. E. Mead. *(Out of print.)*	,,
	166. Stanzaic Life of Christ, ed. Frances A. Foster. *(Out of print.)*	1924
	167. Trevisa's Dialogus inter Militem et Clericum, Sermon by FitzRalph, and Bygynnyng of the World, ed. A. J. Perry. *(Out of print.)*	,,
	168. Caxton's Ordre of Chyualry, ed. A. T. P. Byles. *(Out of print.)*	1925
	169. The Southern Passion, ed. Beatrice Brown. *(Out of print.)*	,,
	170. Walton's Boethius, ed. M. Science. *(Out of print.)*	,,
	171. Pecock's Reule of Cristen Religioun, ed. W. C. Greet. *(Out of print.)*	1926
	172. The Seege or Batayle of Troye, ed. M. E. Barnicle. *(Out of print.)*	,,
	173. Hawes' Pastime of Pleasure, ed. W. E. Mead. *(Out of print.)*	1927
	174. The Life of St. Anne, ed. R. E. Parker. *(Out of print.)*	,,
	175. Barclay's Eclogues, ed. Beatrice White. *(Reprinted 1961.)* 55s.	,,
	176. Caxton's Prologues and Epilogues, ed. W. J. B. Crotch. *(Reprinted 1956.)* 54s.	,,
	177. Byrhtferth's Manual, ed. S. J. Crawford. *(Reprinted 1966.)* 63s.	1928
	178. The Revelations of St. Birgitta, ed. W. P. Cumming. *(Out of print.)*	,,
	179. The Castell of Pleasure, ed. B. Cornelius. *(Out of print.)*	,,
	180. The Apologye of Syr Thomas More, ed. A. I. Taft. *(Out of print.)*	1929
	181. The Dance of Death, ed. F. Warren. *(Out of print.)*	,,
	182. Speculum Christiani, ed. G. Holmstedt. *(Out of print.)*	,,
	183. The Northern Passion (Supplement), ed. W. Heuser and Frances Foster. *(Out of print.)*	1930
	184. The Poems of John Audelay, ed. Ella K. Whiting. *(Out of print.)*	,,
	185. Lovelich's Merlin, ed. E. A. Kock. Part III. *(Out of print.)*	,,
	186. Harpsfield's Life of More, ed. Elsie V. Hitchcock and R. W. Chambers. *(Reprinted 1963.)* 105s.	1931
	187. Whittinton and Stanbridge's Vulgaria, ed. B. White. *(Out of print.)*	,,
	188. The Siege of Jerusalem, ed. E. Kölbing and Mabel Day. *(Out of print.)*	,,
	189. Caxton's Fayttes of Armes and of Chyualrye, ed. A. T. Byles. 63s.	1932
	190. English Mediæval Lapidaries, ed. Joan Evans and Mary Serjeantson. *(Reprinted 1960.)* 50s.	,,
	191. The Seven Sages, ed. K. Brunner. *(Out of print.)*	,,
	191A. On the Continuity of English Prose, by R. W. Chambers. *(Reprinted 1966.)* 25s.	,,
	192. Lydgate's Minor Poems, ed. H. N. MacCracken. Part II, Secular Poems. *(Reprinted 1961.)* 75s.	1933
	193. Seinte Marherete, re-ed. Frances Mack. *(Reprinted 1958.)* 50s.	,,
	194. The Exeter Book, Part II, ed. W. S. Mackie. *(Reprinted 1938.)* 42s.	,,
	195. The Quatrefoil of Love, ed. I. Gollancz and M. Weale. *(Out of print.)*	1934
	196. A Short English Metrical Chronicle, ed. E. Zettl. *(Out of print.)*	,,
	197. Roper's Life of More, ed. Elsie V. Hitchcock. *(Reprinted 1958.)* 35s.	,,
	198. Firumbras and Otuel and Roland, ed. Mary O'Sullivan. *(Out of print.)*	,,
	199. Mum and the Sothsegger, ed. Mabel Day and R. Steele. *(Out of print.)*	,,
	200. Speculum Sacerdotale, ed. E. H. Weatherly. *(Out of print.)*	1935
	201. Knyghthode and Bataile, ed. R. Dyboski and Z. M. Arend. *(Out of print.)*	,,
	202. Palsgrave's Acolastus, ed. P. L. Carver. *(Out of print.)*	,,
	203. Amis and Amiloun, ed. McEdward Leach. *(Reprinted 1960.)* 50s.	,,
	204. Valentine and Orson, ed. Arthur Dickson. *(Out of print.)*	1936
	205. Tales from the Decameron, ed. H. G. Wright. *(Out of print.)*	,,
	206. Bokenham's Lives of Holy Women (Lives of the Saints), ed. Mary S. Serjeantson. *(Out of print.)*	,,
	207. Liber de Diversis Medicinis, ed. Margaret S. Ogden. *(Out of print.)*	,,
	208. The Parker Chronicle and Laws (facsimile), ed. R. Flower and A. H. Smith. *(Out of print.)*	1937
	209. Middle English Sermons from MS. Roy. 18 B. xxiii, ed. W. O. Ross. *(Reprinted 1960.)* 75s.	1938
	210. Sir Gawain and the Green Knight, ed. I. Gollancz. With Introductory essays by Mabel Day and M. S. Serjeantson. *(Reprinted 1966.)* 25s.	,,
	211. Dictes and Sayings of the Philosophers, ed. C. F. Bühler. *(Reprinted 1961.)* 75s.	1939
	212. The Book of Margery Kempe, Part I, ed. S. B. Meech and Hope Emily Allen. *(Reprinted 1961.)* 70s.	,,
	213. Ælfric's De Temporibus Anni, ed. H. Henel. *(Out of print.)*	1940
	214. Morley's Translation of Boccaccio's De Claris Mulieribus, ed. H. G. Wright. *(Out of print.)*	,,
	215. English Poems of Charles of Orleans, Part I, ed. R. Steele. *(Out of print.)*	1941
	216. The Latin Text of the Ancrene Riwle, ed. Charlotte D'Evelyn. *(Reprinted 1957.)* 45s.	,,
	217. The Book of Vices and Virtues, ed. W. Nelson Francis. *(Reprinted 1968.)* 75s.	1942
	218. The Cloud of Unknowing and the Book of Privy Counselling, ed. Phyllis Hodgson. *(Reprinted 1958.)* 40s.	1943
	219. The French Text of the Ancrene Riwle, B.M. Cotton MS. Vitellius. F. VII, ed. J. A. Herbert. *(Reprinted 1967.)* 55s.	,,
	220. English Poems of Charles of Orleans, Part II, ed. R. Steele and Mabel Day. *(Out of print.)*	1944
	221. Sir Degrevant, ed. L. F. Casson. *(Out of print.)*	,,
	222. Ro. Ba.'s Life of Syr Thomas More, ed. Elsie V. Hitchcock and Mgr. P. E. Hallett. *(Reprinted 1957.)* 63s.	1945
	223. Tretyse of Loue, ed. J. H. Fisher. *(Out of print.)*	,,
	224. Athelston, ed. A. McI. Trounce. *(Reprinted 1957.)* 42s.	1946
	225. The English Text of the Ancrene Riwle, B.M. Cotton MS. Nero A. XIV, ed. Mabel Day. *(Reprinted 1957.)* 50s.	,,

226. Respublica, re-ed. W. W. Greg. (*Out of print.*)		1946
227. Kyng Alisaunder, ed. G. V. Smithers. Vol. I, Text. (*Reprinted* 1961.) 75s.		1947
228. The Metrical Life of St. Robert of Knaresborough, ed. J. Bazire. (*Reprinted* 1968.) 42s.		,,
229. The English Text of the Ancrene Riwle, Gonville and Caius College MS. 234/120, ed. R. M. Wilson. With Introduction by N. R. Ker. (*Reprinted* 1957.) 35s.		1948
230. The Life of St. George by Alexander Barclay, ed. W. Nelson. (*Reprinted* 1960.) 40s.		,,
231. Deonise Hid Diuinite, and other treatises related to *The Cloud of Unknowing*, ed. Phyllis Hodgson. (*Reprinted* 1958.) 50s.		1949
232. The English Text of the Ancrene Riwle, B.M. Royal MS. 8 C. 1, ed. A. C. Baugh. (*Reprinted* 1958.) 30s.		,,
233. The Bibliotheca Historica of Diodorus Siculus translated by John Skelton, ed. F. M. Salter and H. L. R. Edwards. Vol. I, Text. (*Reprinted* 1968.) 80s.		1950
234. Caxton: Paris and Vienne, ed. MacEdward Leach. (*Out of print.*)		1951
235. The South English Legendary, Corpus Christi College Cambridge MS. 145 and B.M. M.S. Harley 2277, &c., ed. Charlotte D'Evelyn and Anna J. Mill. Text, Vol. I. (*Reprinted* 1967.) 63s.		,,
236. The South English Legendary. Text, Vol. II. (*Reprinted* 1967.) 63s.		1952
[E.S. 87. Two Coventry Corpus Christi Plays, re-ed. H. Craig. Second Edition. (*Reprinted* 1967.) 30s.]		,,
237. Kyng Alisaunder, ed. G. V. Smithers. Vol. II, Introduction, Commentary, and Glossary. 50s.		1953
238. The Phonetic Writings of Robert Robinson, ed. E. J. Dobson. (*Reprinted* 1968.) 30s.		,,
239. The Bibliotheca Historica of Diodorus Siculus translated by John Skelton, ed. F. M. Salter and H. L. R. Edwards. Vol. II. Introduction, Notes, and Glossary. 30s.		1954
240. The French Text of the Ancrene Riwle, Trinity College, Cambridge, MS. R. 14, 7, ed. W. H. Trethewey. 55s.		,,
241. Þe Wohunge of ure Lauerd, and other pieces, ed. W. Meredith Thompson. 45s.		1955
242. The Salisbury Psalter, ed. Celia Sisam and Kenneth Sisam. (*Reprinted* 1969.) 90s.		1955–56
243. George Cavendish: The Life and Death of Cardinal Wolsey, ed. Richard S. Sylvester. (*Reprinted* 1961.) 45s.		1957
244. The South English Legendary. Vol. III, Introduction and Glossary, ed. C. D'Evelyn. 30s.		,,
245. Beowulf (facsimile). With Transliteration by J. Zupitza, new collotype plates, and Introduction by N. Davis. (*Reprinted* 1967.) 100s.		1958
246. The Parlement of the Thre Ages, ed. M. Y. Offord. (*Reprinted* 1967.) 40s.		1959
247. Facsimile of MS. Bodley 34 (Katherine Group). With Introduction by N. R. Ker. 63s.		,,
248. Þe Liflade ant te Passiun of Seinte Iuliene, ed. S. R. T. O. d'Ardenne. 40s.		1960
249. Ancrene Wisse, Corpus Christi College, Cambridge, MS. 402, ed. J. R. R. Tolkien. With an Introduction by N. R. Ker. 50s.		,,
250. Laȝamon's Brut, ed. G. L. Brook and R. F. Leslie. Vol. I, Text (first part). 100s.		1961
251. Facsimile of the Cotton and Jesus Manuscripts of the Owl and the Nightingale. With Introduction by N. R. Ker. 50s.		1962
252. The English Text of the Ancrene Riwle, B.M. Cotton MS. Titus D. xviii, ed. Frances M. Mack, and Lanhydrock Fragment, ed. A. Zettersten. 50s.		,,
253. The Bodley Version of Mandeville's Travels, ed. M. C. Seymour. 50s.		1963
254. Ywain and Gawain, ed. Albert B. Friedman and Norman T. Harrington. 50s.		,,
255. Facsimile of B.M. MS. Harley 2253 (The Harley Lyrics). With Introduction by N. R. Ker. 100s.		1964
256. Sir Eglamour of Artois, ed. Frances E. Richardson. 50s.		1965
257. Sir Thomas Chaloner: The Praise of Folie, ed. Clarence H. Miller. 50s.		,,
258. The Orchard of Syon, ed. Phyllis Hodgson and Gabriel M. Liegey. Vol. I, Text. 100s.		1966
259. Homilies of Ælfric: A Supplementary Collection, ed. J. C. Pope. Vol. I. 100s.		1967
260. Homilies of Ælfric: A Supplementary Collection, ed. J. C. Pope. Vol. II. 100s.		1968
261. Lybeaus Desconus, ed. M. Mills. 50s.		1969
262. The Macro Plays, re-ed. Mark Eccles. 50s.		,,

Forthcoming volumes

263. Caxton's History of Reynard the Fox, ed. N. F. Blake. (*At press.*) 50s.		1970
264. Scrope's Epistle of Othea, ed. C. F. Bühler. (*At press.*) 50s.		,,
265. The Cyrurgie of Guy de Chauliac, ed. Margaret S. Ogden. Vol. I, Text. (*At Press.*) 100s.		1971
266. Wulfstan's Canons of Edgar, ed. R. G. Fowler. (*At press.*) 50s.		1971
267. The English Text of the Ancrene Riwle, B. M. Cotton MS. Cleopatra C. vi, ed. E. J. Dobson. (*At press.*) 50s.		,,

Other texts are in preparation.

Supplementary Texts

The Society proposes to issue some Supplementary Texts from time to time as funds allow. These will be sent to members as part of the normal issue and will also be available to non-members at listed prices. The first of these, Supplementary Text 1, expected to appear in 1970, will be *Non-Cycle Plays and Fragments* ed. Norman Davis (about 50s.). This is a completely revised and re-set edition of the texts in Extra Series 104 with some additional pieces. Supplementary Text 2, expected to appear in 1971, will be *Caxton's Knight of La Tour Landry*, ed. M. Y. Offord (at press, about 50s.).

April 1969

Publisher: LONDON · THE OXFORD UNIVERSITY PRESS, ELY HOUSE, 37 DOVER ST., W. 1

The manufacturer's authorised representative in the EU for product safety is Oxford University Press España S.A. of El Parque Empresarial San Fernando de Henares, Avenida de Castilla, 2 - 28830 Madrid (www.oup.es/en or product.safety@oup.com). OUP España S.A. also acts as importer into Spain of products made by the manufacturer.
Printed and bound by CPI Group (UK) Ltd, Croydon, CR0 4YY

20/03/2026

02075339-0007